LEGENDARY LOCALS

OF

COHOES

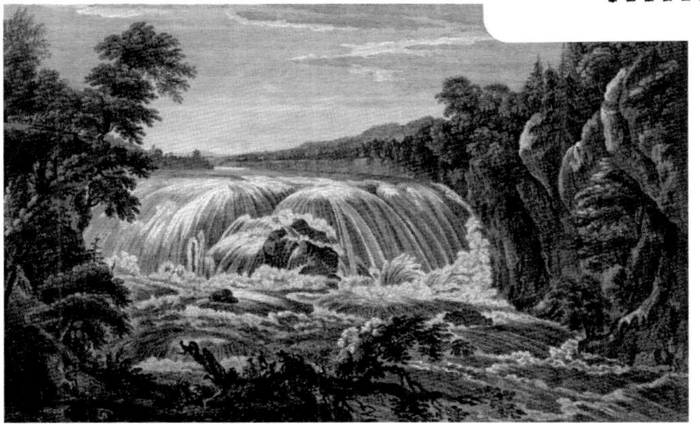

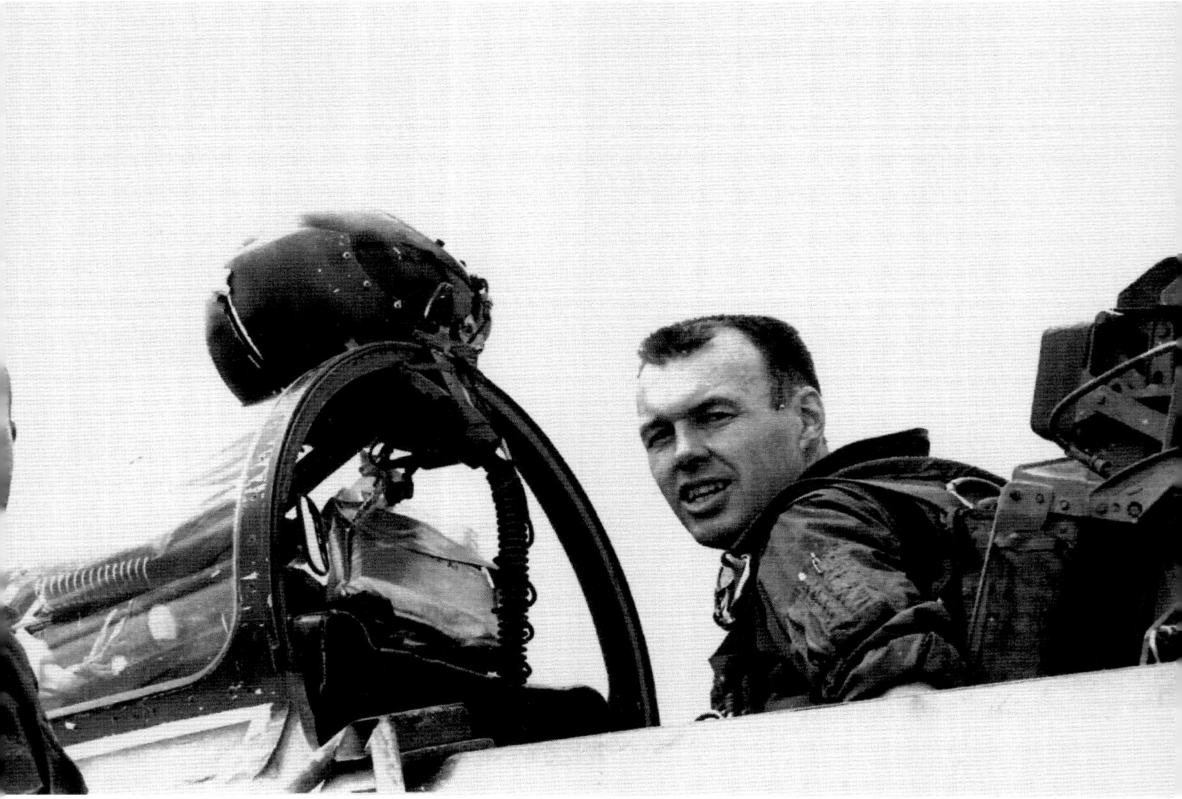

Robert Craner sits in the cockpit of an F-100 fighter jet. Craner was shot down over North Vietnam in 1967 and spent several years as a POW, along with Sen. John McCain. (See page 113.) (Courtesy of the Spindle City Historic Society.)

Page 1:
This is a sketch by Thomas Pownall, governor of the Province of the Massachusetts Bay Colony, upon his visit to Cohoes in 1760. (Courtesy of the Library of Congress.)

LEGENDARY LOCALS

OF

COHOES

RANDY S. KONIOWKA

LEGENDARY LOCALS

ISBN 978-1-4671-0091-5

Legendary Locals is an imprint of Arcadia Publishing
Charleston, South Carolina

Printed in the United States of America

Library of Congress Control Number: 2013932584

For all general information, please contact Arcadia Publishing:
Telephone 843-853-2070
Fax 843-853-0044
E-mail sales@arcadiapublishing.com
For customer service and orders:
Toll-Free 1-888-313-2665

Visit us on the Internet at www.arcadiapublishing.com

Dedication
For Anthony Koniowka Jr.

On the Cover: Clockwise from top left:
Paul Van Buskirk, leader of the Cohoes Citizens movement (courtesy of Paul Van Buskirk, page 45); Madelon K. Hickey, principal (courtesy of the author, page 66); children march down Remsen Street (courtesy of Tom Bessette, page 75); Eva Tanguay, Vaudeville performer (courtesy of the Library of Congress, page 130); George Stacey Davis, baseball hall of famer (courtesy of the National Baseball Hall of Fame and Museum, page 131); Chester A. Arthur, president of the United States (courtesy of the Library of Congress, page 58).

On the Back Cover: From left to right:
The Cohoes Drum Corps (courtesy of Sue Baird, page 117); Thomas O'Connor (right) and the management team of Mohawk (courtesy of Mohawk, page 35).

Randy Koniowka, in profiling legendary locals from the past and the present, creates a picture of how these personalities fit into their eras, exerting their influence, in varying degrees, on the changes that have punctuated the evolution of our city of Cohoes.

The history of Cohoes can be traced from an early Albany Dutch farmstead, through a dynamic industrial period, to eras of urban rise and decline, and finally marching forward to today's period of renaissance.

Cohoes, a speck of land at the confluence of the Hudson and Mohawk Rivers, has evolved from clay hills, outcroppings of shale, and river marshes into what it is today—a city in rejuvenation. A few decades ago, following World War II and the Korean War, Cohoes had, in effect, reached the bottom of the barrel. But it was rescued from the grip of an entrenched political machine during a time of overwhelming urban decay by a group of wise and independent thinkers who set as an enduring objective embodying the mindset of "An All-American City."

Several decades before that, Cohoes was at the zenith of 19th-century industrial strength, only to slide into serious decline caused by advances in technology, the emergence of unions, and the impact of the Great Depression.

At Cohoes' historic beginning were the early pioneers, who came to build on the clay hills. They carved canals and built factories and humble dwellings on the shale outcroppings. Over a broad stretch of time, Koniowka's legends influenced the course of events, applying their own particular aptitudes.

For instance, very few people in Cohoes, or elsewhere for that matter, recognize the name David Wilkinson. This mechanical genius, a native of Pawtucket, Rhode Island, who lived and worked briefly in Cohoes, exerted a profound and lasting effect, launching Cohoes into the Industrial Revolution. Charles H. Adams was not only a rich Cohoes industrialist, but also the first mayor of Cohoes, a state and federal representative, and a relative of the famous presidential Adams family. Grace Reavy, a brilliant resident, was the first woman in New York state to be appointed to a municipal public office, eventually becoming deputy secretary of New York. And these are just three of Koniowka's legendary locals.

As a local history buff, former Cohoes schoolteacher, and former city historian, I think this book is a must for both the interested public and local schoolteachers, who could use samples from it to relate the history of Cohoes with the development of the nation.

—Walter Lipka

This book would not have been possible without the assistance of the many individuals who shared their photographs and their stories. I am truly grateful and would like to thank the following for their contributions to this book: John and Jackie Reavy, Paul Van Buskirk, Bob Signoracci, Ralph Signoracci IV, Ralph Signoracci III, Mary Donlon, George Primeau, Lisa Lewis and the *Troy Record*, Gerry Rymanowski, John McDonald, Barbara McDonald, Sue Baird, Tom Bulger, Ed Niles, Stacie Waters, Robert Langely, Robert Gullie Jr., Diane O'Connor, Thomas O'Connor, Ed Tremblay, Linda Tremblay, Kelly Tremblay Brady, Mike Carey, Kathy Duval Beattie, and Teigan Powell.

Thanks also go to Kathleen Coleman and the Saratoga County Historical Association, Michele Bemis, Donald Sevigny and the Old Slater Mill Association, Harry Robinson, Herb Hyde, Darrell Beattie, Katherine Collett and the Hamilton College Library, the National Baseball Hall of Fame and Museum, The Cohoes Public Library, Adeline Rand, and Bill Robinson.

I am also grateful to Brig. Gen. Edward Clark, Mike Brooks, Tom Bessette, Miriam Biskin, April Kennedy, Paul Dunleavy, Dave Sequin, Bernard Ouimet, Dane Vore, Theresa Thibodeau, Dean Plowman, Linda Plowman, Mark Dufresne, the Gleason family, Rev. Nick Tebordo, the Columbia County Historical Society, Shawn Morse, Darlene Koniowka, Pam McGrath, Alana and Jesse Matulis, Matt Stevens, Rich Devoe, Dave Berdar, Pastor Rick Colquhoun, Daniele Cherniak, Bill Fazioli, Bill Robinson, and Gil Ethier.

A special thank-you goes to Walter Lipka, for reopening the door on Cohoes history, and to the Spindle City Historic Society for its years of dedication and commitment to preserving the history and heritage of Cohoes.

Unless otherwise noted, all photographs are courtesy of the author.

The great modern-day historian David McCullough was once quoted as saying "history is about human beings." It is a simple yet profound statement. For history is less about the collection and retention of dates and facts and more about us, about people. My love for the human story, and the story of Cohoes in particular, developed at a very early age. It was a copy of the *Cohoes Centennial*, a booklet celebrating the 100th anniversary of the incorporation of Cohoes as a city, tucked away in a cubbyhole in my third-grade classroom, that ignited a spark for which a burning flame is still lit. In that booklet were a host of fascinating characters from all walks of life. It was these individuals that I wanted to bring back into the public consciousness. And while the history of Cohoes may not be unlike that of any small town in America, for those of us who call Cohoes home and are tied to it by the mystic cords of generations long past, it is indeed special.

When setting out to do this book, I knew almost immediately that I would not be able to include all of the people who have left profound and distinctive marks on the community. With that in mind, I set out to portray a wide variety of individuals that would be representative of the greater whole. Many of those profiled have lived their entire lives in Cohoes. For others, Cohoes was their adopted hometown. And for some, Cohoes was just a brief stop along the road of life. But each made contributions that continue to constitute the fabric of the community.

I hope that this book will perhaps light a spark in some young person's mind and encourage them to explore their local history, as there is so much yet to discover. I hope it brings those who have dissipated from the public consciousness back into our modern-day discourse. And I hope this book serves as a reminder that we are nothing more than stewards. It is up to us and future generations to carry on what those before us have laid down. All of the hopes and dreams of generations past now lay on our shoulders. It is our turn to pick up the torch and become the legends of tomorrow.

—Randy S. Koniowka
Cohoes, New York
April 7, 2013

Nestled in the Mohawk and Hudson River Valleys and surrounded by the Adirondack, Catskill, and Taconic Mountains, the city of Cohoes sits at the geographic center of the greater Capital Region. Its long and storied history has spanned the course of centuries, playing a prominent role in the seminal events in American history. Her land was home to both Iroquois and Algonquin Indians, who established agricultural villages and an advanced system of governance. By the mid-to-late-17th century, these native populations were beginning to be pushed out by Dutch settlers. By the middle of the 18th century, the area was primarily a Dutch farming community and would remain so until the completion of the Erie Canal in 1825. An early attempt at manufacturing was initiated in 1811 when the Cohoes Manufacturing Company was established to produce wood screws. The factory burned down in 1815, and subsequent attempts to revive the operation failed. As the Cohoes Falls essentially disrupted east-west travel, Cohoes was a transshipment point, a place where transportation paused. Here also was where the Erie and Champlain Canals would meet, forming a junction. And while the industrial potential of the area had been envisioned as early as the middle of the 17th century, it was not until the construction of the Erie Canal that the vision would become a reality. The power of water would be harnessed to industrialize, as it had been done in England.

During the 100 years between 1830 and 1930, Cohoes would rise and fall as a major industrial powerhouse. Her factories at one time employed thousands of people in the textile industry, and the town was dubbed the "spindle city." Her population had soared to nearly 25,000 people by the end of World War I. Immigrants from French Canada, England, and Ireland poured into the streets, seeking work in the textile mills. Later immigrants came from Poland, Italy, and Russia, all looking for a better life and new opportunity. But by the time the Depression hit, Cohoes was on a steep decline. The rise of labor unions and the electrification of factories convinced textile companies to move their operations to the American South, as it was no longer necessary to situate textile manufacturing near water. By the late 1940s, the suburban experiment in America had begun. Cities were deemed dirty and inhospitable. The American Dream was now home ownership, far removed from the center of town. Locally, the construction of the Thruway and Adirondack Northway in the 1950s saw the once-rural areas to the north and west become populated with former city-dwellers.

During this time, Cohoes was also starting to decline physically. Her canals, once the lifeblood of the textile industry, had become open sewers. The housing stock, roads, and water systems were in dire need of repair. Public buildings and parks were forlorn and neglected. But the citizens of Cohoes would rise up and begin to demand a new tomorrow. In 1963, the Democratic machine that had controlled Cohoes for decades was thrown out of power by an upstart grassroots political movement dubbed the Citizens Party. Federal money began to pour into the city. The canals were filled, new housing was built, and a new firehouse was constructed. Parks were cleaned, and plans were drawn up for a new community center and senior housing. In 1967, Cohoes was named an All-America City in recognition for all that it was and all that it became. But those rather miraculous achievements did not stop the phenomenon known as suburban flight. The 1970s and 1980s saw further decline in the population base of the city. By the early 1990s, the suburban exodus had claimed nearly 10,000 people and left the downtown business district a shadow of its former self. But, while Cohoes was down, it was not out. During this period, a movement to reclaim old industrial cities was born. By later in the same decade, Cohoes started to see interest and investment along its riverfront and in its former industrial corridor, North Mohawk Street. By the end of the first decade of the 21st century, the city's residential base was reviving. The once-empty shrines of the Industrial Revolution were now being occupied by single professionals and empty nesters, as high-end loft apartments became the rage. The Hudson Riverfront, a once-industrial waterway, was giving itself over to luxury condominiums. And while one can no longer purchase a pair of shoes on Remsen Street, they can sip on an espresso, attend a yoga class, and view the latest modern art. Many have claimed that the urban renaissance taking place in Cohoes is putting it back on the map. However, it can be argued that the town never left. It has stood strong through its darkest days. Cohoes has been bruised and battered and has the scars to show it. But that is perhaps what gives the place its character. It is not perfect, not cookie-cutter. And it is as all-American now as it ever was. The people of Cohoes have been the town's greatest strength, never giving up, never giving in. This is their story, a story of a place and of a people uniquely, and unequivocally, American.

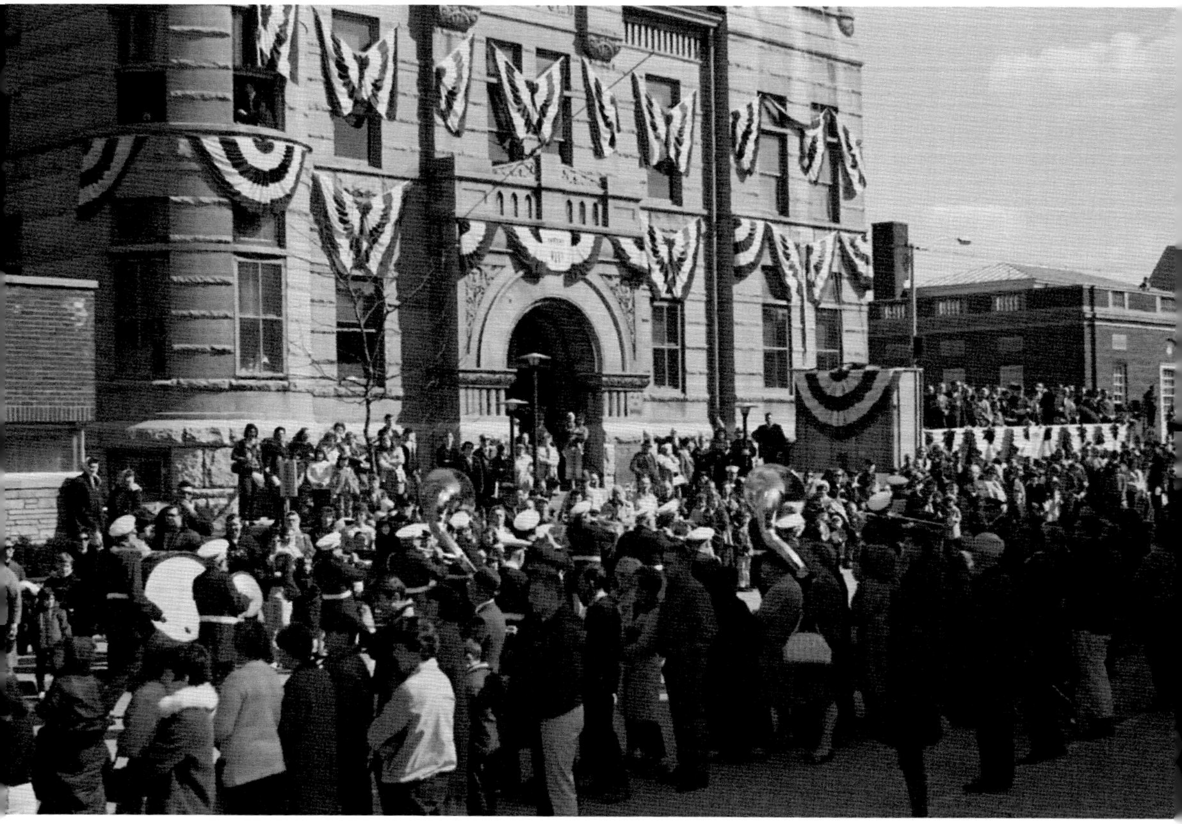

April 8, 1967, was one of the proudest days in the history of Cohoes. Thousands lined the city streets in celebration of Cohoes being proclaimed an "All-America City." (Courtesy of Paul Van Buskirk.)

Early Locals

Long before Europeans sailed up the Hudson River, the area now called Cohoes had been populated by native peoples. Those who perhaps first called Cohoes home were Paleo-Indians who arrived around 10,500 B.C., following the most recent Ice Age, when mammoths and mastodons were among the region's inhabitants. Native American agricultural villages were not established until around 1,000 A.D. During this period, the native population had discovered the transportation advantages of the area. They developed highly efficient and advanced trading networks that extended their reach far beyond the Cohoes area. By the 16th century, a system of political governance was established among the nations of the Iroquois. In 1609, Henry Hudson discovered the area on a voyage intended to find the Northwest Passage. Soon after, the Dutch began to colonize the area, purchasing land from the Indians. The entire Cohoes region would come under the patroonship of Kiliaen Van Rensselaer. As Europeans increased in numbers, the native population was pushed farther west, north, and east. By the turn of the 19th century, the area had become a predominantly Dutch farming community. This chapter highlights both Native American and Dutch locals who played a prominent role in the early development of what is now known as Cohoes.

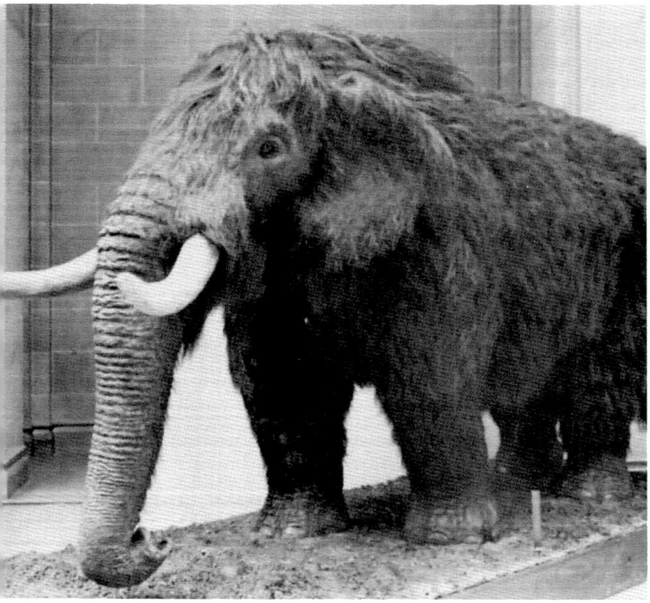

Mastodon americanus, now simply known as the Cohoes Mastodon, inhabited present-day Cohoes during the Pleistocene period, which ended nearly one million years ago. It was not until the dawn of the last Ice Age that these six-ton mammals became extinct. As a result of that ice, many mastodons were frozen and then preserved for tens of thousands of years. This was the case with the Cohoes Mastodon when, in 1866, workmen excavating for the foundation of Harmony Mill No. 3 discovered the skeletal remains. A massive hunt for more bones ensued, which became "the talk of the town" according to the *Cohoes Cataract* newspaper. Today, the full skeleton (below) can be found in the south hall lobby of the New York State Museum. A life-sized reproduction (left) can be found at the Cohoes Public Library.

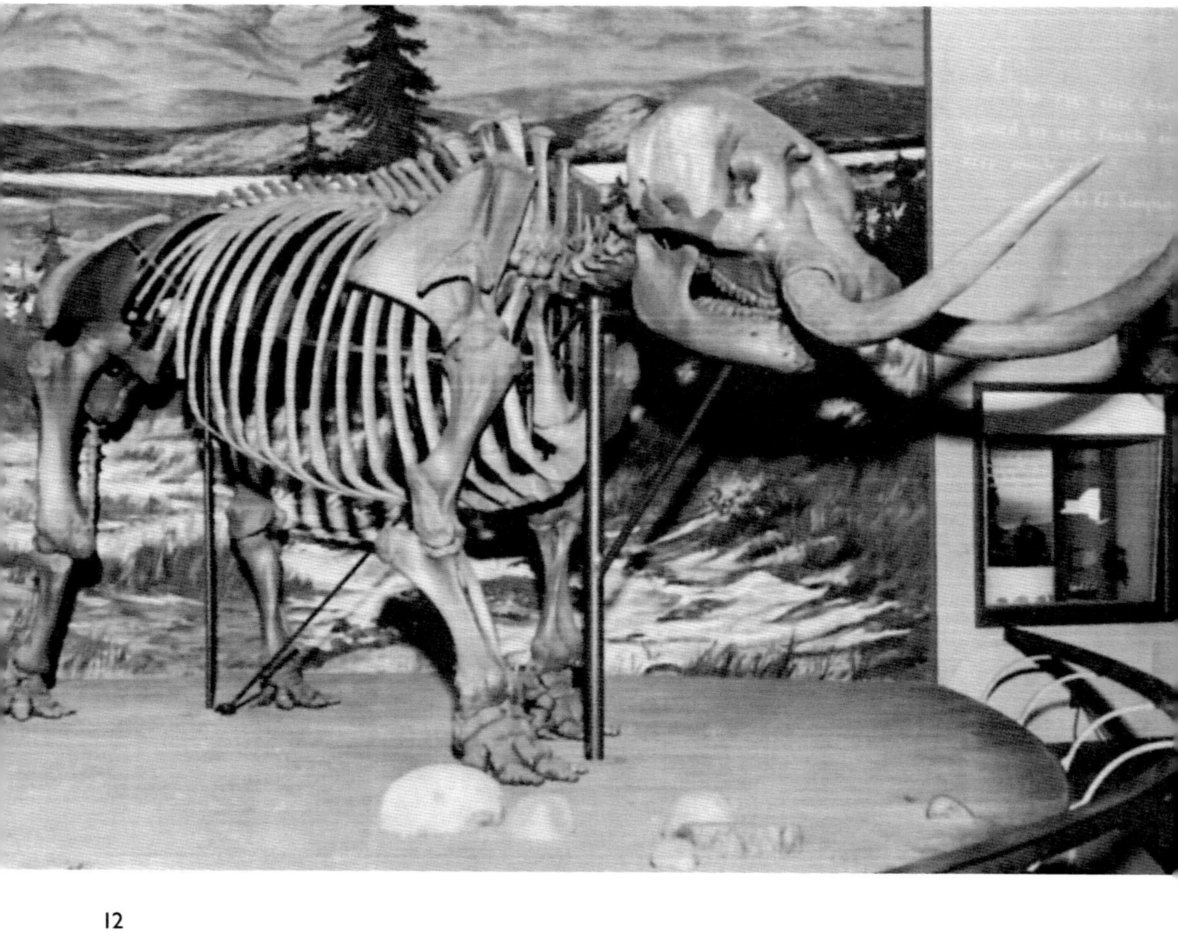

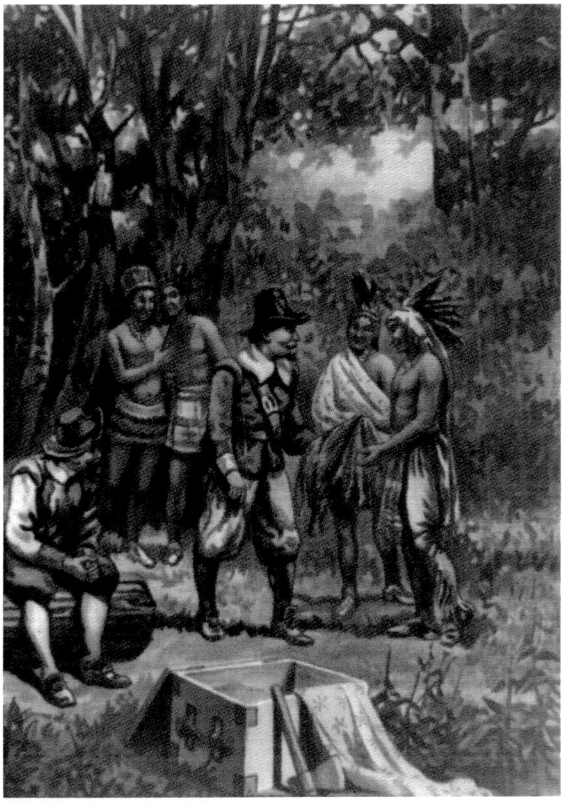

The Mohican are a nation of the Algonquian that largely settled on the eastern side of the Hudson River but also had settlements in present-day Cohoes. The Mohican were part of a confederation comprising four other nations. In the early part of the 17th century, the Mohican established trade with the Dutch. However, as the trade of beaver and other furs began to intensify, the scarcity of fur began to affect relations between themselves and the Mohawk, with the Mohawk ultimately gaining dominance in the area. Shown here is the 1893 painting *Dutch Traders in New Netherlands*. (Courtesy of the Library of Congress.)

When Henry Hudson sailed up the river that would ultimately bear his name, he was entering a land already rich in tradition, culture, and history. For thousands of years prior to Hudson's "discovery," aboriginal populations had called the Cohoes area home. The Mohawk are a nation of the Iroquois Confederacy and were known as "Keepers of the Eastern Door." Their nation stretched along what is now the Mohawk Valley from Central New York to Cohoes.

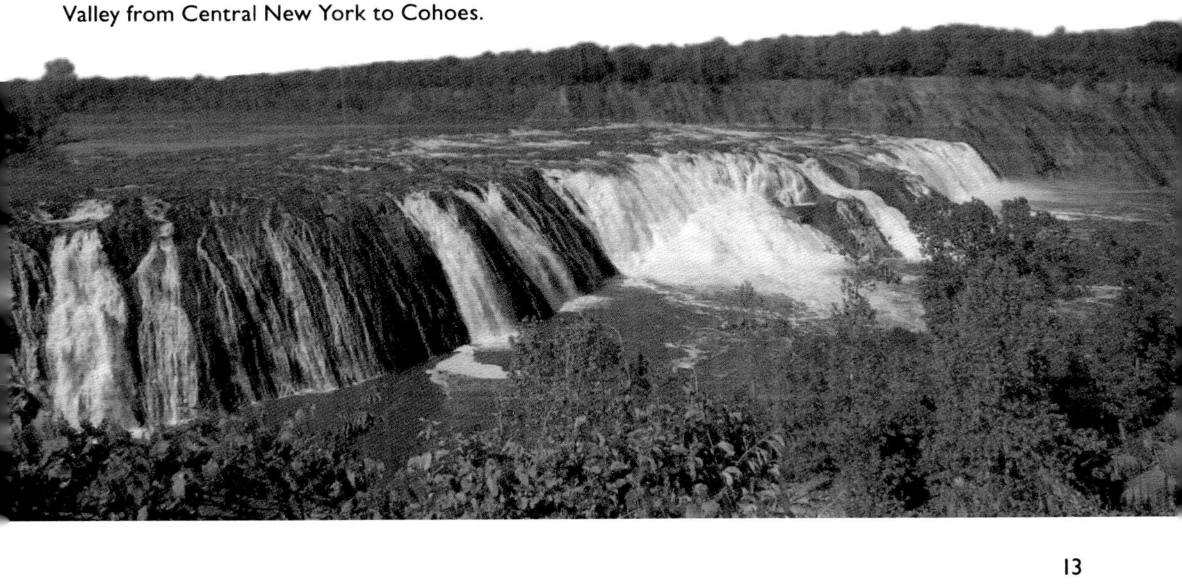

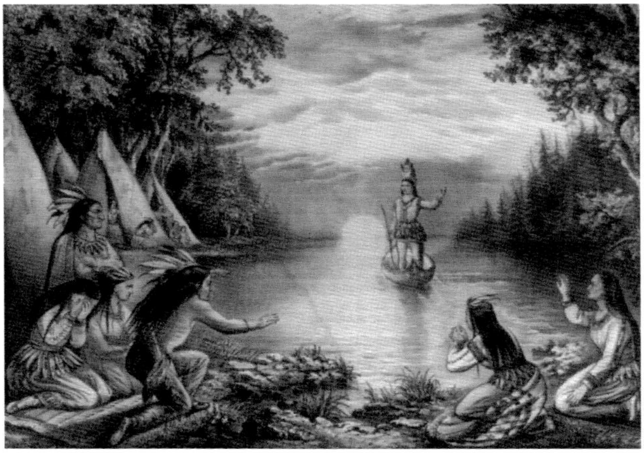

Hiawatha, or Ayenwatha, was a statesman, lawmaker, and man of peace who lived during the latter part of the 16th century. He was of the Onondaga Nation and had exceptional oratorical skills. However, some accounts claim he was actually born a Mohawk, but fled to the Onondagas after his teachings of peace and unity were rejected. He joined forces with the Great Peacemaker, who convinced him of his prophecy of an Iroquois confederacy. Together, they traveled throughout Upstate New York and brought the warring tribes of the Iroquois together as one nation. According to legend, Hiawatha went over the Cohoes Falls in a white canoe, never to be seen again. The very name *Cohoes*, or ga-ha-oose, is said to be a Mohawk term for "falling canoe." In 2012, understanding the sacredness of the site, Brookfield Power gave a portion of land near the Cohoes Falls to the Hiawatha Institute of Syracuse University. The inset image above is the 1868 Currier & Ives painting *Hiawatha's Departure*. (Courtesy of the Library of Congress.)

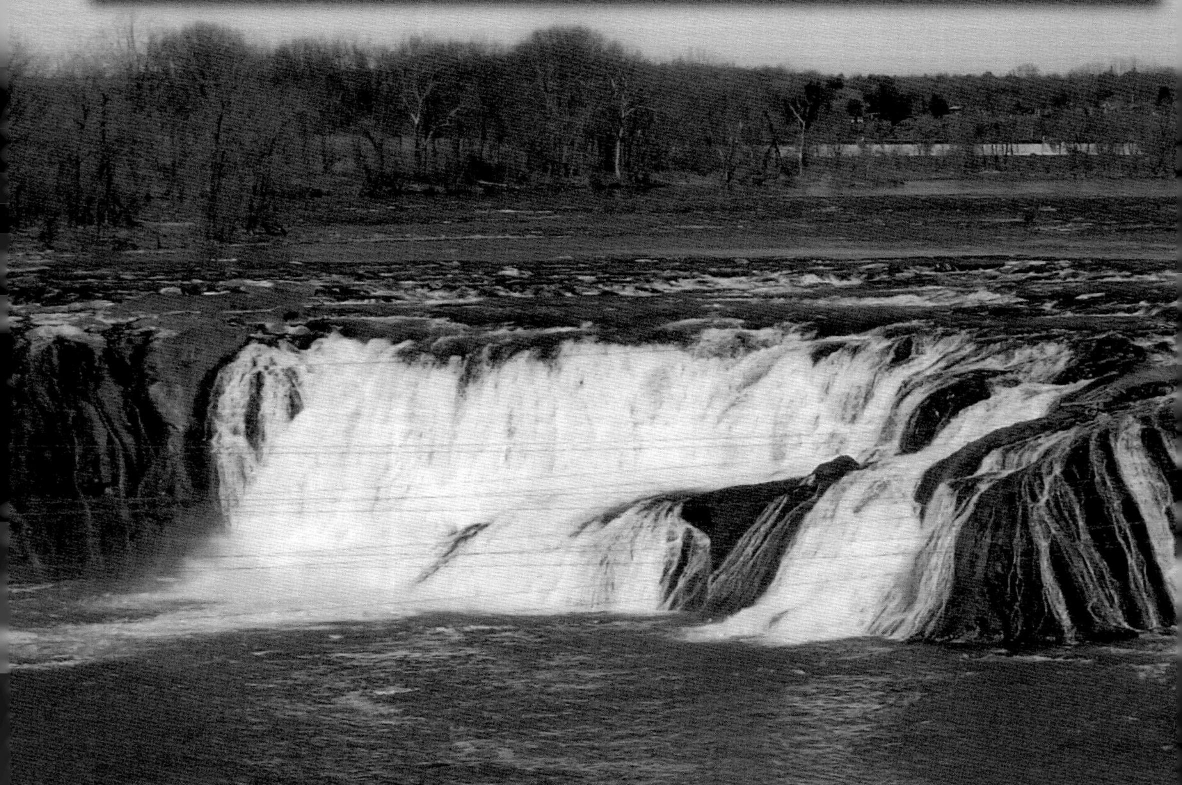

It is often said by historians that the American republic was based largely upon that of the Iroquois Confederacy. That confederacy, or the League of the Five Nations, was formed by Seneca, Cayuga, Onondaga, Mohawk, and Oneida during the latter part of the 16th century. It was the vision of Deganawidah, or "The Great Peacemaker," a Huron prophet who, according to legend, was born of a young virgin woman. Because of this, her mother was convinced that the baby had to be killed and made several attempts to do so. When the baby did not die, the population was convinced of his spiritual powers. As he reached adulthood, he realized that his mission was to restore peace to the warring nations of the Iroquois. Deganawidah came to Cohoes in order bring his message of peace to the Mohawk Nation. However, the Mohawk initially rejected his concepts of peace and unity. In order to convince them of his spiritual power, legend has it that he climbed a tree above the Cohoes Falls (shown here) and then plummeted into the roaring cataract, disappearing in the mist. Deganawidah was believed to be dead, until he appeared the next morning. Convinced of his miraculous abilities, the Mohawk joined the confederacy. A "great binding law" or constitution was established, and a governing council was instituted. As early as 1751, Benjamin Franklin advised that the American colonies form a confederacy like the Iroquois. Franklin had traveled to Cohoes to witness firsthand how the confederacy functioned. In 1775, John Hancock declared that "the Five Nations are a wise people. Let us harken to their council and teach our children to follow it."

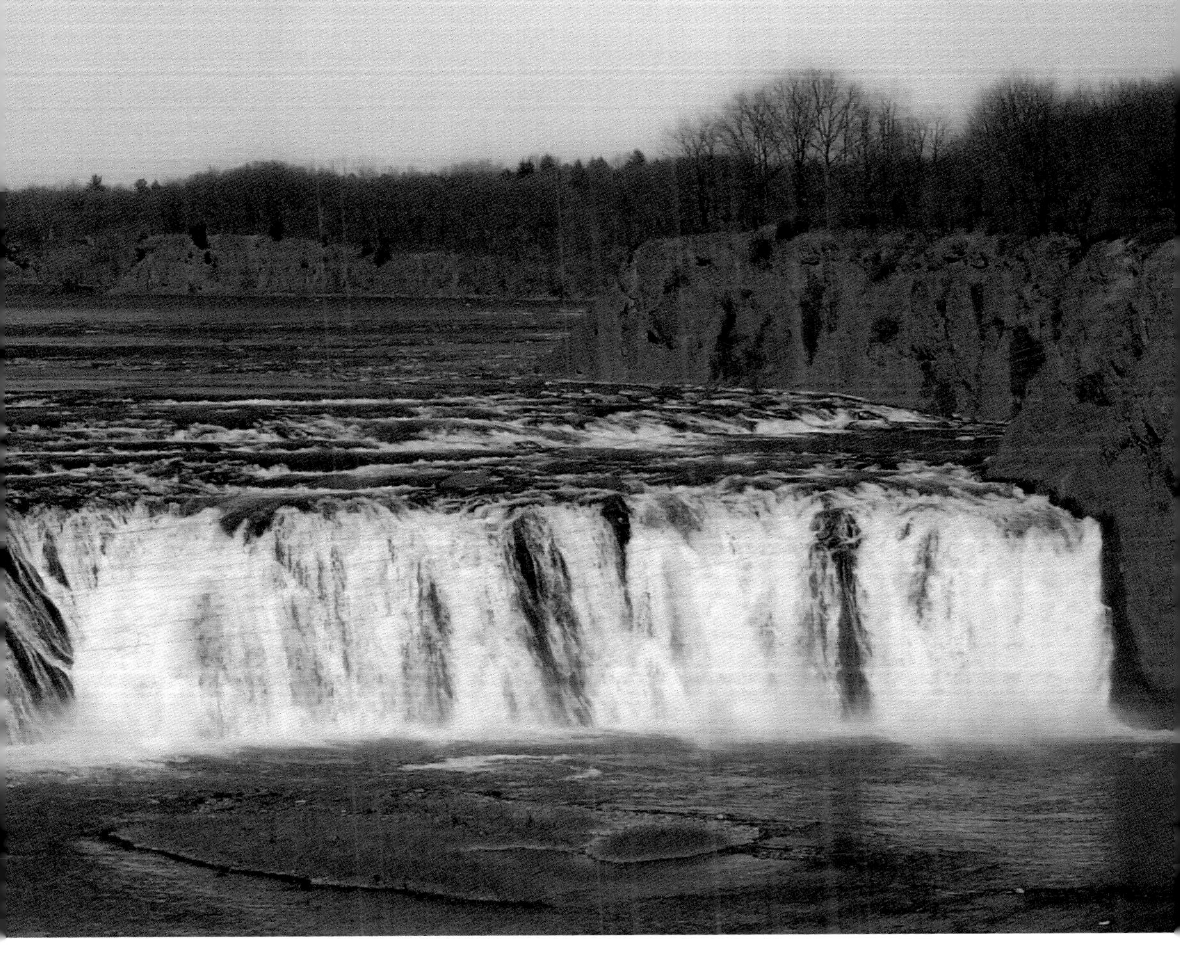

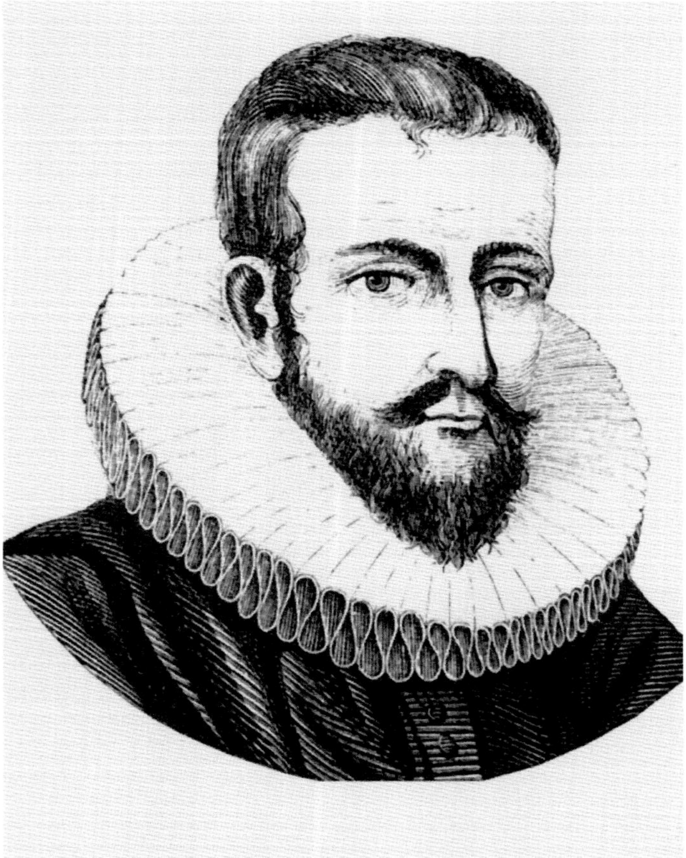

In September 1609, Henry Hudson, an English navigator sailing for the Dutch East India Company, sailed up the body of water that would come to bear his name. He was in search of an expedited trade route to the Far East, dubbed the Northwest Passage. On September 19, he reached the point beyond which he could sail no more, the mouth of the Mohawk River. It was then that Hudson became convinced that the shallow body of water was not the Northwest Passage. From that time on, Hudson would be forever tied to Cohoes. The below image shows Hudson sailing into New York Harbor. (Courtesy of the Library of Congress.)

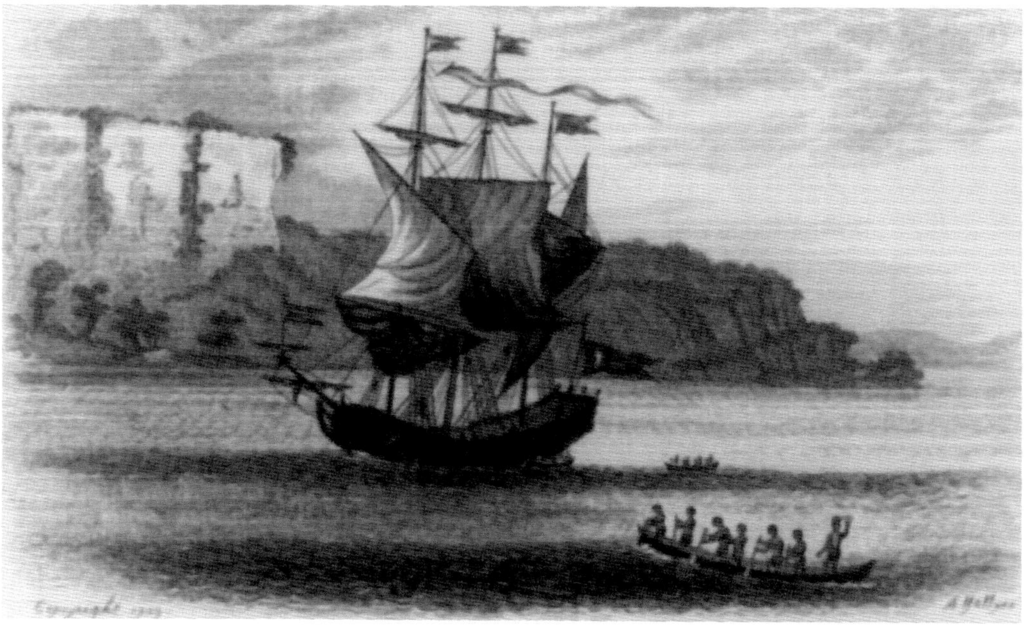

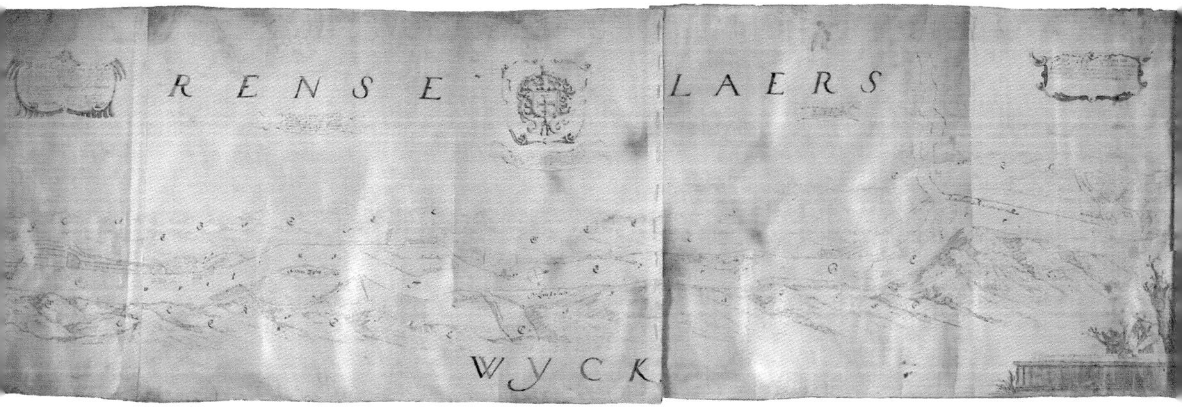

Born in 1586, Kiliaen Van Rensselaer was a Dutch merchant and one of the founders of the Dutch West India Company. Often referred to as the "Good Patroon," Van Rensselaer was the first European landholder in the Cohoes area, then called Rensselaerswyck. In fact, Van Rensselaer owned much of the greater Capital District after he purchased the area from the Mohicans in 1630. Van Rensselaer died in 1643 but the family retained control of the area as the title of patroon was passed down the family line. By the 1660s, the Van Rensselaer family had begun to lease land to newly arriving Dutch settlers. However, they maintained control of most of the Cohoes area until the 1690s when more leases were extended. But the family held on to the area around the Cohoes Falls, having understood its great potential for water power. It is said that Rensselaerwyck was the only successful patroonship in New Netherland. Pictured is an original map of Rensselaerwyck created around 1632.

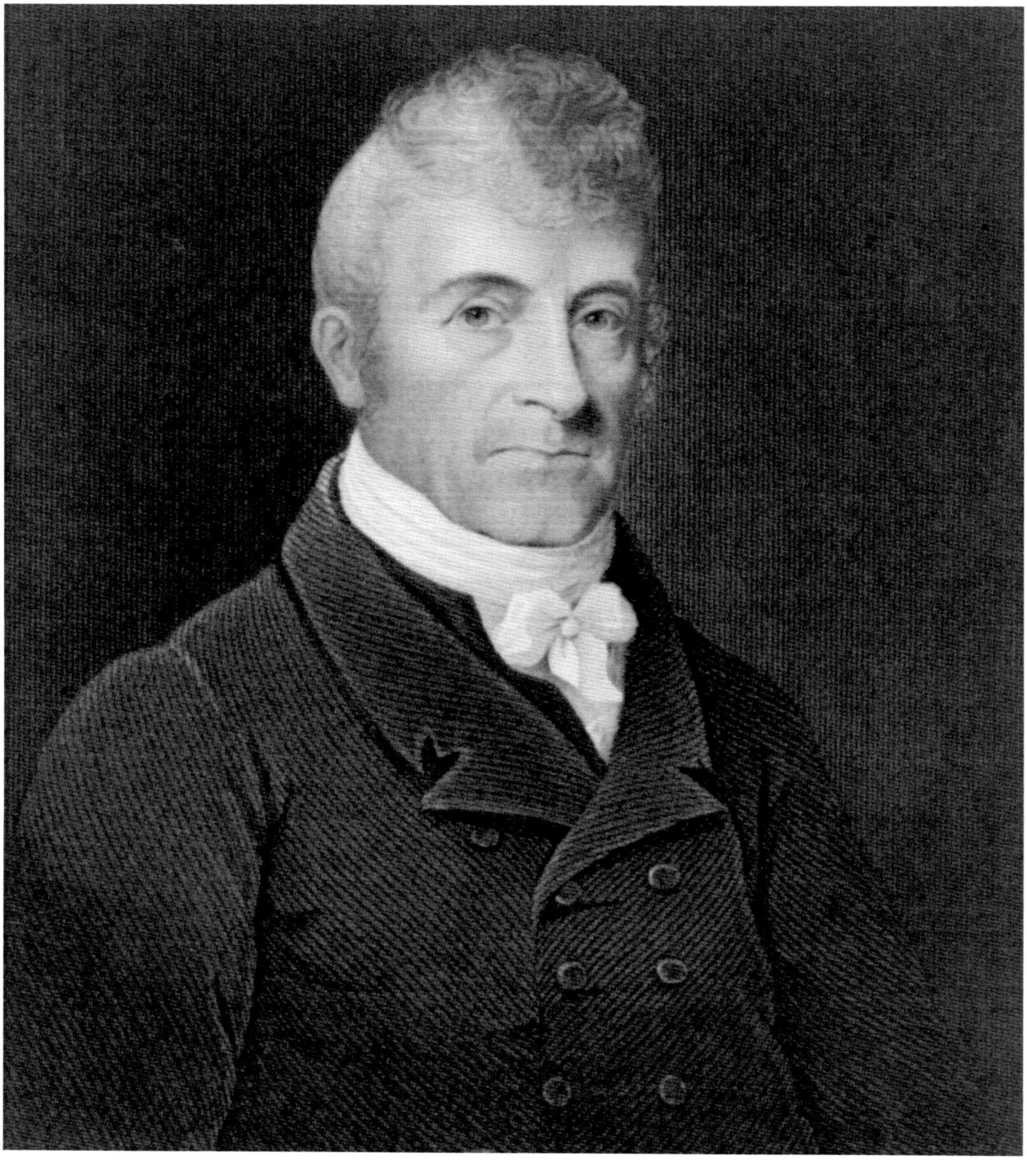

In 1785, marking the occasion of his 21st birthday, Stephen Van Rensselaer, a direct decedent of Kiliaen Van Rensselaer, was given control of his family's 1,200-square-mile estate, becoming the Ninth Patroon of Rensselaerswyck. Determined to profit from these vast land holdings, but not wanting to sell off the land, he granted perpetual leases and became landlord to some 3,000 tenants. Van Rensselaer was known as a fair and honest landlord who had the respect and admiration of his tenants. Through his landholdings, he would become one of the richest men in American history. In 1795, he was elected lieutenant governor of New York state. In 1824, he established the Rensselaer School, now known as Rensselaer Polytechnic Institute. And in 1826, he became one of the original incorporators of the Cohoes Company, which was established to harness the power of the Mohawk River for industrial use. (Courtesy of the Library of Congress.)

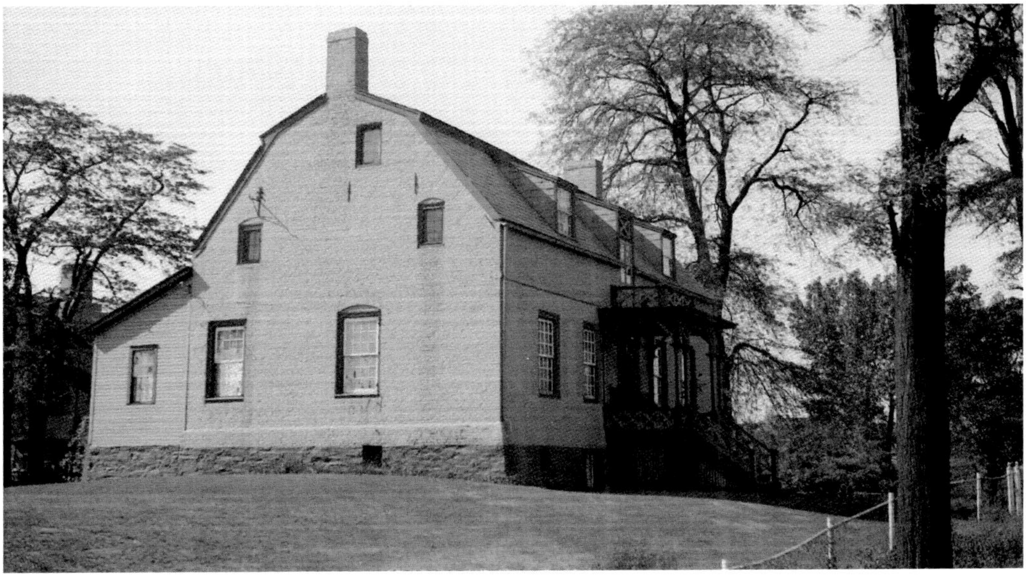

In 1664, Goosen Gerritsz Van Schaick, along with Philip Pietersen Schuyler, purchased the islands at the mouth of the Mohawk River from the Van Rensselaer family. A decade later, Schuyler deeded his portion of the land to Van Schaick, making him the sole landowner of the island that would ultimately bear his name. When he died two years later, Van Schaick willed the island to his second wife, who then conveyed it to her son, Anthony. The island then became known as Anthony's Island. Between 1735 and 1755, Van Schaick constructed a home (above) on the banks of the Hudson River that still stands today. During the American Revolution, the family not only financed the war effort, but gave over their home to serve as a military headquarters. The family retained a presence on the island well into the 19th century; to this day, it is their final resting place (below). (Above, courtesy of the Library of Congress.)

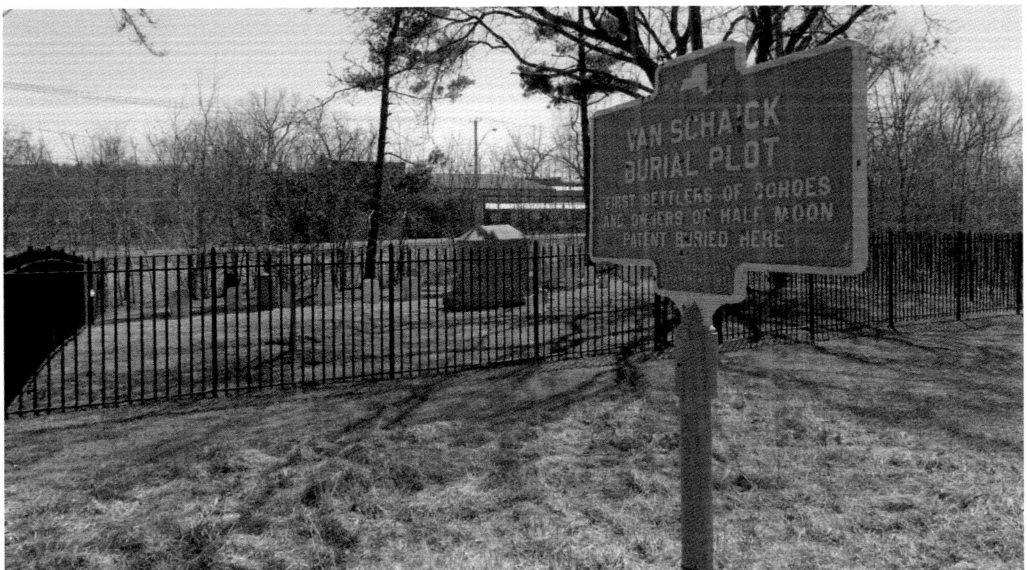

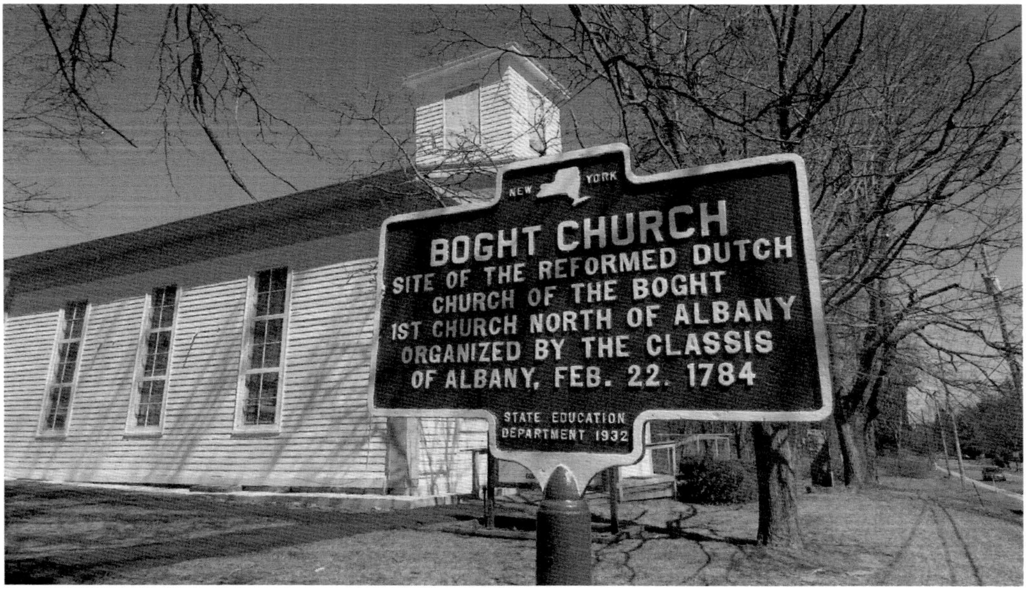

The Lansing family arrived in Cohoes in the early part of the 18th century. They would come to own large portions of land in the southern and northern portions of the city, with the first parcels being purchased in 1731. For the next 150 years, the family was very prominent in the civic and business affairs of the area. In 1784, the family helped establish the Reformed Church of the Boght (above), the first church erected north of Albany. The Lansings later became active in the Dutch Reformed Church of Cohoes, on Mohawk Street. In the early part of the 19th century, the family operated a sawmill and later a gristmill near the Cohoes Company dam. The family was also among those who incorporated the Cohoes Savings Institution in 1851. During the mid-1850s, the Lansings were instrumental in erecting the city's first waterworks.

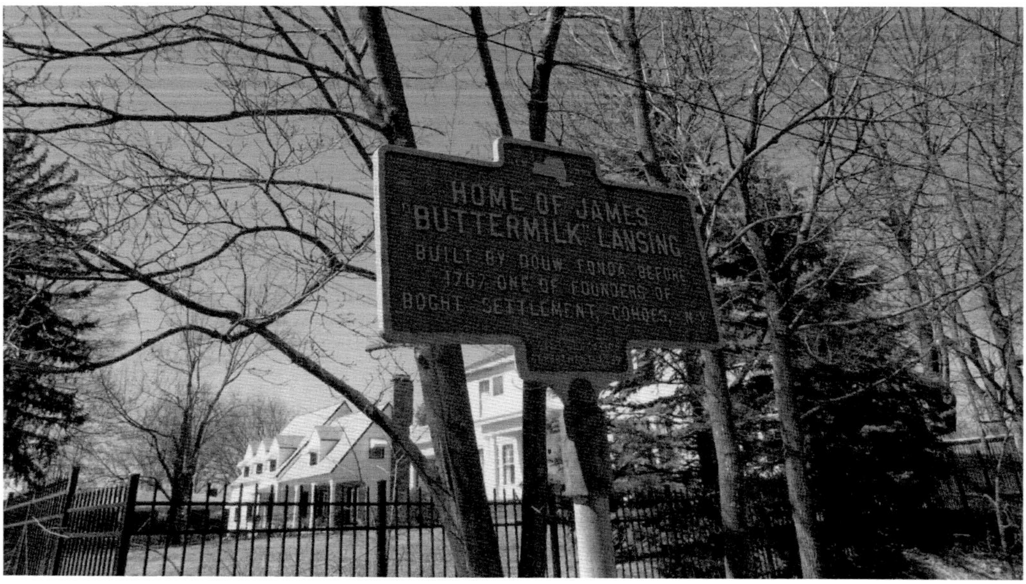

Industrialists

Before Silicon Valley gave rise to the Internet revolution, the Hudson Valley of New York state, and Cohoes in particular, gave birth to the Industrial Revolution in the United States. While fully under way in England, the Industrial Revolution would not begin in America until the early 19th century. Although men had foreseen the potential for industrial capacity in Cohoes as far back as the early 18th century, it would not be until the completion of the Erie Canal in 1825 that industrialists began to set their sights and their wallets on Cohoes. A small Dutch farming hamlet prior to the canal, Cohoes would become an important transportation hub. Cohoes was situated where the Erie and Champlain Canals formed a junction. But economic success in Cohoes was not a given. Establishing an industrial empire in Cohoes took an incredible amount of vision and courage, along with the backing of financial interests based in New York City, which, during the early 19th century, was becoming one of the biggest and most successful ports in the nation. In the decades that followed, many fortunes were made, and some others were lost. The spinning loom reigned supreme in Cohoes for decades and employed thousands. Cohoes had become a true company town, and the men who built their industrial empires in Cohoes possessed great civic commitment. They established hospitals and waterworks and erected public buildings. In addition, these industrialists were involved in the political and religious affairs of the area, organizing and constructing churches and running for political offices at the local, state, and national levels. It was a time when company and town were one and the same—the town was the company and the company was the town.

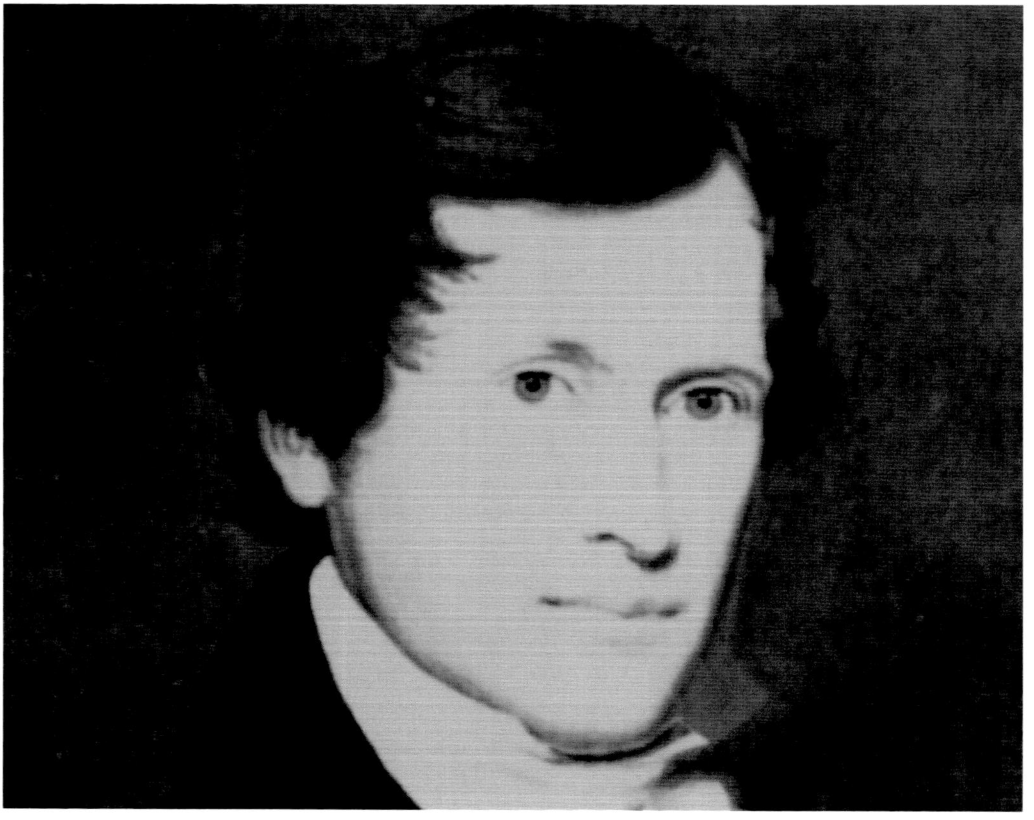

Canvass White was born in Whitestown, New York, on September 8, 1790. Unlike many young men of the era, he was able to complete school. Upon graduation, he enlisted in the Army as a second lieutenant and fought the British during the War of 1812. Wounded, he returned to New York to resume his studies in engineering. In 1816, he joined the Army Corps of Engineers for the Erie Canal, which, at the time, was the largest public works project ever attempted in the United States. One year later, he convinced canal commissioners to send him to England, where industrialization had been under way for several decades. White returned with a trove of documents and drawings. His documentation of the English canals provided canal commissioners with a blueprint for a way forward in New York. But what perplexed engineers most of all was how to construct the locks. What they lacked was cement that would be suitable for lock construction. White developed what was called hydraulic cement and received a patent in 1820. When he arrived in Cohoes to begin work on the section of canal that needed to rise above the Cohoes Falls, he marveled at not only the incredible natural beauty of the area, but also the immense potential for waterpower. The English had used water to power their industrialization, and White knew the same could be done in America. When the Erie Canal was completed in 1825, White devoted all his attention to that very concept. In 1826, with the financial backing of De Witt Clinton, Stephen Van Rensselaer, and Peter Remsen, the Cohoes Company was officially incorporated. According to its charter, the company was to "have full right, power and authority to cut, construct, and make a canal or canals from said river, to supply water for the purposes of said corporation." This system of waterpower would bring Cohoes into the industrial age in a big way. In 1830, White turned over daily operations of the company to his brother Hugh. And in 1834, due to failing health, he moved to Florida, where he soon died. He was just 44 years old. Henry Clay once said of Canvass White, "no man more competent, no man more capable. And while your faith in his ability and fidelity increases, your friendship will grow into affection."

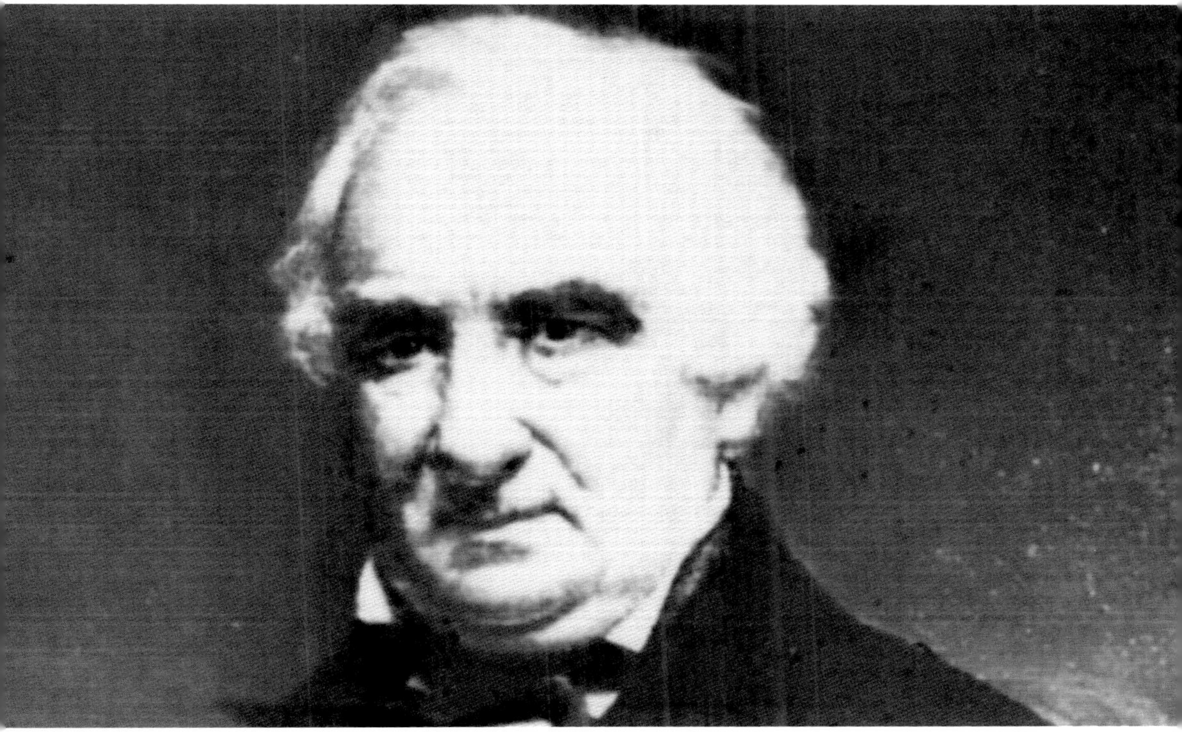

In 1831, an Albany merchant named Egbert Egberts had an idea. He wanted to improve the processes of making knit goods, which, at the time, were only made by hand. He also thought that the power of water could be used to operate the machinery. In 1832, Egberts partnered with a young machinist from Ballston Spa named Timothy Bailey. The two immediately began experimenting with various methods of production. A hand-crank machine was quickly developed that greatly improved output. But Egberts was certain that an even greater method of production could be had. Shortly thereafter, Bailey invented a power-knitting loom run by waterpower. Also in 1832, the Ontario Knitting Mill was established in Cohoes, on Ontario Street, employing some 250 people. Previously, knitting a pair of drawers took an entire day. With the new technology, 20 pairs could be produced in the same amount of time. Large fortunes began to develop for both men, and Egberts would soon turn his attention to the civic life of the city. In the 1850s, he assisted in the creation of the Cohoes Savings Institution, the Cohoes Gas Light Company, and the Cohoes Water Works Company. In 1863, Egberts Institution, a public high school, was incorporated, with the land and building donated by Egberts. In 1866, the board of education leased the building, which became known as Egberts High School. Egberts also purchased land and constructed the Dutch Reformed Church on Mohawk Street at a cost of $30,000. He died in 1869, leaving behind a lasting legacy of industrial vision and civic commitment.

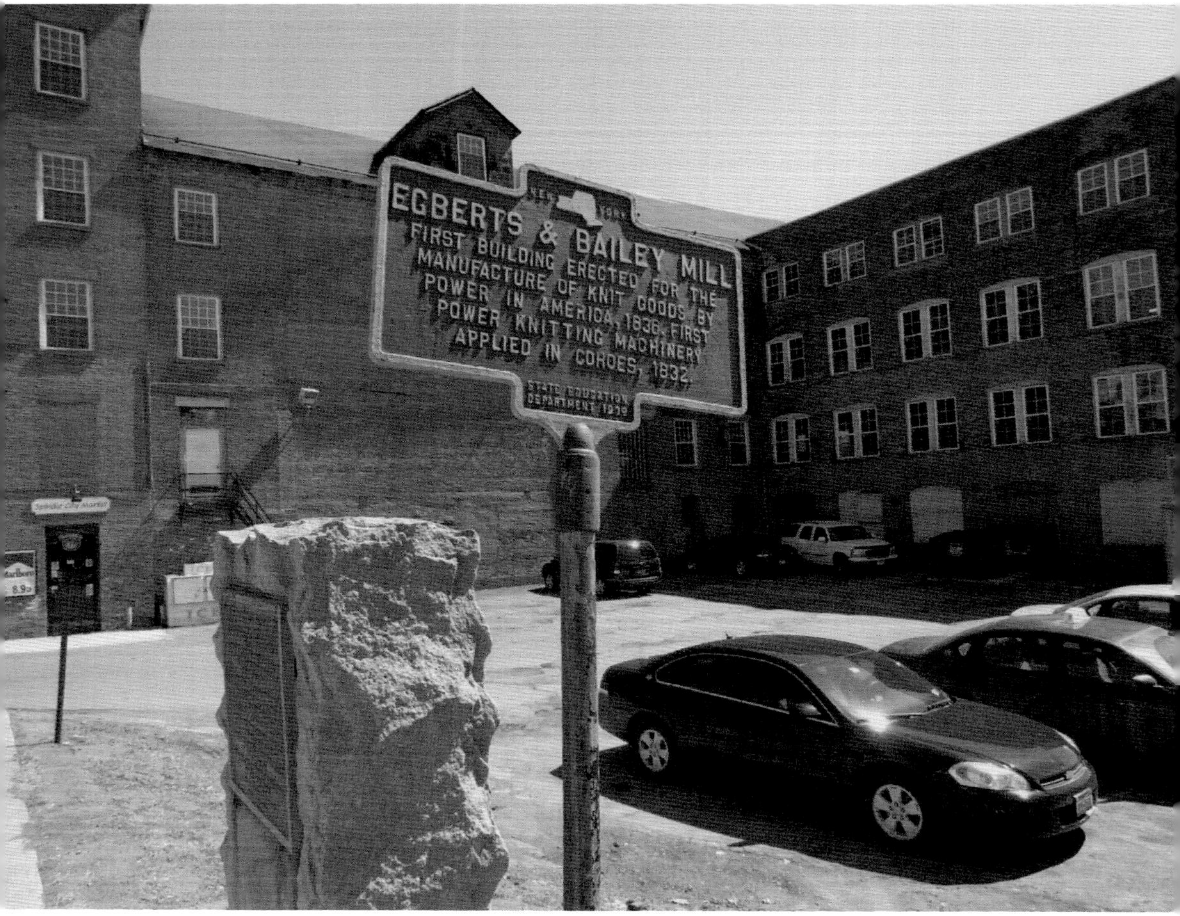

Timothy Bailey had shown himself to be a highly capable machinist from an early age, even before Egbert Egberts approached him in Albany about improving knitting machinery. With the financial backing of Egberts, Bailey was able to fully develop his talents, soon creating the industry's first power-knitting loom. In 1832, Egberts, Bailey, and his younger brother Joshua moved their operation from Albany to Cohoes. At the time, the Cohoes mill was the only facility in the world where shirt and drawer knitting was done by machinery. Bailey, who retired from the company before profits were fully realized, left with just $20,000. Pictured here is the site of the former Egbert and Bailey Mill on Ontario Street.

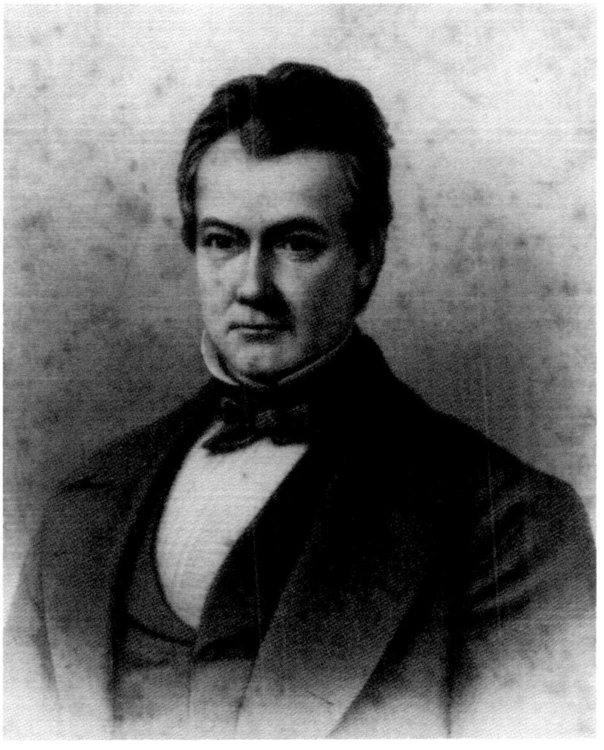

Hugh White (left) was the younger brother of Canvass White. Hugh pursued the law, graduating from Hamilton College in 1823. But he soon devoted his attentions to his brother and worked in his mill, which manufactured waterproof cement. Upon his brother's untimely death in 1834, Hugh took over as president of the Cohoes Company. In 1836, he became one of the founding members of the Harmony Manufacturing Company. By the mid-1840s, White had entered the world of politics, becoming a US congressman. When he left Congress in 1851, he ventured back into the world of business, where, in 1863, he helped organize the Waterford & Cohoes Railroad. White's home in Waterford (below), still standing, is the home of the Waterford Historical Museum. (Left, courtesy of the Hamilton College Library.)

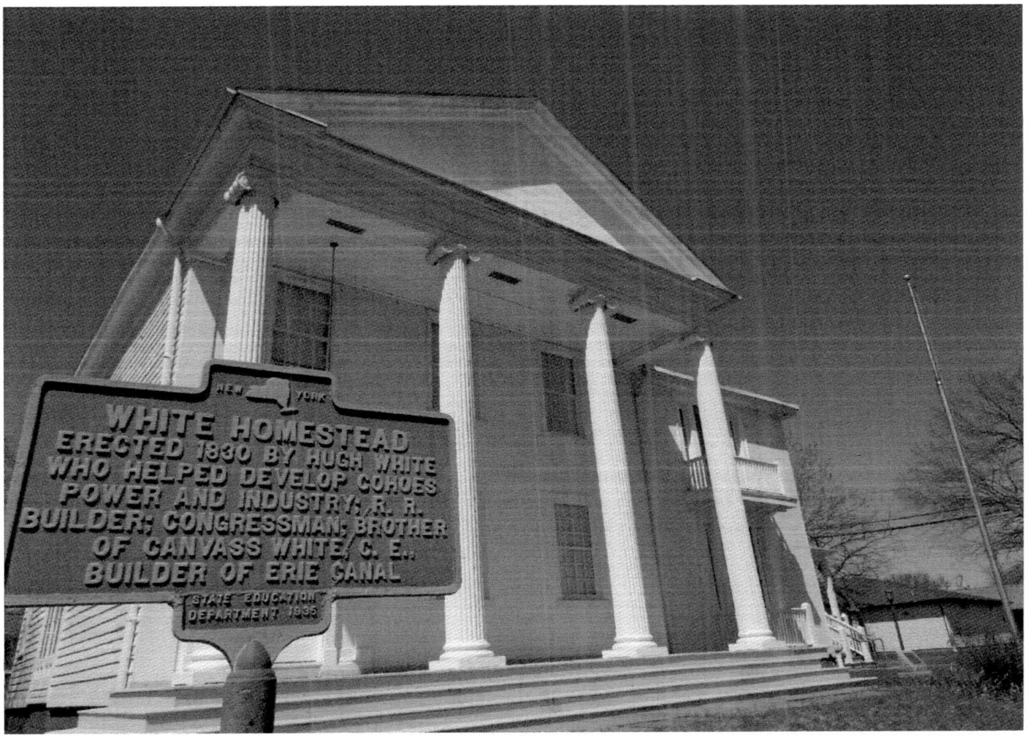

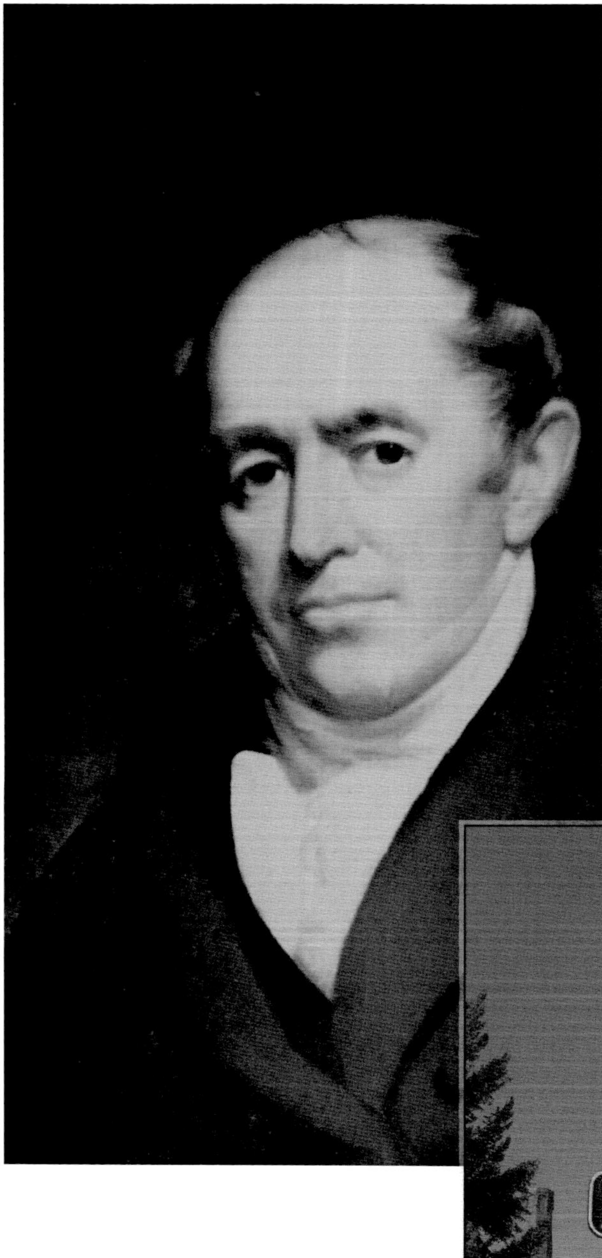

Peter Remsen was born in 1771 on his family's farm in Queens. He became a successful merchant in New York City and served as president of the Merchant's Bank of New York. Remsen then developed many business interests in Cohoes. He was one of the original trustees of the Cohoes Company, the company most responsible for developing waterpower for industrial use in the area. He was also one of the original directors of the Harmony Manufacturing Company. His gravestone is inscribed: "Beneath this monument are deposited the mortal remains of Peter Remsen, who for upwards of 40 years was an eminent merchant in the city of New York and attained a standing for intelligence, decision of character and integrity which few have surpassed."

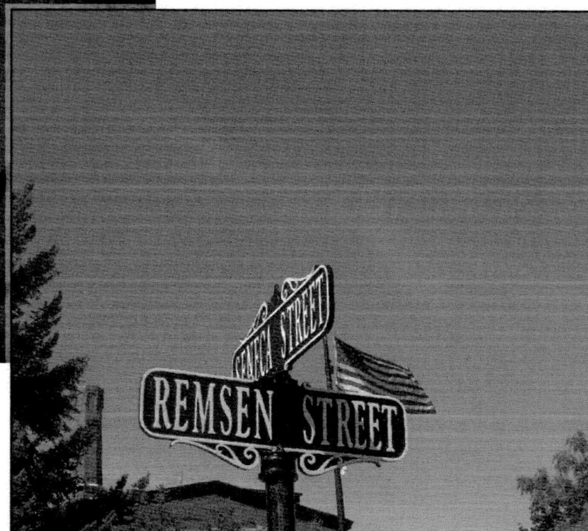

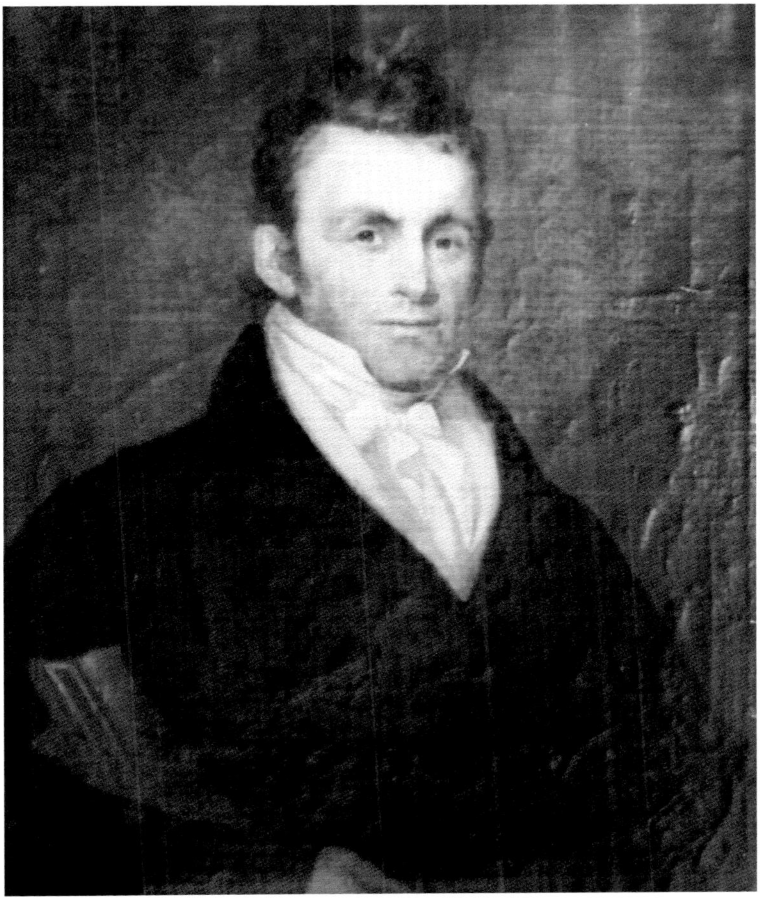

One of the great pioneers of the American textile industry, David Wilkinson began his career in machine tools at the age of six. By age 13, he was working in a rolling mill in Pawtucket, Rhode Island. He became a protégé of Samuel Slater, the father of the textile industry in America, providing machinery for Slater's Mill in Pawtucket. In 1810, Wilkinson and Slater constructed a mill in Pawtucket for the purposes of constructing textile machinery. By 1812, the two men were producing machinery for dozens of mills throughout the Northeast. They would remain successful until a severe financial panic in 1829 left Wilkinson with nothing. Slater sold his properties to pay off debt, but Wilkinson, who was 58 years old, was not quite ready to retire.

The following year, he settled in Cohoes, which at the time was a small canal village. Wilkinson set up shop at the foot of Mohawk Street, where he could obtain waterpower from the Erie Canal via a small ditch. In 1832, he constructed the Cohoes Iron Foundry at the corner of Oneida and Mohawk Streets. It was here that he invented the vertical lathe, a device for cutting screw threads. The lathe would prove extremely valuable in the machine tool industry. However, it was not until 1848 that Wilkinson was awarded $10,000 by Congress for his invention. Like many Cohoes industrialists, Wilkinson was devoted to the social and religious affairs of the community. Shortly after his arrival in town, he worked to establish an Episcopal church and helped organize St. John's, on Mohawk Street. Wilkinson was a paternalistic mill owner, believing that his employees should be well fed, clothed, and educated. While none of his Cohoes buildings remain, the Wilkinson Mill in Pawtucket still stands and has recently undergone a complete renovation. (Courtesy of the Slater Mill Historic Site.)

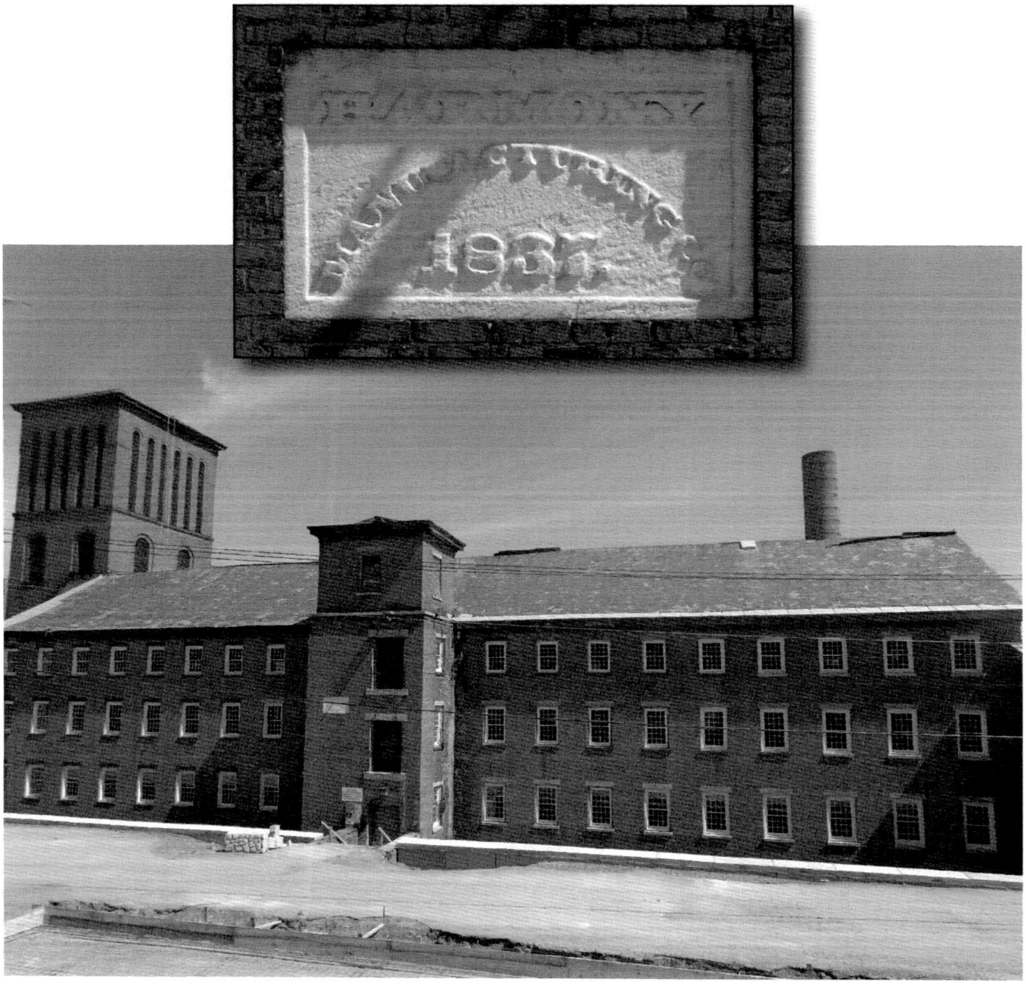

Born in Cadiz, Spain, in 1776, Peter Harmony came to the United States, arriving in Philadelphia in 1801. He made his way to New York City in 1805, where he is listed as a "mariner." While in New York, Harmony was engaged in the slave trade, common for someone in the shipping industry during the early part of the 19th century. In 1836, he founded the Harmony Manufacturing Company with an initial investment of $100,000 and constructed its first mill the following year. The mill employed 250 workers, mostly of English and Irish descent. However, the company was ultimately a failure, as it only recorded one profit-earning year. In 1850, it was sold at auction to Thomas Garner and Nathan Wild. Just one year later, Harmony died in New York City. Pictured is the mill constructed by Peter Harmony in 1837. It is currently under renovation and will contain loft-style apartments.

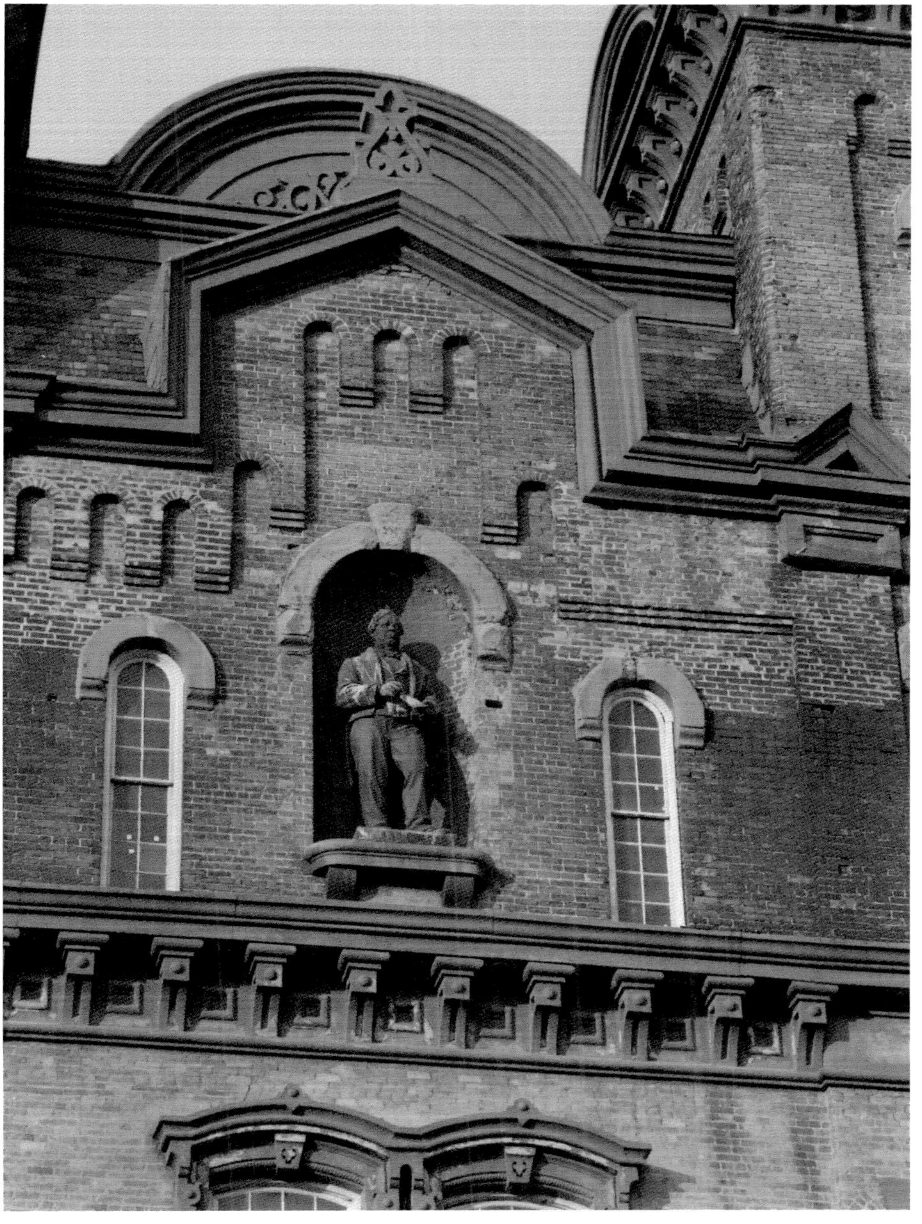

In 1850, Thomas Garner, a New York City merchant, purchased the beleaguered Harmony Manufacturing Company at a sheriff's auction. Garner quickly began to invest in and expand the mills, bringing in new equipment, building additional factories, and hiring the premier cotton spinner of the day, Robert Johnston. He remained president and principal stockholder until his death in 1867, at which time his son, William, assumed control of his father's holdings. Under Thomas Garner and his partner, Nathan Wild, the Harmony Mills became one of the largest textile manufacturing companies in the United States. Garner is immortalized by a life-sized bronze statue, by Martin Milmore of Boston, in the niche of the central tower of Harmony Mill No. 3. (Courtesy of the Library of Congress.)

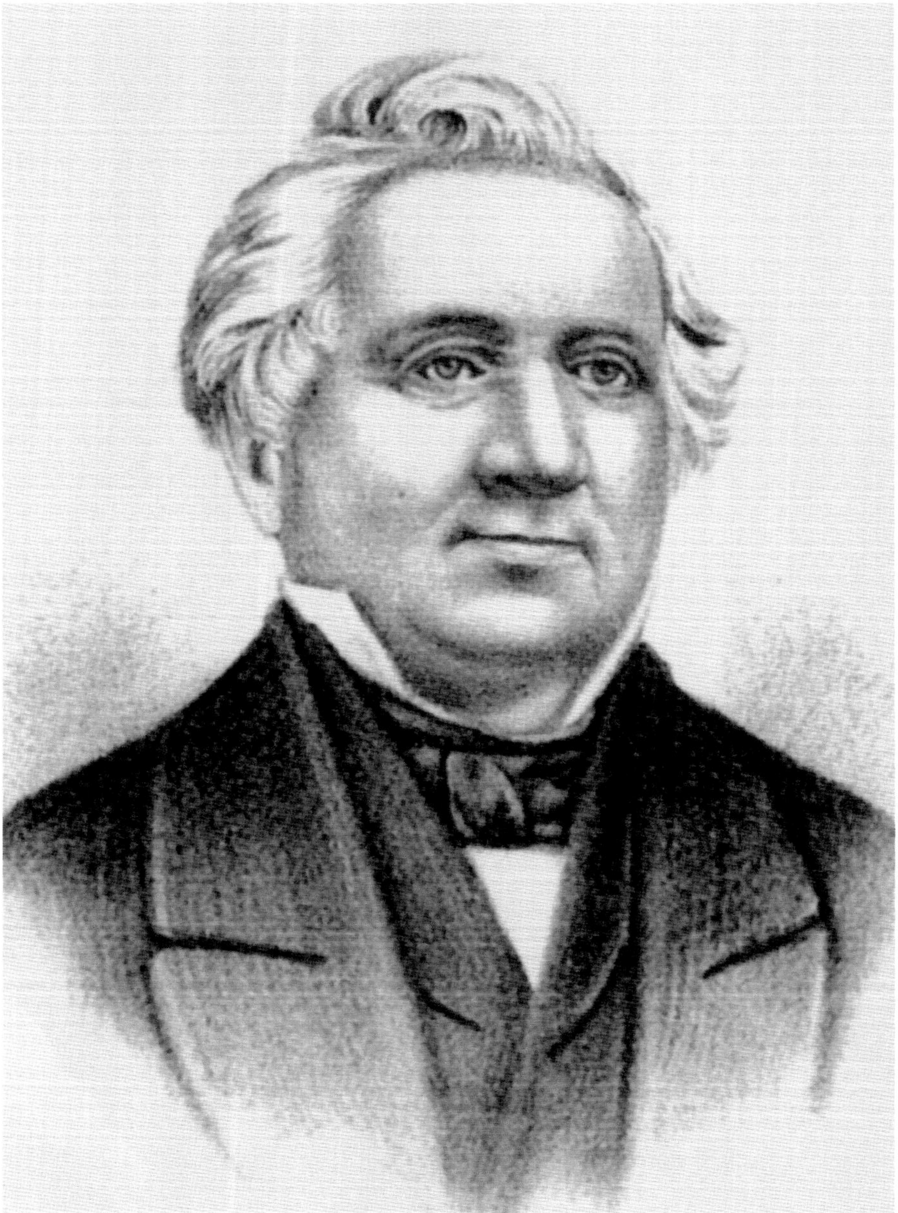

Nathan Wild immigrated to the United States from Manchester, England, in 1800. He settled in Rhode Island and worked under Samuel Slater. In the 1820s, Wild would make his way to Columbia County, where he established the Wild Mill Complex in Valatie, which employed some 175 people. In 1850, he teamed with Thomas Garner of New York City and purchased the beleaguered Harmony Manufacturing Company in Cohoes. Under the ownership of Garner and Wild, the Harmony Company saw its biggest success and was transformed into the largest textile manufacturing company in the nation. Wild continued in the textile industry until 1858. He died in 1867 at the age of 77.

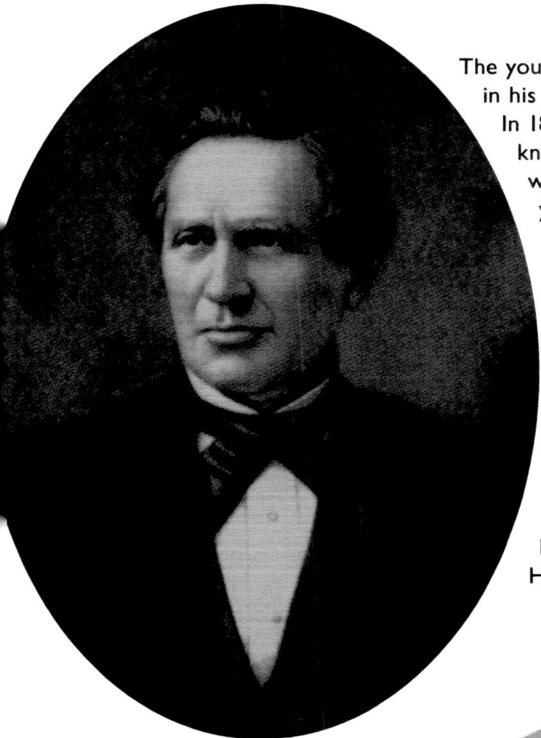

The younger brother of Timothy Bailey, Joshua would follow in his brother's footsteps and go into the textile industry. In 1832, he joined his brother and Egbert Egberts in their knitting-mill operation in Cohoes. But while the older Bailey would retire early before profits were fully realized, the younger Bailey continued in the business with Egberts until the firm was dissolved in 1850, leaving both men considerably wealthy. Like Timothy, Joshua put his inventive skills to good use. In 1845, he drew up a system of using steam to heat buildings. His design worked beautifully and was the model for steam heating systems in the United States. In 1852, Bailey constructed the Mohawk Knitting Mill at 122 Remsen Street, which at the time was the largest knitting mill in the nation. In 1860, Bailey sold the mill to A.E. Stimson. He then retired to Waterford, where he died in 1875. Pictured below is the former Mohawk Knitting Mill on Remsen Street. (Left, courtesy of the Saratoga County Historical Association.)

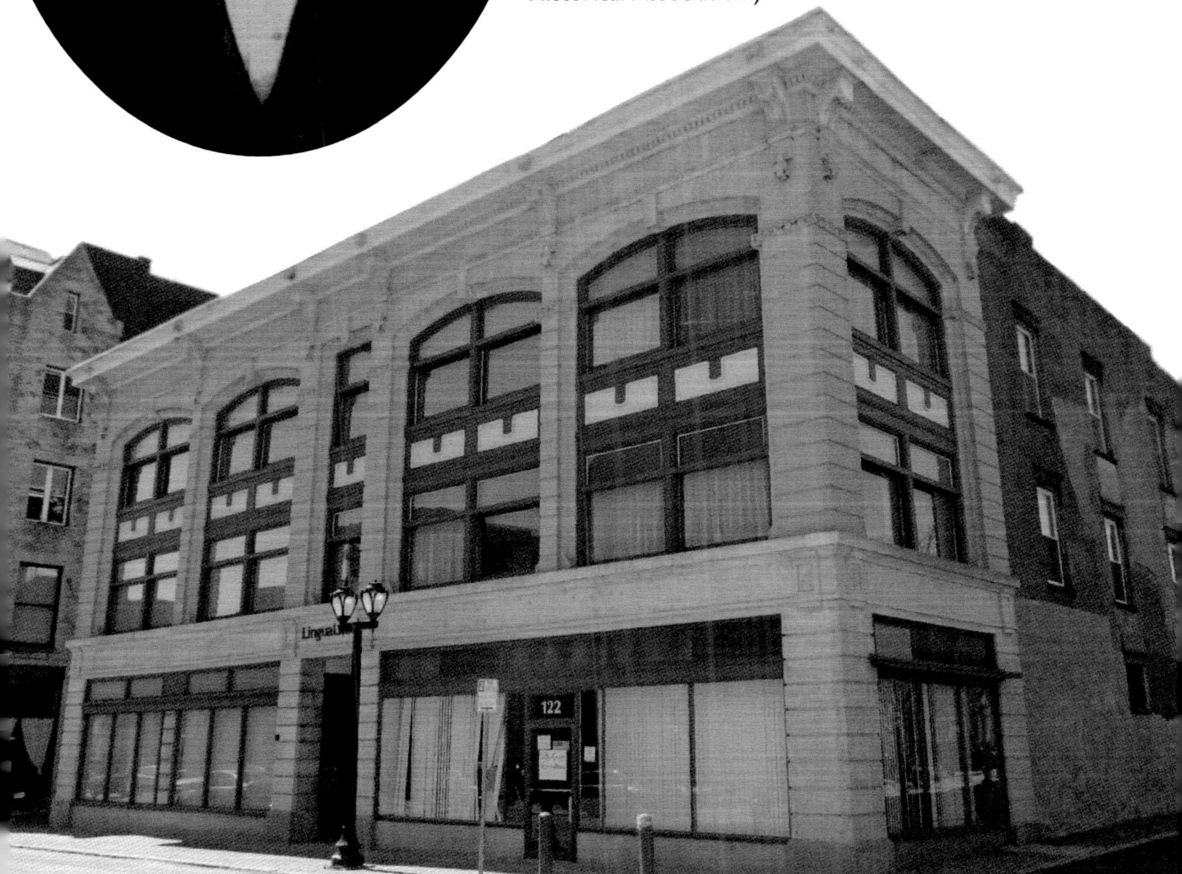

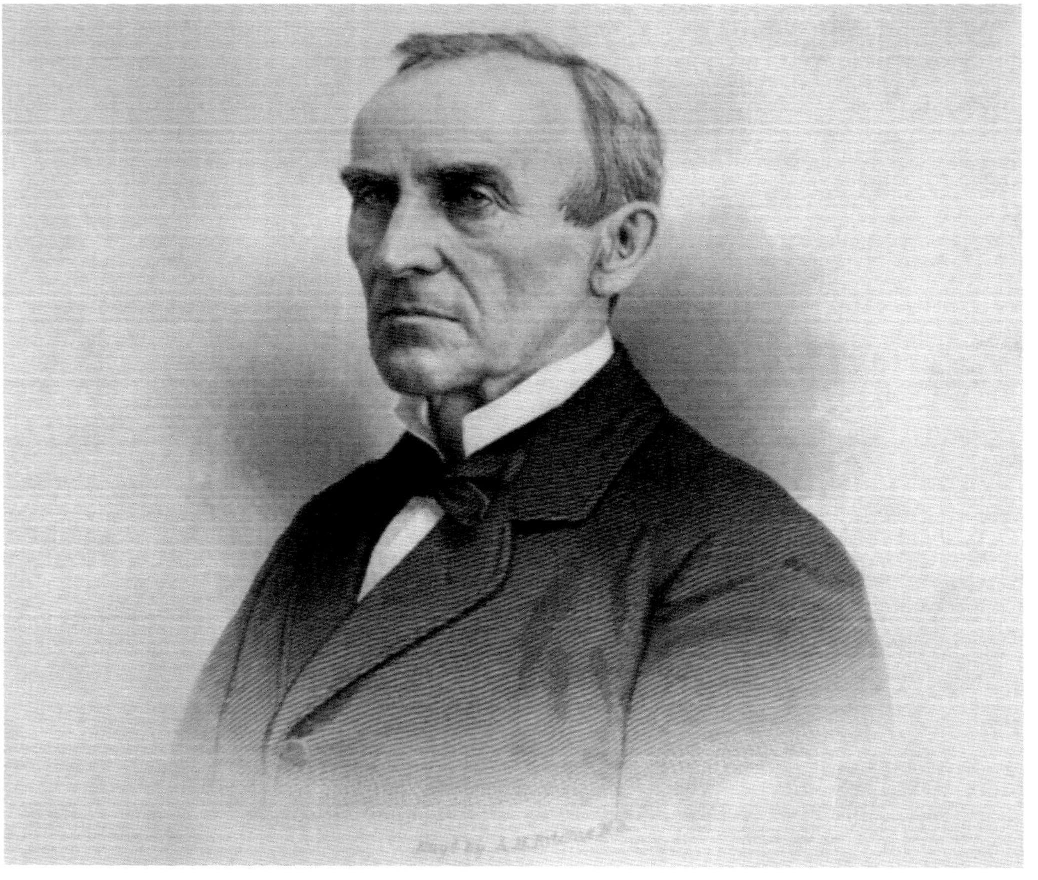

During the middle to latter part of the 19th century, the Harmony Mills saw its greatest economic success. This was due in no small part to the leadership of one family and, more specifically, that family's patriarch, Robert Johnston. Born in Carlisle, England, in 1807, Johnston got his start in the textile industry at the age of seven, working in the mills of Dalston-Carlisle. When he came to America in 1830, he was already an expert in what was the most advanced textile machinery of the period, the spinning mule. Johnston went to work in Providence, Rhode Island, at the Providence Steam Mills, where he observed Samuel Slater, the preeminent spinner of the time. In 1834, Johnston moved to Valatie and was employed by Nathan Wild, managing his cotton mill. Realizing the potential of the fledgling Harmony Mills, Johnston convinced Wild and his partner, Thomas Garner, to purchase the operation at auction in 1850. Soon after the purchase, Garner and Wild appointed Johnston to be the superintendent, overseeing the daily operations. Johnston began expanding the facilities almost immediately. In 1853, an addition to mill No. 1 was built, and in 1856, mill No. 2 was constructed. Workers' tenements were built along Cataract Street, and land was purchased on what would become Harmony Hill for hundreds of additional tenements. Johnston continued expanding the operations during the Civil War, with the construction of the massive mill No. 3, or mastodon mill. Also during this time, he made many trips to England, bringing back additional workers and the latest in textile machinery. While tensions existed between management and labor during Johnston's leadership, he was beloved by many of the workers. The *Cohoes Cataract* of 1871 described Johnston as a "patriarch, prudent in council, active in philanthropy and devoted to the public good." At his death in 1890, Johnston left behind one of the largest textile manufacturing operations in the world, with a book value of $22 million. (Courtesy of the Spindle City Historic Society.)

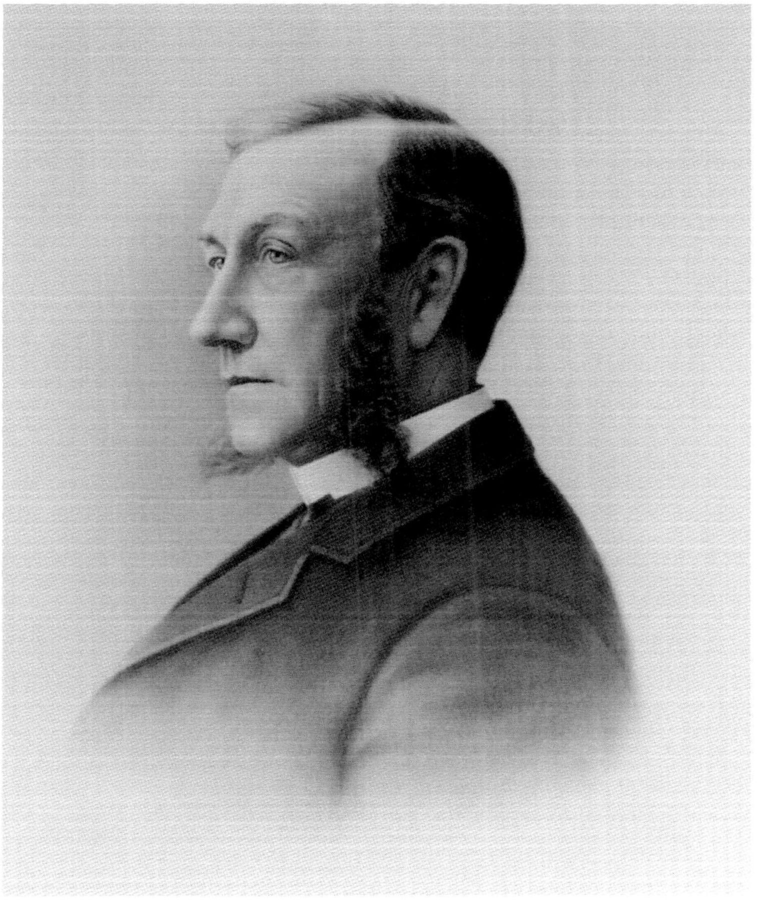

The son of Robert Johnston, David Johnston began working for the Harmony Company at the age of 16 as an office clerk. In 1866, he was named superintendent and quickly began to expand mill operations, just as his father had done a decade prior. Johnston oversaw the design and construction of mill No. 3, the largest textile mill in the United States. The building contained some 130,000 spindles and 2,700 looms. Like his father, David formed personal relationships with many of the mill workers. He would often start his day walking with his employees down Harmony Hill. A very religious man, Johnston believed it a moral duty to provide more than just a wage for his employees, especially the many children who toiled in the mills. He would serve as general superintendent of the Harmony Mill Union Sabbath School, which operated out of the company's offices at the corner of Vliet and North Mohawk Streets. He was remembered by a worker in the 1890s as "a very kind man, loved by all the mill hands, as his father was before him." But, while David was always willing to hear the plight of the mill worker, he was very much aware of his duty to the owners. Johnston would fight numerous battles with labor unions during his time as superintendent. But Johnston did not confine himself to the office. He would involve himself in the political and banking affairs of the city as well, serving as an alderman, president of the National Bank of Cohoes, trustee of the Cohoes Savings Bank, president of the Cohoes Gas Light Company, and as the city's mayor from 1872 to 1874 and from 1876 to 1878. Johnston died while on vacation in Quebec in 1894. The *Cohoes Cataract* said in 1871, "he stands foremost in regard of our citizens. As a civic administrator, a merchant and a philanthropist, he is second to none." (Courtesy of the Spindle City Historic Society.)

A native of Guilderland, New York, David Van Auken resided in Cohoes for some 35 years. He was the chief engineer of the Harmony Company and the engineer and secretary for the Cohoes Company. He was also director of the United Traction Company and a director of the Manufactures Bank of Cohoes. Van Auken designed the Cohoes Company gatehouse (below), which was constructed in 1866. But perhaps his greatest work was the design of Harmony Mill No. 3, a massive Victorian-style building with elaborate Second Empire features. When it was completed, mill No. 3 contained 130,000 spindles and had the capacity to produce 100,000 yards of cloth every 60 hours. According to Cohoes historian William Bean, the mill "was the largest cotton mill in the country and probably in the world." (Courtesy of the Library of Congress.)

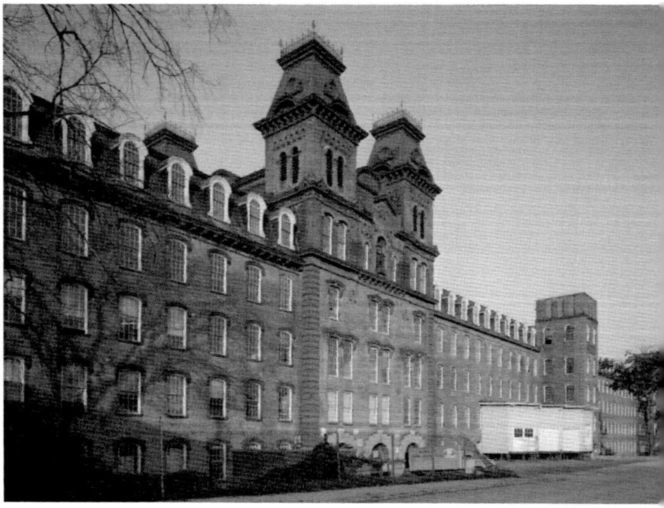

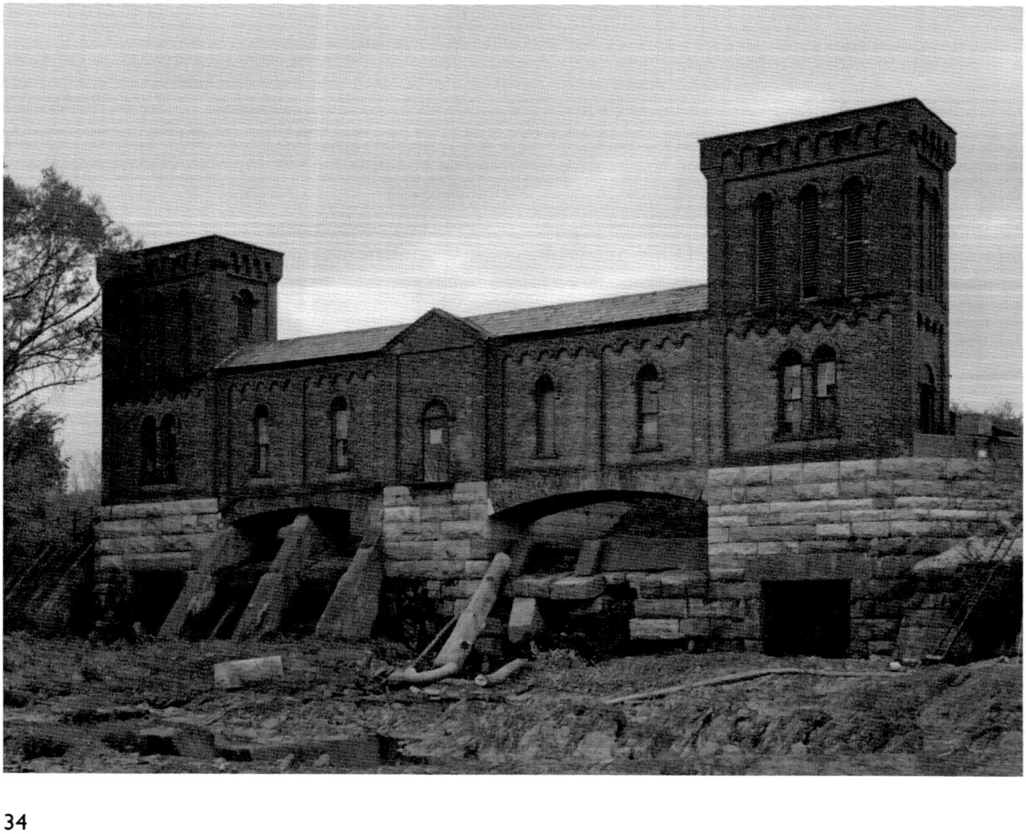

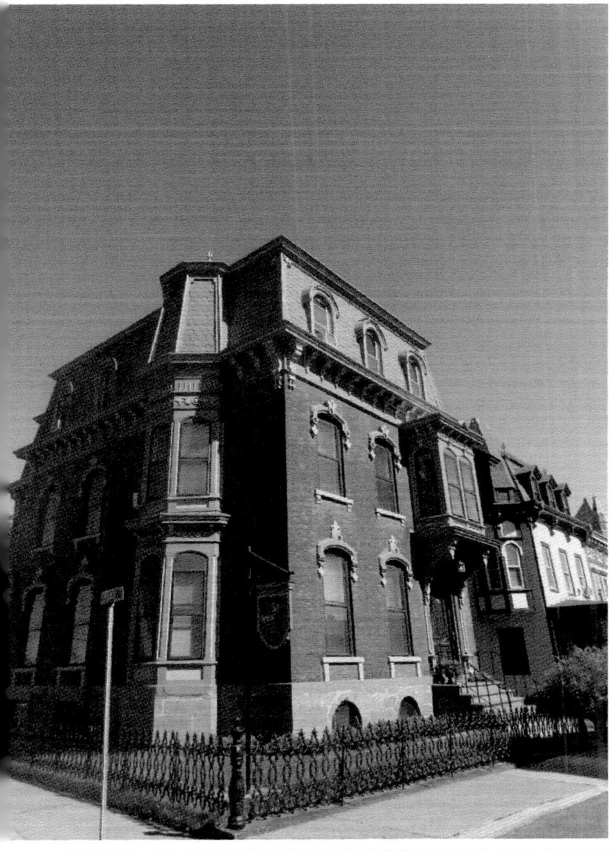

Moore was a millionaire who made his fortune in the textile industry in Cohoes during the latter part of the 19th century. He was president of the Erie Knitting Mill and a partner in the William Moore Knitting Company and the Moore & Tierney Company. He was also a founder and president of the Manufactures Bank of Cohoes. In 1874, Moore had a home constructed at 115 Mohawk Street. The beautiful Second Empire Victorian house, seen here, was sold to the Cohoes YWCA in 1892. The building is now the home of Spiral Design Studio.

Over the last half century, as manufacturing in Cohoes slowly declined, Mohawk stood strong and grew to become an industry leader. The story of Mohawk and of the O'Connor family is one of dedication and risk-taking. The members of the current management team are, from left to right, Edward G. O'Connor, John B. O'Connor, F. Joseph O'Connor, and chairman and CEO Thomas D. O'Connor Jr. (Courtesy of Mohawk.)

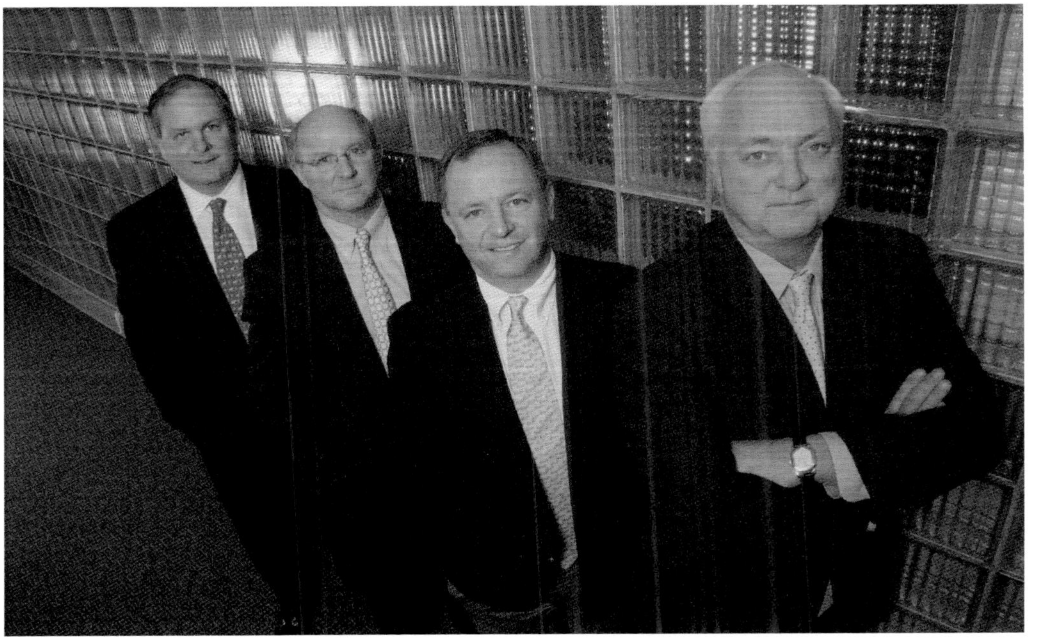

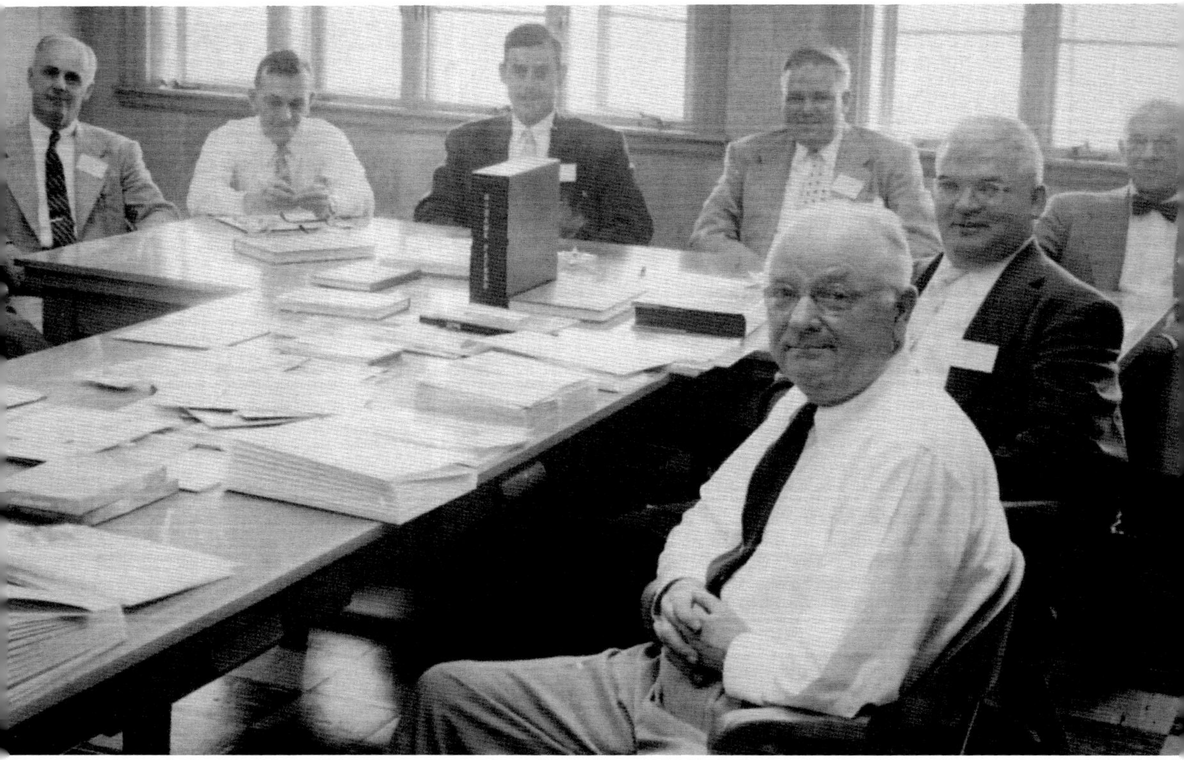

In 1931, a young attorney named George O'Connor inherited from his father, Thomas, the investment of debt in the Frank Gilbert Paper Company. Having never set foot in a mill in his life, O'Connor relied on good instincts and sound judgment. Upon assuming control of the company, he began to diversify its operations. The concept of diversification, along with perseverance, has come to define Mohawk to this day. Throughout the Depression and the war years, O'Connor was able to not only maintain operations but create innovate products. A fiber shortage during the war led to the production of a premium paper called superfine, which is still manufactured today. George O'Connor also set a precedent when it came to his employees. For O'Connor, they were not simply employees, but an extended family, a concept that is also very much alive today. O'Connor led the company until his beloved wife, Annabel, died in 1968. Heartbroken, he decided to sell the firm to the Regal Paper Company for between $5 million and $6 million. However, in 1972, the company was bought back by the O'Connors, to be led by George's son Thomas. Tom O'Connor began to invest millions of dollars in new equipment. He also made it a point to stay far ahead of the relatively new environmental regulations that were just starting to come into place. O'Connor led the company into the digital printing era in the mid-1990s, once again diversifying the company's operations to stay ahead. In 2004, Thomas O'Connor Jr. became president upon the death of his father. The younger O'Connor never hesitated, understanding and embracing the notion that this was to be his life's work. He acquired International Fine Paper in 2005 and, in 2010, diversified operations yet again, investing heavily in a new photograph-sharing software called Pinhole Press. Like the risky investments made by his father and grandfather, it paid off. Mohawk is now an industry leader, with approximately $300 million in annual sales. Although George O'Connor has long since passed on, his presence is very much alive. His office, off the main lobby of the Cohoes mill, remains as it was when he walked out for the last time in 1969. It is a shrine of sorts to a man whose guiding principles remain alive and well. George O'Connor (foreground) is seen here with members of the Mohawk management team in the 1960s. (Courtesy of Mohawk.)

Politicians

Former Speaker of the House of Representatives Tip O'Neill once proclaimed that "all politics is local." Indeed, local government is often where democracy is at its most pure form. It is the level of government at which the people have the most access to their representatives. But the history of American politics and the history of Cohoes politics has not always been what our founders intended. Yes, there has been corruption and graft. But there has also been a tremendous commitment to public service and the public good. Throughout the 19th and early 20th centuries, Cohoes was governed by the Republican industrialists who ran the textile industry. This is not to say that the early political leaders of Cohoes took advantage of the populace. In fact, many of these individuals saw to it that public improvements in infrastructure, education, and the overall public welfare were made. But as the textile industry moved southward during the early part of the 20th century, the political control of the Republicans waned. In 1921, the Albany County Republican machine, led by William Barnes, was taken out by the O'Connell brothers in Albany. Cohoes saw the election of Daniel Cosgro, a young attorney and the first Democrat elected mayor. The Democrats, led by party boss Mike Smith, would reign in Cohoes until 1963, when a group of young reformers ousted the machine, then led by William Dawson. The Citizens Party held power until 1975, when the Democrats took back city hall with the election of Ron Canestrari. The city of Cohoes has remained under Democratic control ever since. This chapter highlights the more notable politicians who have left their mark over the decades.

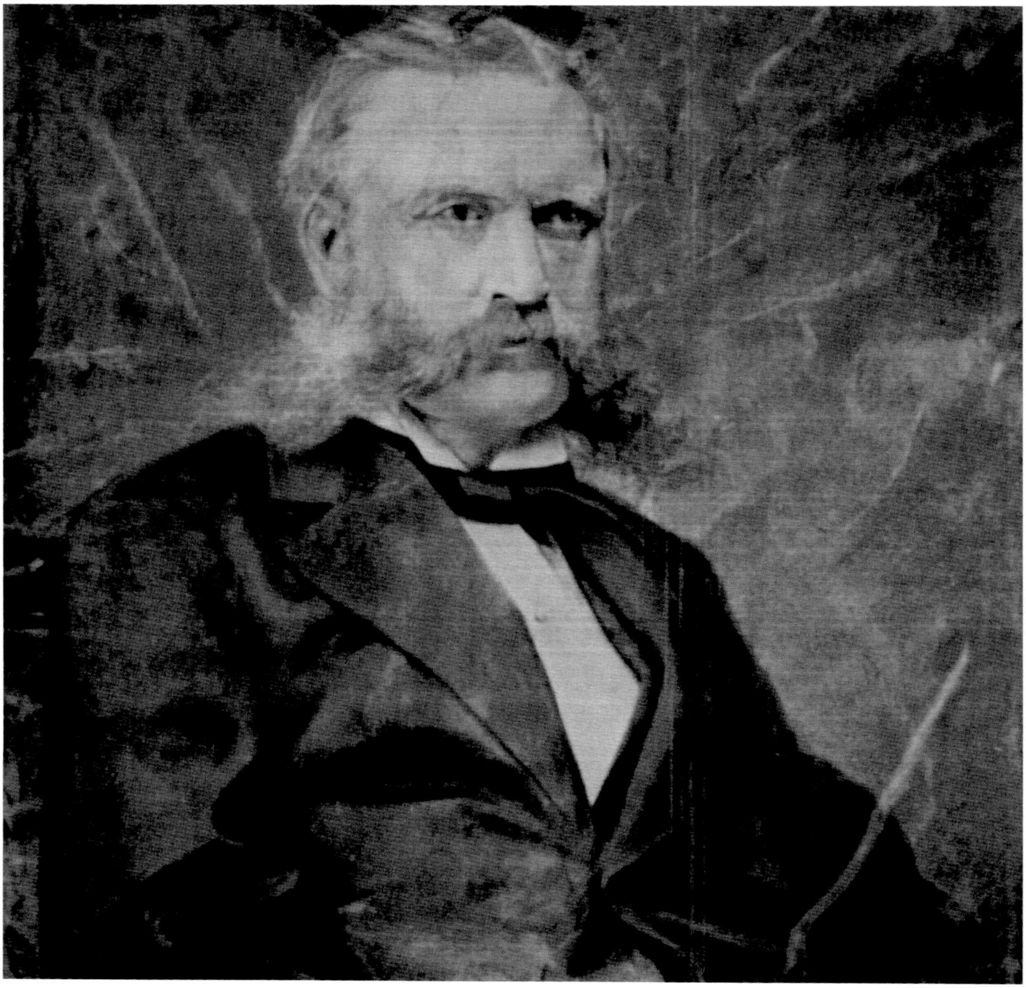

Born in 1824 in Coxsacki, New York, Charles Adams could boast of such ancestors as Samuel Adams, John Adams, and John Quincy Adams. His father, Dr. Henry Adams, fought in the War of 1812. Adams attended Albany Academy and, following his graduation, began to practice law. However, he soon developed an interest in the growing knitting industry in Cohoes, which had been started by his uncle, Egbert Egberts. In 1852, when Egberts dissolved his partnership with Timothy Bailey, he gave his nephew the newly constructed Watervliet Mill as a Christmas present. The mill adjoined the original Ontario Mill located on Ontario Street. Like his uncle, Adams devoted himself to the civic affairs of the community. In 1859, he assisted in establishing the National Bank of Cohoes. Adams was a director of the Waterford & Cohoes Railway, and in 1867, he donated a piece of fire apparatus to the community that became known as the Adams steamer. In 1869, he financed the construction of a block of buildings on Remsen Street known as the Adams Block, which remains today. That same year, Cohoes was incorporated as a city, and the first city elections were held the following year. Adams, the Republican candidate, defeated Democrat Charles Doyle by just 12 votes. Aside from his business and local interests, Adams was also involved in statewide politics. He served as an aide to Gov. Washington Hunt and was a state assemblyman and state senator. In 1876, Adams became a member of the US House of Representatives. He retired from business and politics in 1892 and moved to New York City, where he died in 1902.

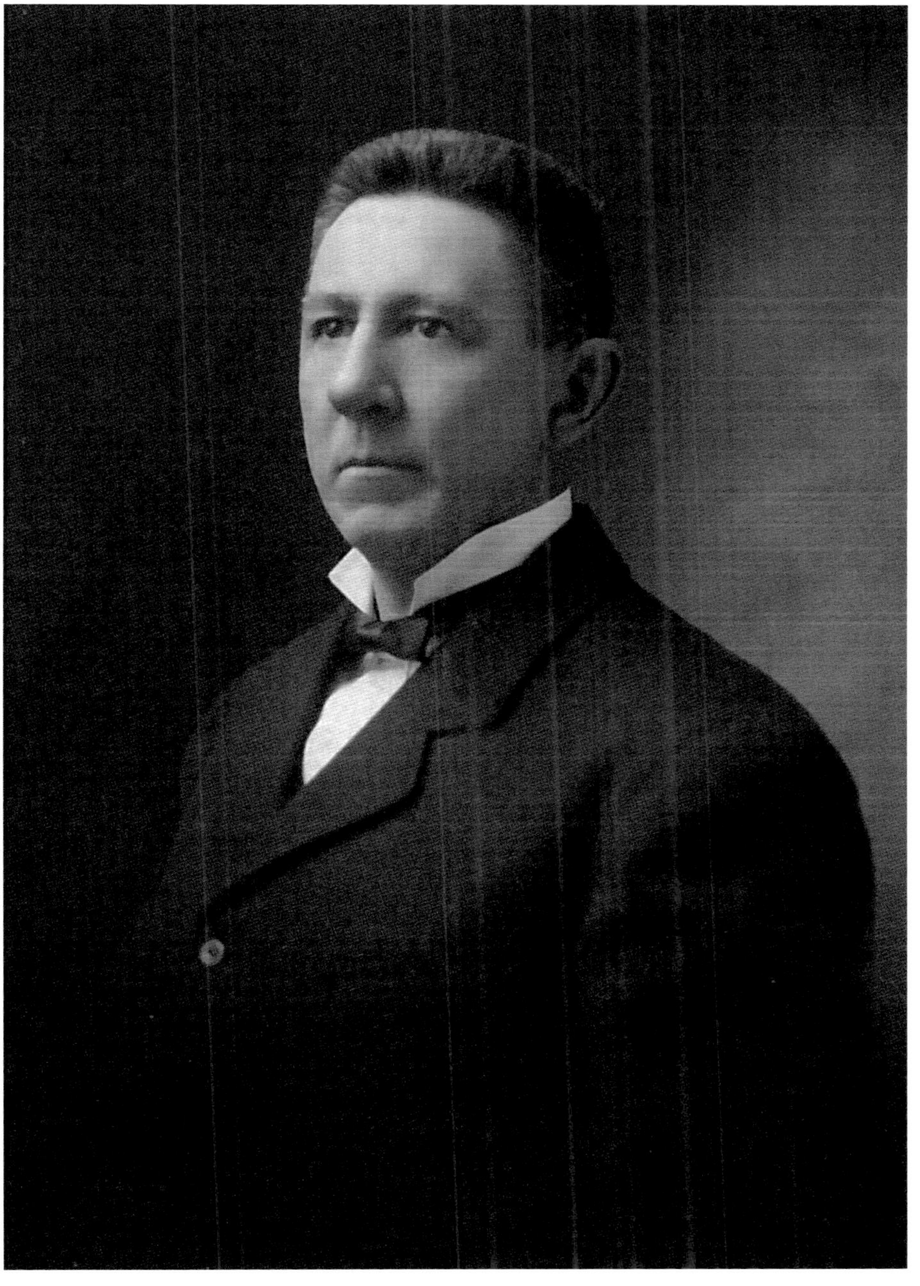

Born in 1862, George Conboy was the son of Irish immigrants who came to Cohoes in the middle part of the 19th century. The Conboys settled in an area off Manor Avenue, along the Erie Canal. Conboy opened a grocery store/tavern/inn on what is now Conboy Avenue. It became a popular stop for canal boats and served the needs of the neighborhood. Conboy became a community leader and served as alderman for the First Ward. He was also an advocate for hydroelectric power in the area and worked for Niagara Mohawk Power Company as a gatehouse operator. (Courtesy of Sue Baird.)

In 1921, Daniel P. O'Connell ousted the Republican machine in Albany County, which was led by William Barnes. Thus began the era of what was known as the Albany Democratic machine. In Cohoes, it was Cosgro who led the Democrats to victory over Republican mayor James H. McDonald. Born in 1866, Cosgro became an attorney and formed a partnership with Henry Strong. One of the most interesting stories during Cosgro's time in office is that of the replica of Henry Hudson's ship, *Half Moon* (below). In 1924, Cosgro got the state legislature to have the boat towed to Cohoes, citing the fact that Cohoes was the northernmost point that Hudson had traveled. The ship was destroyed by vandals eight years later. Many believe that the destruction was political payback for a falling-out between Cosgro and Democratic boss Mike Smith. Cosgro died in 1946 at the age of 80.

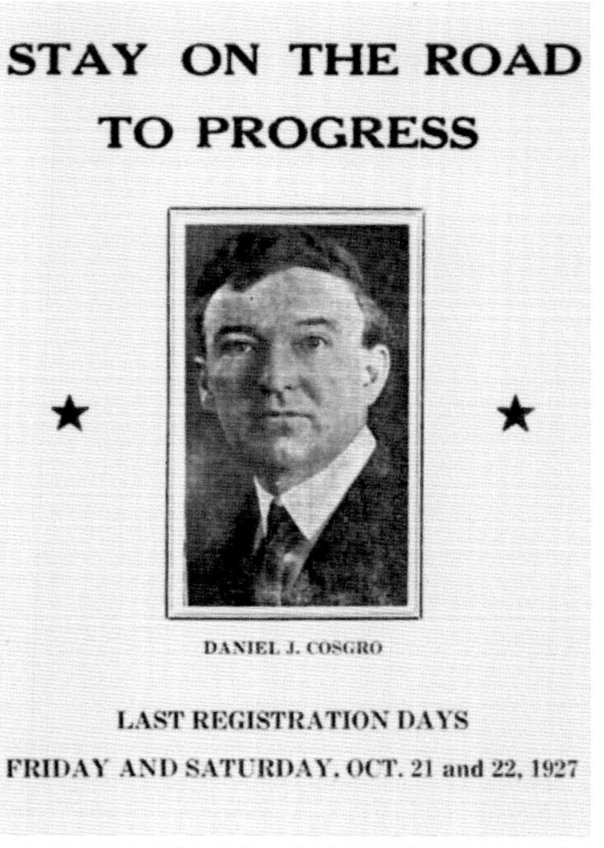

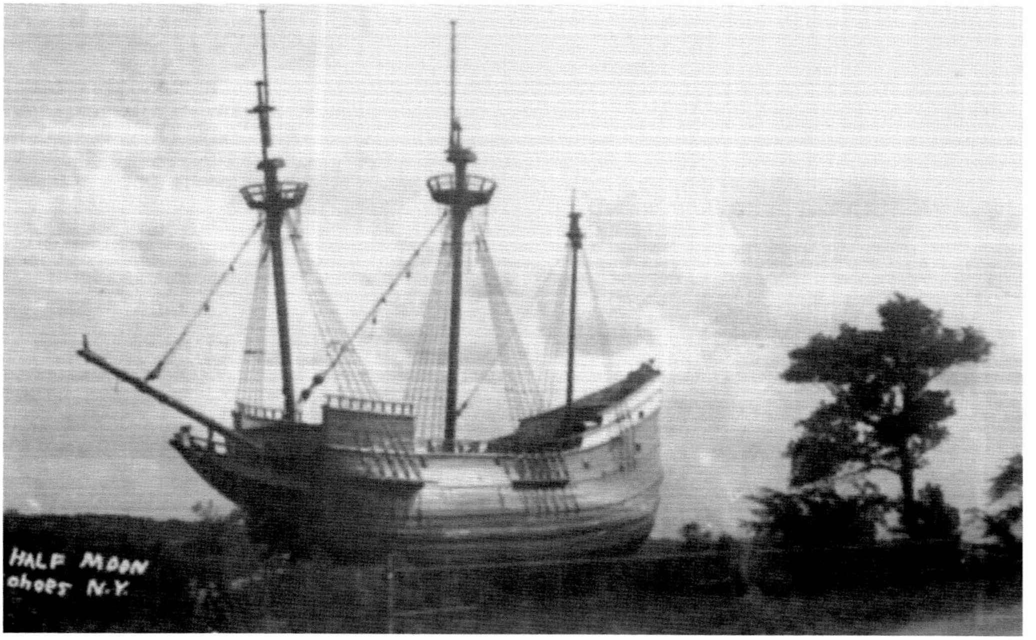

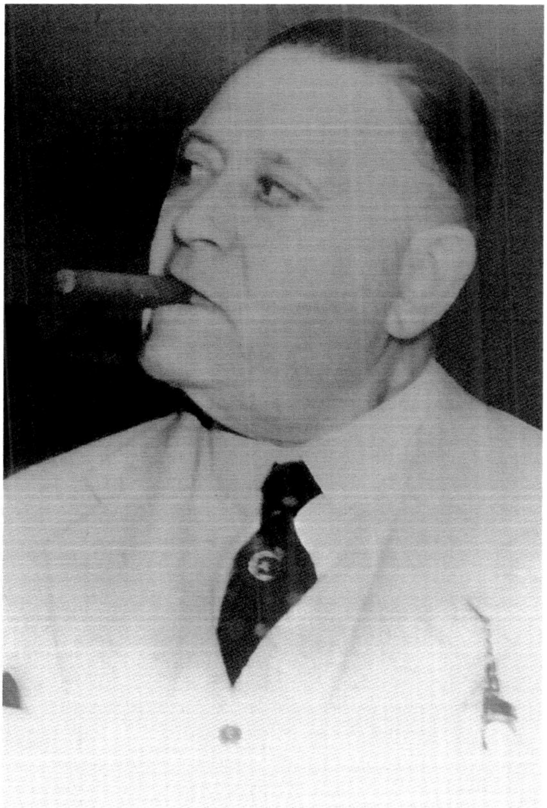

In June 1936, at the Democratic National Convention in Philadelphia, the arrival of the Democratic leader from Cohoes was announced over national radio. The man in the white suit and white hat and brandishing a fat cigar had made quite an entrance. At six feet, four inches tall and weighing nearly 300 pounds, Michael T. "Big Mike" Smith was larger than life, both literally and figuratively. Despite not being able to read or write, he rose to become one of the most powerful men in Albany County, second only to party boss Daniel P. O'Connell. Regarding his relationship with Smith, O'Connell said, "Mike Smith and I put all this together." Cohoes was essentially a client state of the Albany machine. However, in many ways, Cohoes was its own machine, and Smith was its king. His political methods were not unlike those being used in New York City, Chicago, Kansas City, and the other machine towns across the United States. Smith would be the first to aid the poor, especially immigrants, whether it was giving away a piece of coal or a piece of beef, which he would distribute from his "beef house" on the corner of Vliet and Garner Streets. But when one received assistance from Smith, loyalty was owed in return, especially when it came to the voting booth. In 1944, as part of Gov. Thomas Dewey's investigation into the O'Connell machine, Smith was indicted on charges related to his methods of governance, including voter fraud and tampering with property tax assessments. But, like O'Connell, he was never convicted. Aside from politics, Smith owned a restaurant on Remsen Street aptly named Smith's. The establishment was considered one of the finest in Albany County and became a popular political hangout. On December 31, 1949, Mike Smith died in his home, dubbed "the Big House," on Hamilton Place. On the day of his funeral, schoolchildren in Cohoes were given the day off. Nearly 60 years since his death, Smith's legacy lives on. The Democratic Party in Cohoes is as strong as ever and has not faced a serious challenge in nearly 40 years. And Smith's Restaurant serves as a venerable shrine to one of the most legendary figures in the city's history. (Courtesy of Brig. Gen. Edward J. Clark.)

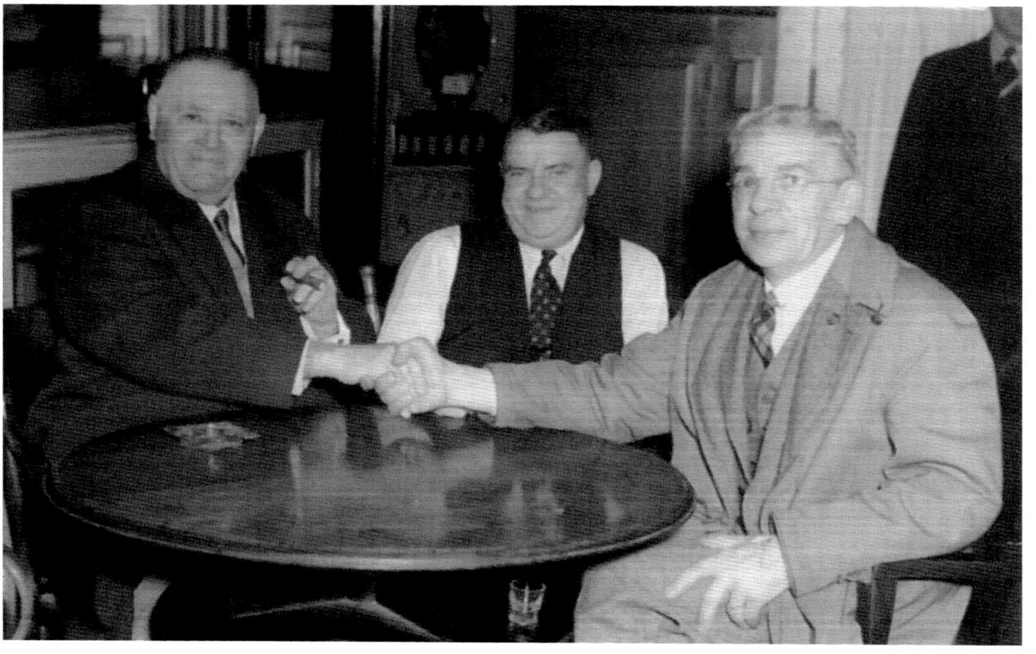

Rudolph Roulier was born in Lacadie, Quebec, in 1883 and moved to Cohoes when he was in his early teens. He was a laborer at the Eddy Valve Plant in Waterford and then went on to open Roulier & Chamberland Furniture on Remsen Street. Roulier served as commissioner of welfare and commissioner of public safety in Cohoes before being elected to the state assembly, where he served from 1927 to 1932. He was elected mayor of Cohoes in 1939 and held the office for the next 19 years. He is the longest-serving mayor in the history of the city. The above photograph shows Mayor Roulier (right) shaking the hand of Cohoes Democratic Party boss Mike Smith upon his victory in 1939. Cohoes schools treasurer George Reed looks on. (Above, courtesy of Brig. Gen. Edward J. Clark; below, courtesy of Michele Bemis.)

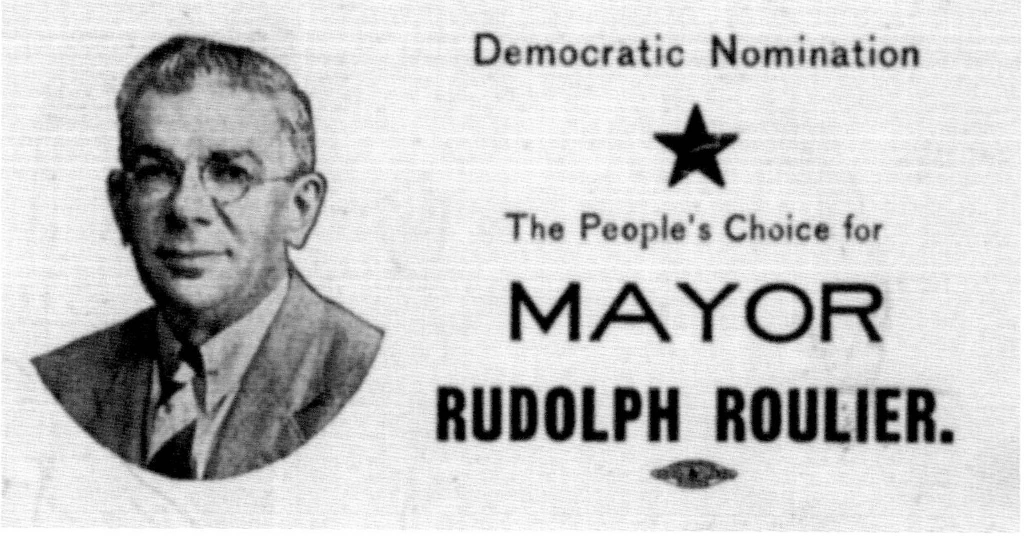

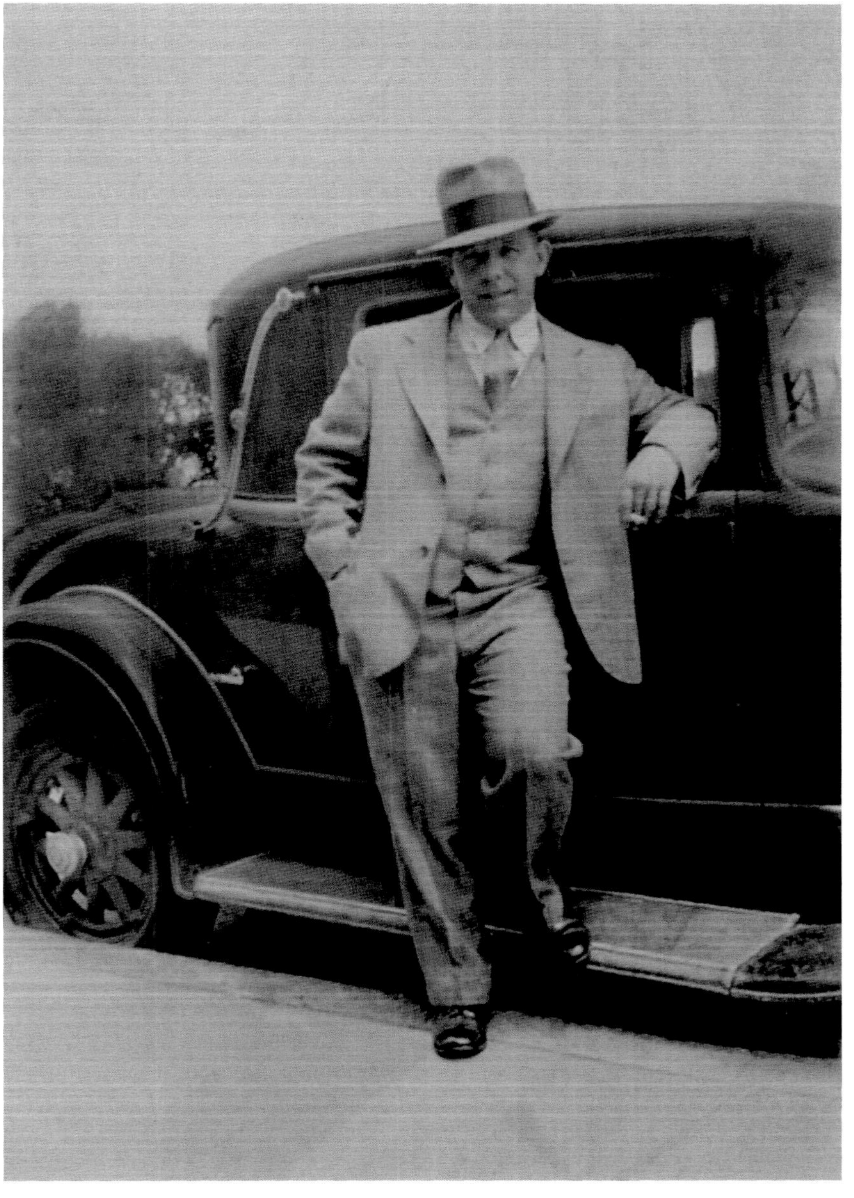

When Andrew Santspree was elected mayor in 1959, it was with the largest majority in the history of the city. When asked about his interests, he famously stated that he had 20,000 of them, meaning the people of Cohoes. Prior to his involvement in politics, Santspree spent decades in business. Among his establishments were Santspree's Luncheonette on White Street and Spree's Stationery Store on Remsen Street. He also spent 10 years as commissioner of the Cohoes Housing Authority. In 1963, he and the entire Democratic machine were defeated by Dr. Jay McDonald and the Citizens Party movement. And while charges of corruption were leveled against party boss Bill Dawson, there is no evidence to suggest that Santspree was anything less than honorable. Santspree is seen here in the 1930s. (Courtesy of Adeline Rand.)

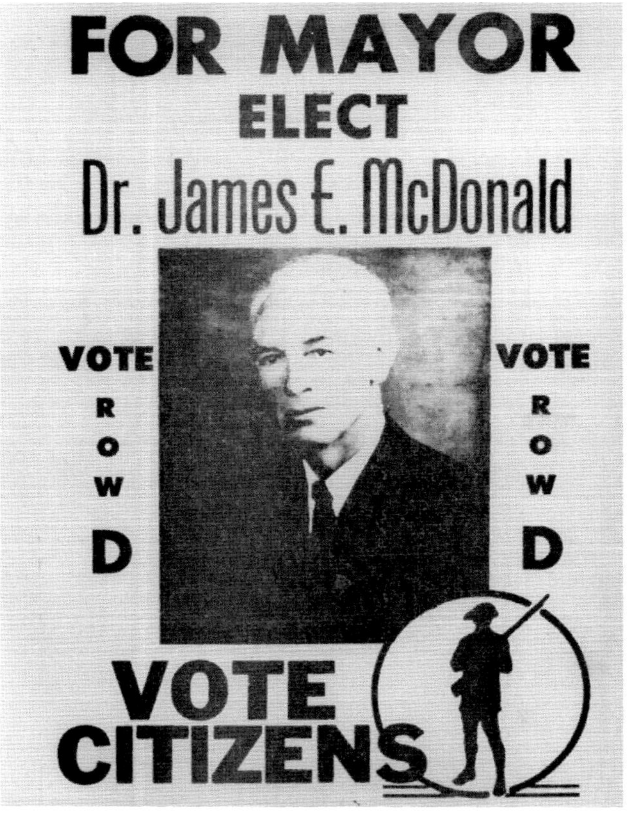

The headline read, "Upstate City in Revolt, Reformers in Cohoes Demonstrate that City Hall Can Be Fought and Captured." That was what millions of Americans woke up to on April 10, 1967, as the Citizens Party graced the cover of the *New York Times*. The Citizens Party was a collection of young idealists of all political stripes who had managed to overthrow a political machine that had held power for over 40 years. That machine, led by boss William Dawson, was a satellite of the Dan O'Connell Democratic machine that ran all of Albany County. It all started with a young engineer named Paul Van Buskirk. Tired of living under the yoke of what was described at times as a corrupt and oppressive regime, Van Buskirk decided to do what was considered impossible: fight city hall. He started attending city budget meetings, asking questions and gathering like-minded citizens of all political stripes. Together, they became the Citizens Party, determined to take their city back and take control of their own destinies. Their first victory came in 1961 with a ballot question regarding city assessments. This gave them the credibility to launch a campaign for elective office in 1963. They were able to convince Dr. Jay McDonald, a popular town doctor, to run for mayor. They defeated the incumbent machine mayor Andrew Santspree and won three of the six council seats. But in 1969, the beloved McDonald died of a brain tumor. Council president Frank Colourtolo became acting mayor. The party decided that Jay's wife, Virginia, should run for mayor in the upcoming election. McDonald won and became the first female mayor in New York state. However, by the early 1970s, the party began to become unglued. Van Buskirk had left city government to administer the Model Cities program. Jay McDonald was gone. The party was leaderless and fractured, and infighting took hold. In 1975, Virginia McDonald was defeated by a young attorney named Ron Canestrari. In 1981, a last-ditch effort to reclaim city hall by Herb Hyde met with defeat. The Citizens Party was no more. Paul Van Buskirk sums up the legacy of the Citizens Party this way: "It proved that City Hall could be fought and that a city that was at rock bottom could rise to the top."

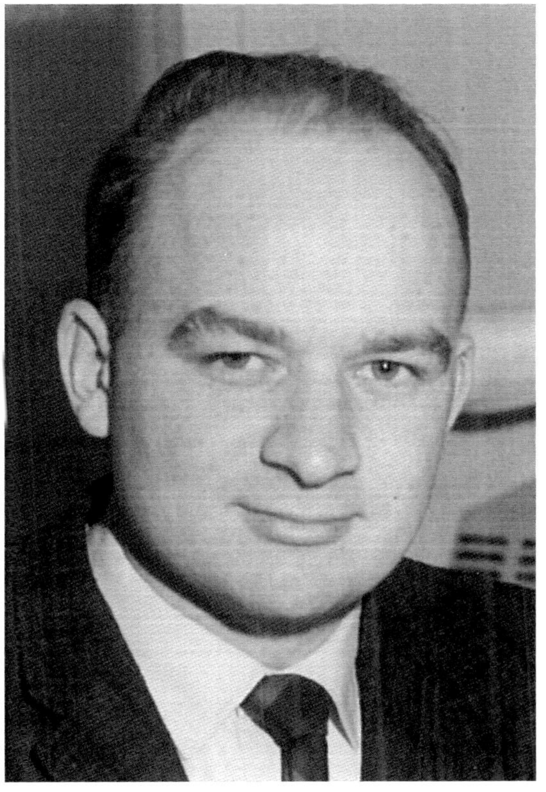

Paul Van Buskirk never wanted to be a politician. As a matter of fact, he disdained politics. But he would become one of the greatest political leaders in the city's history. The old adage "you can't fight city hall" had no bearing on the young engineer or the movement he created. Van Buskirk was born and raised in Cohoes, growing up on Grant Avenue. He attended Cohoes schools and went on to Rensselaer Polytechnic Institute in Troy, where he received his degree in engineering. He became a highway superintendent on the New York State Thruway and taught at Hudson Valley Community College in Troy. While everything seemed to be going well for Van Buskirk, he believed his city was languishing under the oppressive yoke of the Democratic machine, led by William J. Dawson. He began to study politics and statistics in voting trends. He also started attending city budget meetings and began reviewing the budget. By 1961, a full-fledged reform movement was in effect. Van Buskirk started receiving death threats, and members of the group were harassed by city police. He accepted the possibility that he would be thrown in jail. But neither he nor the members of his group backed down. When the scare tactics failed to silence the reformers, Dawson offered Van Buskirk a job as city engineer, which he refused. Van Buskirk and his group of citizen reformers went on to defeat the Democratic machine in the 1963 election, winning three of the six council seats and the mayor's office. Van Buskirk became executive assistant to Mayor Jay McDonald and immediately began working to improve the quality of life in Cohoes. Perhaps his biggest achievement was getting Cohoes selected to participate in the Model Cities program, a Great Society initiative. Cohoes was one of 150 cities selected. The influx in federal money from Model Cities allowed for the rehabilitation of the Cohoes Music Hall, the filling of the polluted canals, and the construction of a new firehouse, community center, and senior housing. But by the early 1970s, the party began to become fractured. In 1975, after a smear campaign from within the party, Van Buskirk had had enough of politics. By 1981, the party was finished. Van Buskirk went on to become a highly accomplished city planner and educator. (Courtesy of Paul Van Buskirk.)

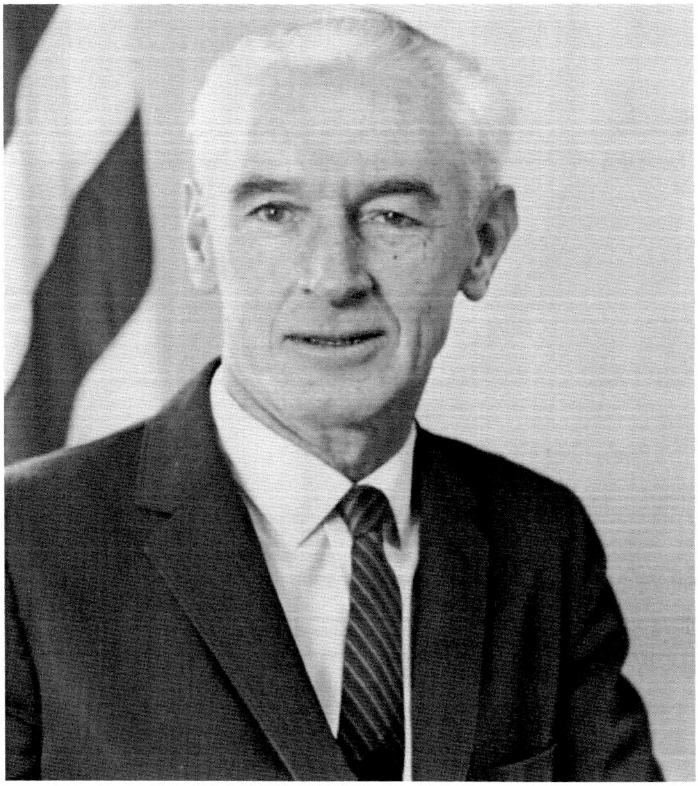

James E. McDonald was the son of James H. McDonald, who served as the city's mayor from 1920 to 1921 and was the last Republican to do so. James McDonald attended Cohoes schools and went on to Union and Albany Medical Colleges. During World War II, he served in both the African and Italian campaigns with the 701st Tank Destroyer Battalion and the 8th Field Artillery. Following the war, he began to practice medicine in his hometown, serving at Cohoes Memorial Hospital and Leonard Hospital in Troy. But in small-town America during the middle part of the 20th century, the house call was how many came to know Dr. McDonald. He became active in politics in 1961, as the newly formed Cohoes Citizens Party began to question the mainline Democratic establishment. McDonald was selected to become the party's standard-bearer in the mayoral election in 1963. He went on to defeat incumbent Andrew Santspree 5,857–4,443, carrying four of the city's six wards. Mayor McDonald would go on to lead the city during an unprecedented period of renewal. In 1965, a new fire headquarters on Central Avenue was constructed. Plans for a new high school and community center were also put in place. Toward the end of the decade, new senior housing downtown was being planned, Cohoes Music Hall was restored, and a new public library was established. Most important, Mayor McDonald restored trust in city government. In 1966, because of the transformation of political and civic life in the city, *Look* magazine honored Cohoes with its All-America City status, noting how Cohoes "nearly took the count at the hands of its crooked government." In 1968, McDonald was offered the Democratic nomination for mayor by Albany County boss Dan O'Connell. He refused and told the *Knickerbocker News* that O'Connell told him "it will be easier for you, your administration and the people of Cohoes if you go along with us." Mayor McDonald died in office of a brain tumor in June 1969. He is one of the most beloved political figures in the city's history. In his last public address, in May 1969, he told the people of Cohoes why he loved his hometown. "I perhaps love Cohoes most of all because she is a plucky little city, brave, stubborn and dogged, lifting her head once again, determined to regain her place in the sun."

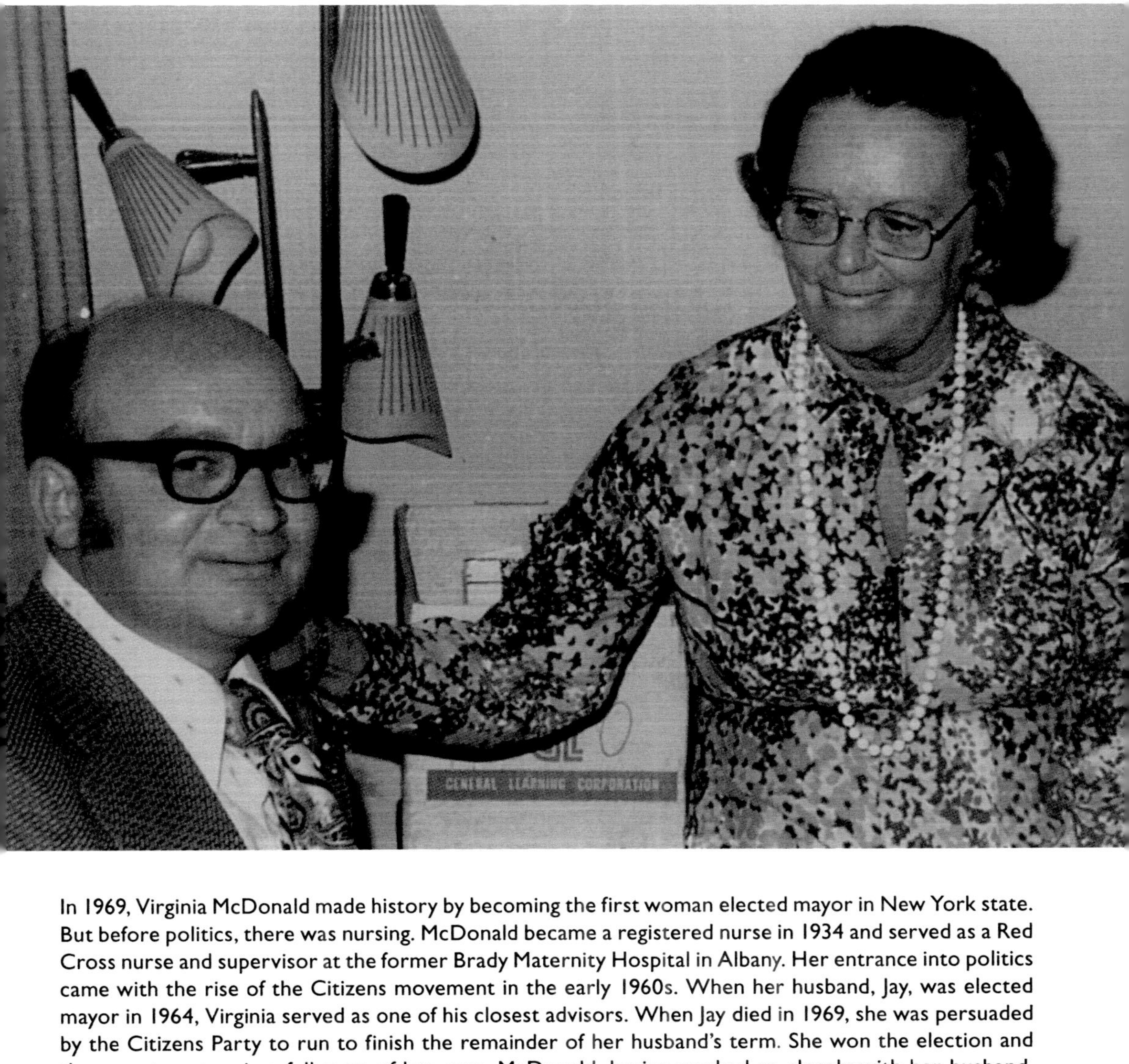

In 1969, Virginia McDonald made history by becoming the first woman elected mayor in New York state. But before politics, there was nursing. McDonald became a registered nurse in 1934 and served as a Red Cross nurse and supervisor at the former Brady Maternity Hospital in Albany. Her entrance into politics came with the rise of the Citizens movement in the early 1960s. When her husband, Jay, was elected mayor in 1964, Virginia served as one of his closest advisors. When Jay died in 1969, she was persuaded by the Citizens Party to run to finish the remainder of her husband's term. She won the election and then went on to win a full term of her own. McDonald, having worked so closely with her husband, was able to see to completion many of the programs that the former administration had started. Chief among these was the establishment of the Cohoes Community Center, for which she served as vice president. She was also responsible for implementing the Model Cities program with Paul Van Buskirk. The federally funded program, which was begun in 1969, would come to transform nearly every aspect of life in the city, including public housing, recreation, and the restoration of the Cohoes Music Hall. In spite of these achievements, McDonald was not able to ward off a resurgent Democratic Party, and in 1975, she lost reelection to a young attorney named Ron Canestrari. She is pictured here with Paul Van Buskirk. (Courtesy of Paul Van Buskirk.)

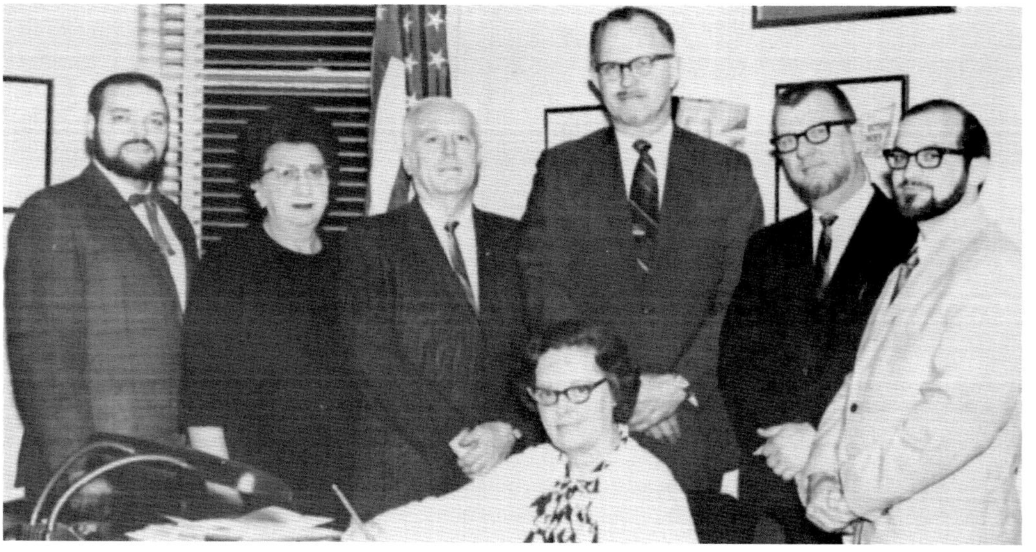

Frank Colaruotolo became a member of the Citizens Party in the early 1960s. He served as a city councilman from the Sixth Ward and later became president of the council. In June 1969, Colaruotolo became mayor of Cohoes upon the death of Jay McDonald. However, Colaruotolo decided not to run to finish out the term, allowing for the election of Virginia McDonald. Colaruotolo remains active in the community, serving on the board of directors of the Cohoes Savings Foundation. Colaruotolo (left) is seen here with members of the Common Council and Mayor Virginia McDonald (seated).

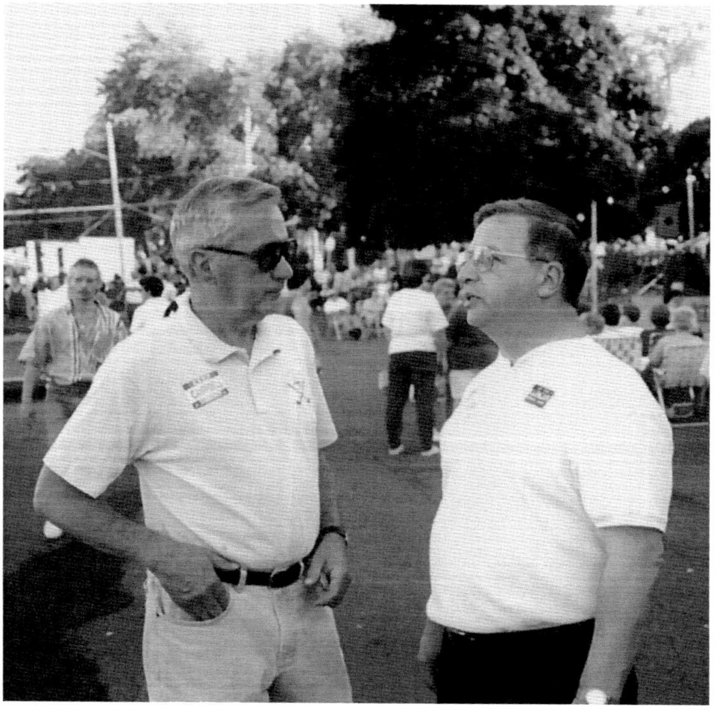

A member of the Common Council representing the Sixth Ward from 1990 to 2000, Ralph Signoracci III was one of the most active councilmen in the city's history. He proposed numerous pieces of legislation over the years, including establishing a city curfew for children. Perhaps his greatest legislative achievement was enacting a review of the city charter, which gave the council a more active role in city government. Signoracci (right) is seen here with former sheriff Jim Campbell.

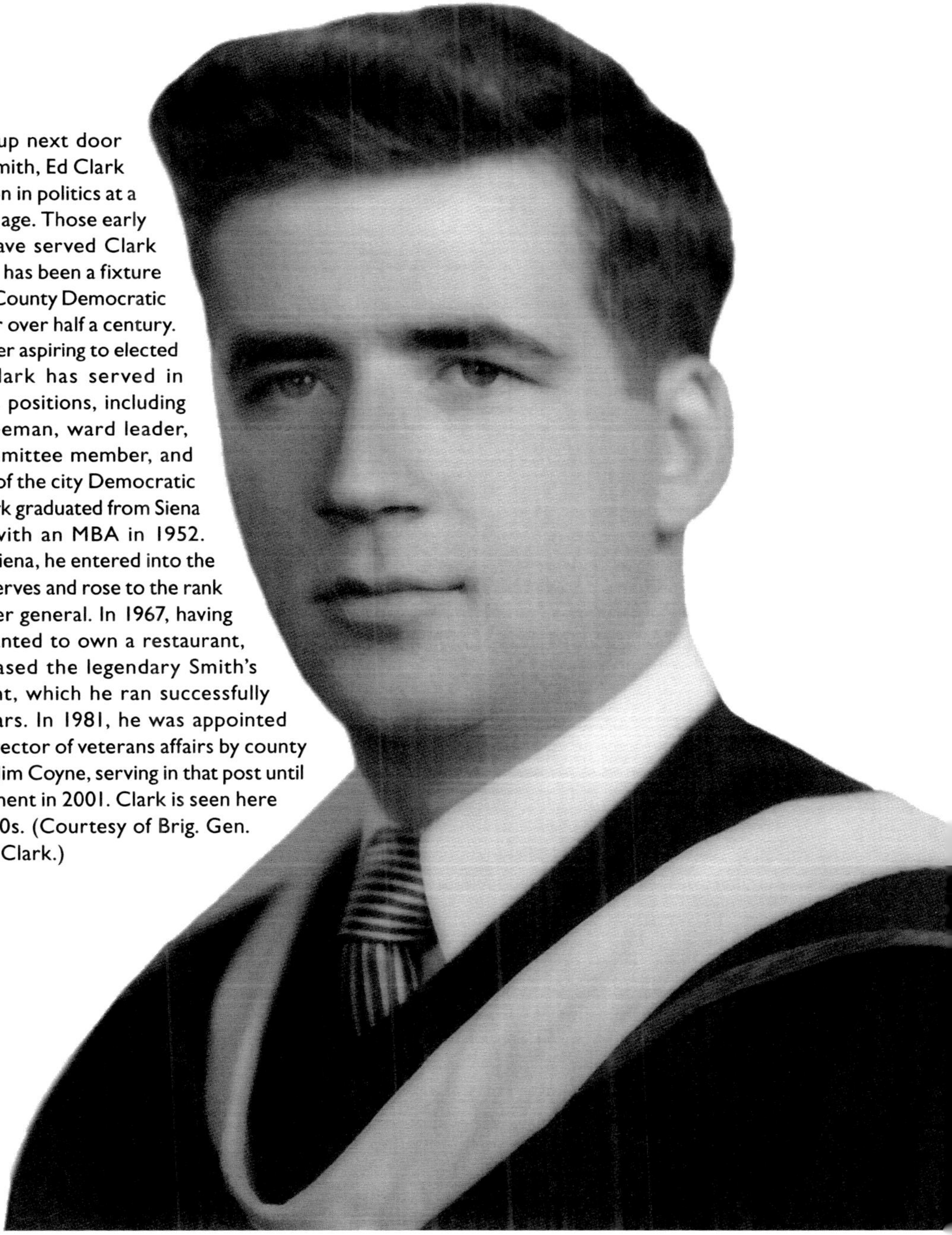

Growing up next door to Mike Smith, Ed Clark got a lesson in politics at a very early age. Those early lessons have served Clark well, as he has been a fixture in Albany County Democratic politics for over half a century. While never aspiring to elected office, Clark has served in numerous positions, including committeeman, ward leader, state committee member, and chairman of the city Democratic Party. Clark graduated from Siena College with an MBA in 1952. While at Siena, he entered into the Army Reserves and rose to the rank of brigadier general. In 1967, having always wanted to own a restaurant, he purchased the legendary Smith's Restaurant, which he ran successfully for 15 years. In 1981, he was appointed deputy director of veterans affairs by county executive Jim Coyne, serving in that post until his retirement in 2001. Clark is seen here in the 1950s. (Courtesy of Brig. Gen. Edward J. Clark.)

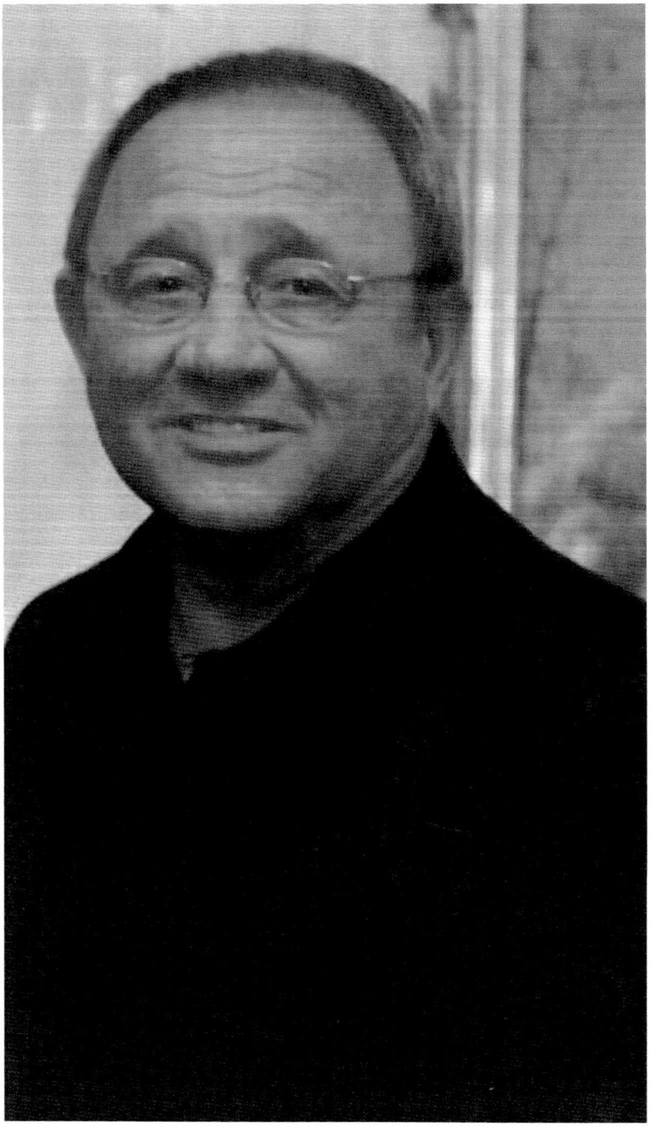

For nearly six decades, Gil Ethier has been at the forefront of Democratic politics in Cohoes. Born and raised in Cohoes, Ethier graduated from Cohoes High School in 1959, where he was a basketball standout. Following high school, he quickly became involved in politics at Matty's Tavern on Bridge Avenue. This was a time when the local taverns served as centers for political and community organization. Ethier was appointed a Democratic committeeman in 1960 at the age of 18. The young Ethier would receive many early lessons when the Democrats went down to defeat by the Citizens Party in 1963. However, he remained in the party; the following year, he started the Albany County Young Democrats. In 1979, he challenged the organization and was elected to the county legislature, where he continues to serve. In 1989, he retired from the Ford Motor Company in Green Island after 30 years. In 2003, he was made chairman of the Cohoes Democratic Committee and is one of the longest-tenured committeemen in the city's history. (Courtesy of Gil Ethier.)

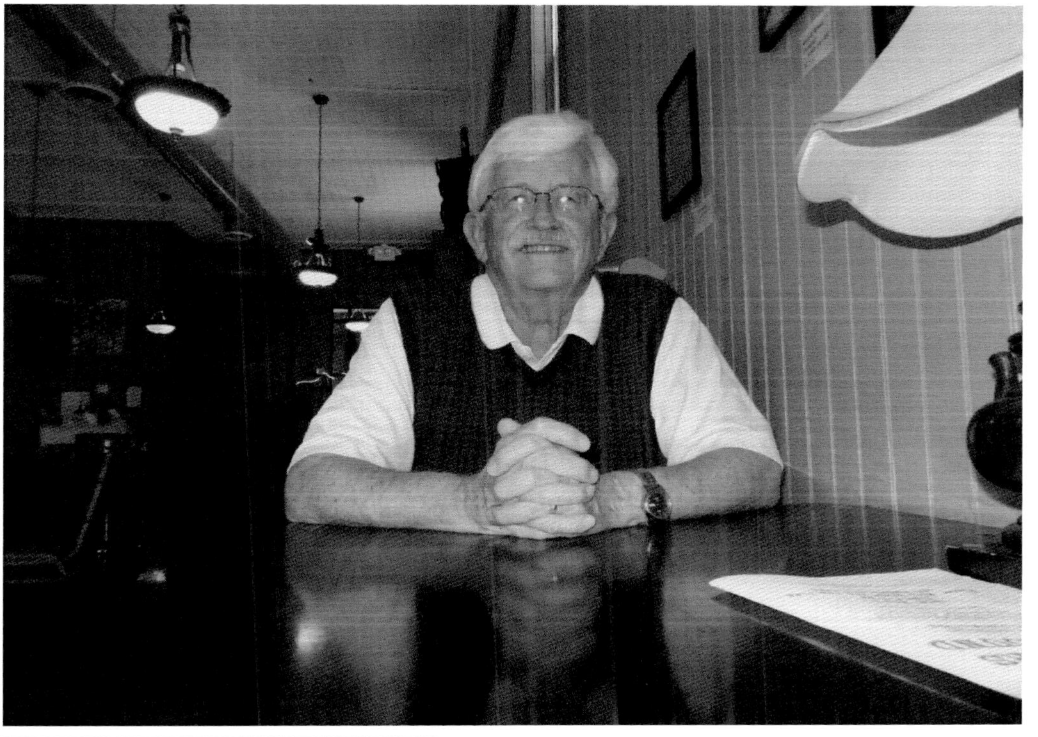

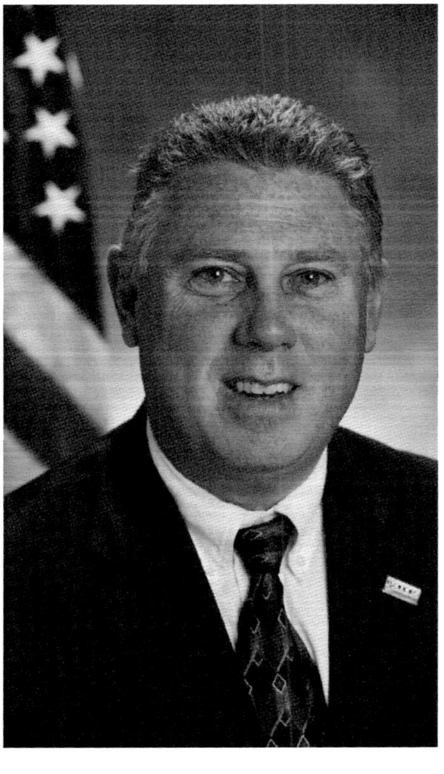

Herb Hyde became involved in politics in the mid-1970s with the Concerned Citizens movement and its efforts to reform the school system. He became chairman of the Citizens Party in 1980 and, in 1983, became the party's candidate for mayor. He wanted a counterbalance to the resurgent Democratic Party and ran on a platform to bring more businesses into the city. Hyde ended up losing by a wide margin to incumbent mayor Ron Canestrari, but not without a fight. Hyde, now a writer, has published his memoir, *College and Eighth*, about growing up in Troy, New York.

John McDonald became mayor of Cohoes in 2000 after defeating Mike Brooks in a Democratic primary. McDonald's devotion to his job and the city was apparent during his 12 years in office, as he seemed to be at every neighborhood meeting and was known to get down and dirty, pulling weeds or trimming trees in the city's parks. During his tenure as mayor, the city grew in population for the first time in decades. In 2012, he was elected to the state assembly, replacing retiring assemblyman Ron Canestrari. (Courtesy of John McDonald.)

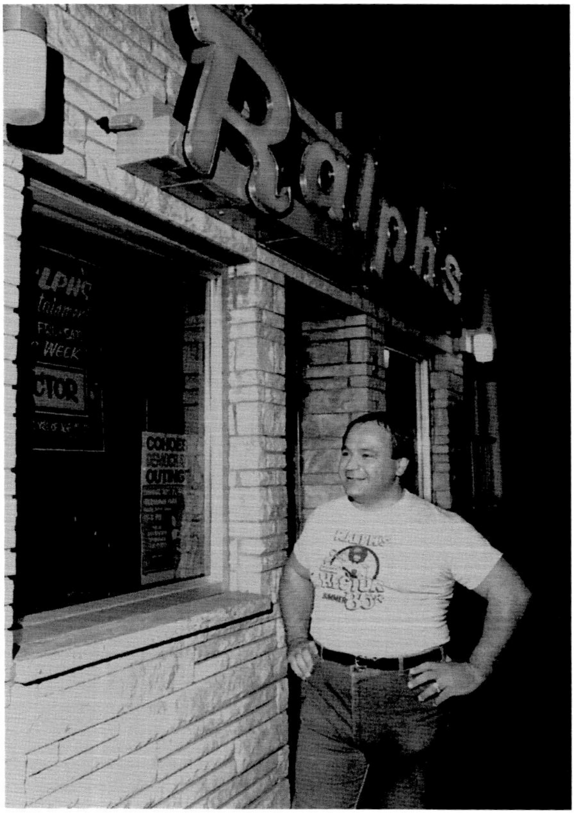

For those who knew him, former mayor Robert Signoracci was simply "Bobby." He grew up in the city's Van Schaick Island neighborhood and went into the family bar business. Ralph's Tavern on Ontario Street was one of the many neighborhood watering holes that dotted the city for decades. But Ralph's was also the scene for neighborhood politics, which Bob Signoracci embraced at an early age. His first run for public office, in 1980, was met with defeat. But he came back in 1984 and won a seat on the city council and was reelected in 1989. During that same year, when the mayor's office became vacant upon Ron Canestrari's departure to the state assembly, Signoracci saw an opportunity. He defeated Frank Valenti and William Malloy in a hotly contested three-way Democratic primary. As mayor, Signoracci began investing in the city's aging infrastructure belowground. He also began investing aboveground, by instituting a code enforcement unit. On the quality-of-life front, he took the issue of drugs in the city head-on, ridding parks of drug activity and creating the DARE program in the schools. Several of the city's current success stories were initiated during Signoracci's administration, including the rebirth of the city's North Mohawk Street corridor and Hudson River waterfront. It was a vision spelled out in a Signoracci-drafted master plan to chart the city's future. However, there were some things that were beyond the control of the mayor's office. The 1990s saw corporate retail abandon small towns. Cohoes saw the departure of Woolworth's and Cohoes Manufacturing. Suburban flight was at its peak, and the New Urbanism movement had yet to take shape. Perhaps the biggest challenge, and one that would forever change Signoracci, was a 30-month FBI probe on the apparent misuse of city funds. The probe, which proved to be a political witch hunt and for which Signoracci was cleared of any wrongdoing, left its mark. Signoracci chose not to run for reelection in 1999, citing a promise he made after his reelection victory in 1994 that he would not seek another term. He became an avid pilot and finished his career in public service with the Department of Housing and Urban Development. (Courtesy of the *Troy Record*.)

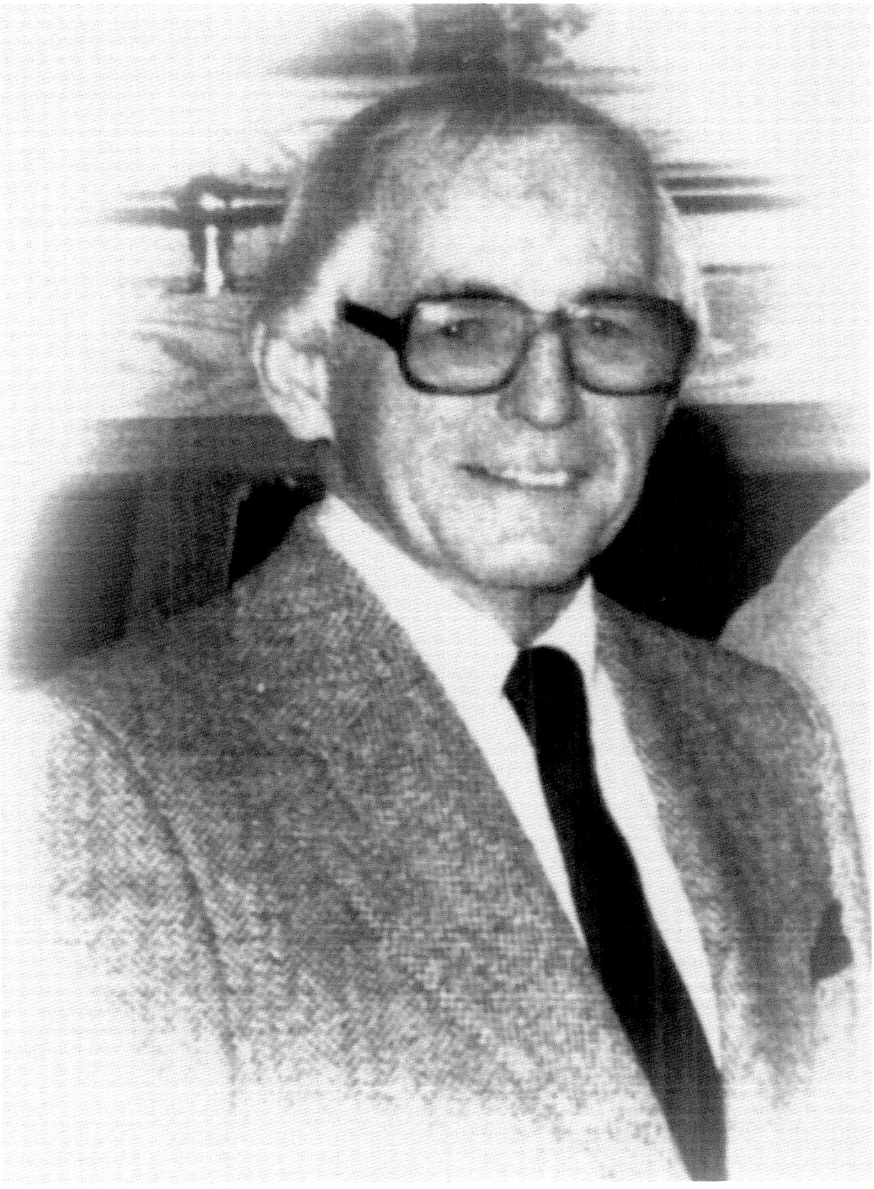

Frank Kennedy could trace his family straight back to the Plymouth Colony. This was just one among many points of pride for a man who dedicated most of his life to public service. Kennedy began that public service during World War II, serving under General Patton. He was wounded during the Battle of the Bulge and received the Purple Heart. Upon returning home, Kennedy became employed with the Mohawk Paper Company, where he remained for 43 years. In 1980, he was elected to serve as First Ward councilman, a position he held for 20 years. As councilman, Kennedy was known for his warm heart and gentle demeanor. Respected by all and enemy of none, Kennedy would often be the first to help and the last to boast. He passed away in 2006. One of his constituents remembered him this way: "he was the epitome of what a man should be." (Courtesy of April Kennedy.)

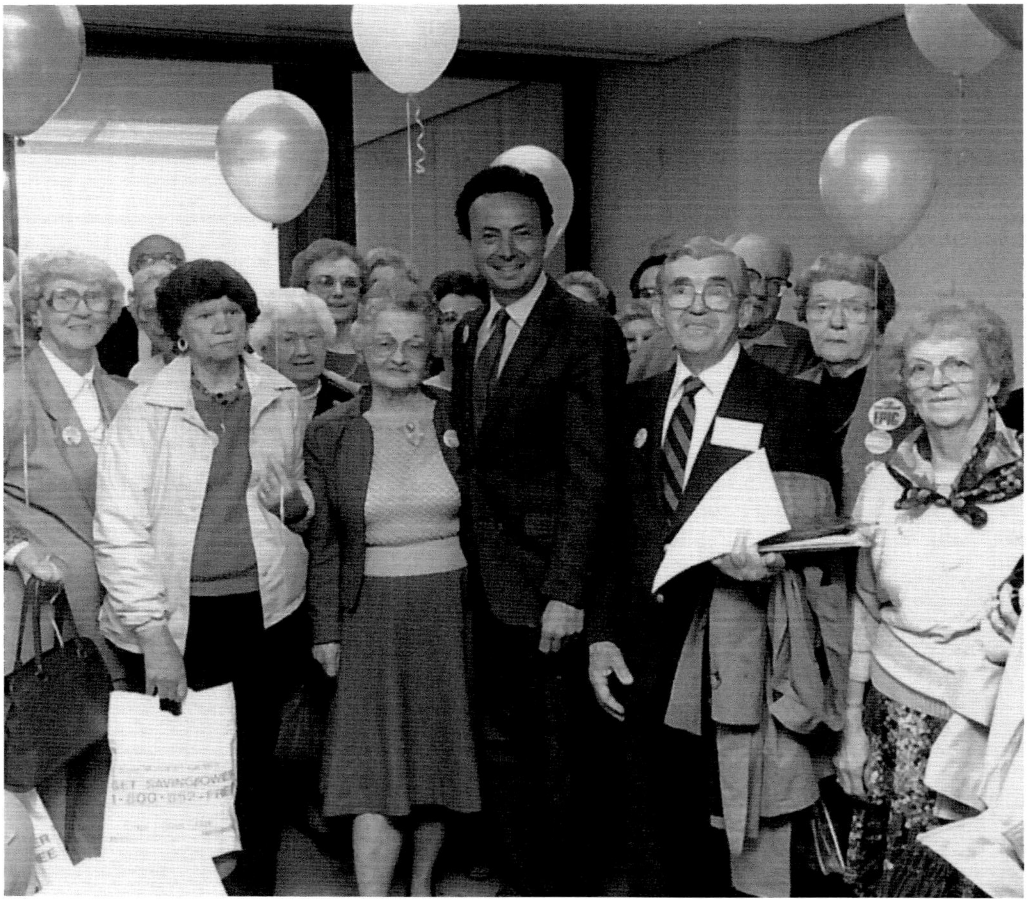

Ron Canestrari has an immense likeability that is rare in politics today. It is a testament to a career devoted to the people he was elected to serve. Ron Canestrari grew up on First Street on Van Schaick Island. He went to Cohoes schools and to Christian Brothers Academy, then graduated from Fordham College in 1965. He went on to Fordham University Law School, graduating in 1968. In 1969, he enlisted in the US Army, serving as an attorney for the Army and the federal government until 1971. He entered the Cohoes political scene in the early 1970s. In 1975, he decided to run for mayor as a Democrat against incumbent Virginia McDonald. Canestrari received the Democratic Party nomination without a challenge. With the Citizens Party mired in internal discord, Canestrari was able to defeat McDonald and restore Democratic rule to the city after an 11-year absence. Canestrari's tenure as mayor saw the construction of a new senior center and a new senior apartment tower (Cayuga Plaza), and infrastructure improvements along Remsen Street including new sidewalks, lighting, and a civic plaza (Canal Square). In 1986, he secured funds to renovate the former St. John's Church into a state-of-the-art library. In 1989, Canestrari was elected to the New York State Assembly and became that body's majority leader in 2007. As an assemblyman, Canestrari was always there for the people of Cohoes, whether it was a new roof for the senior center or new equipment for the Little League. He was also a constituent-minded legislator, making himself available to help the average citizen with whatever issues they were having. In 2012, Canestrari retired from the state assembly, ending a 36-year career in public service. Canestrari (center) is seen here with a group of Cohoes seniors. (Courtesy of Sue Baird.)

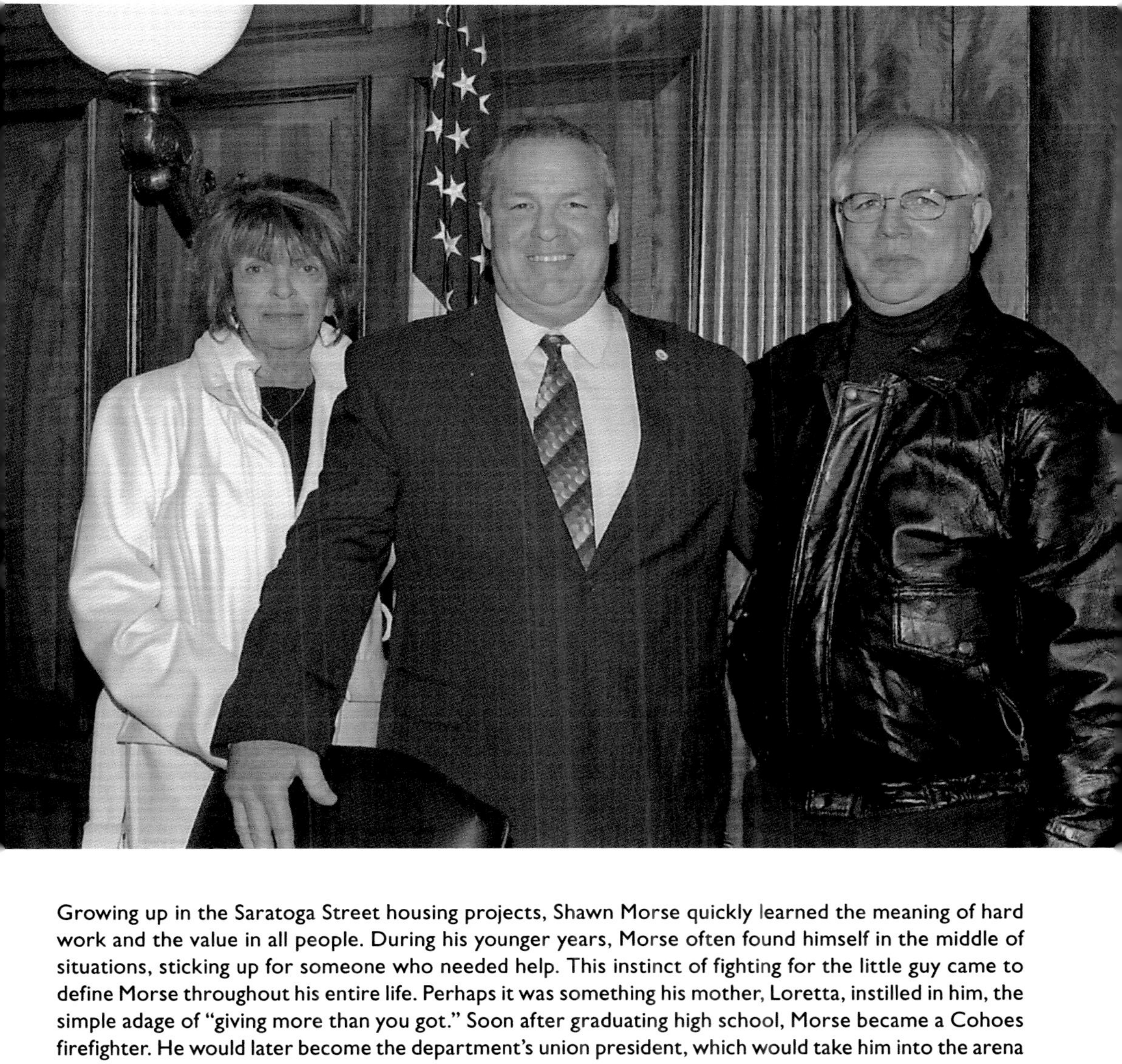

Growing up in the Saratoga Street housing projects, Shawn Morse quickly learned the meaning of hard work and the value in all people. During his younger years, Morse often found himself in the middle of situations, sticking up for someone who needed help. This instinct of fighting for the little guy came to define Morse throughout his entire life. Perhaps it was something his mother, Loretta, instilled in him, the simple adage of "giving more than you got." Soon after graduating high school, Morse became a Cohoes firefighter. He would later become the department's union president, which would take him into the arena of politics. Often finding himself shut out of the political process by city officials, Morse decided the only way to get a seat at the table would be to run for office himself. In 2004, he ran for a seat on the Albany County legislature as an independent, going against the Democratic establishment. Nobody thought he could win, but Morse was relentless. He knocked on doors in the city's poorest neighborhoods, gaining the support of many who had never voted before. He also got the support of the senior community, who were among his biggest supporters. Morse defeated his Democratic challenger, shocking the political establishment. He quickly rose up the ranks of the county legislature, becoming chairman of the Audit and Finance Committee and deputy majority leader. In 2012, he was elected chairman of the legislature, becoming one of the most powerful men in county government. Shawn Morse (center) is shown here with his father, Gary Oliver, and his stepmother, Linda Oliver. (Courtesy of Shawn Morse.)

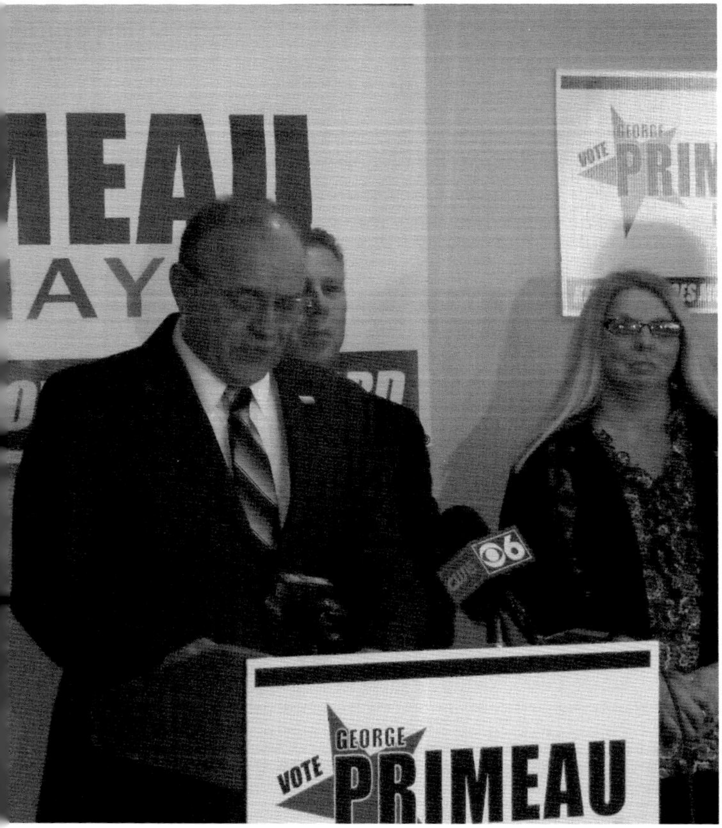

Becoming mayor of Cohoes is certainly not something that George Primeau ever set his sights on. A lover of cars at an early age, Primeau became an automotive mechanic and eventually moved into the field of auto-body restoration. In 1984, he used his life savings and rented a small repair shop on Columbia Street. That same year, he expanded and moved into his own shop on High Street, where his brother Joe came on board as a partner. In 1999, George was elected to the Common Council, representing the Third Ward. He later went on to be president of the council. In 2012, he was sworn in as acting mayor following the vacancy left by John McDonald. Primeau is currently campaigning to serve out the remainder of the term. In addition to his automotive and political work, Primeau can be found from time to time rocking out on the bass guitar in a local band, Backbeat. (Below, courtesy of Rich DeVoe.)

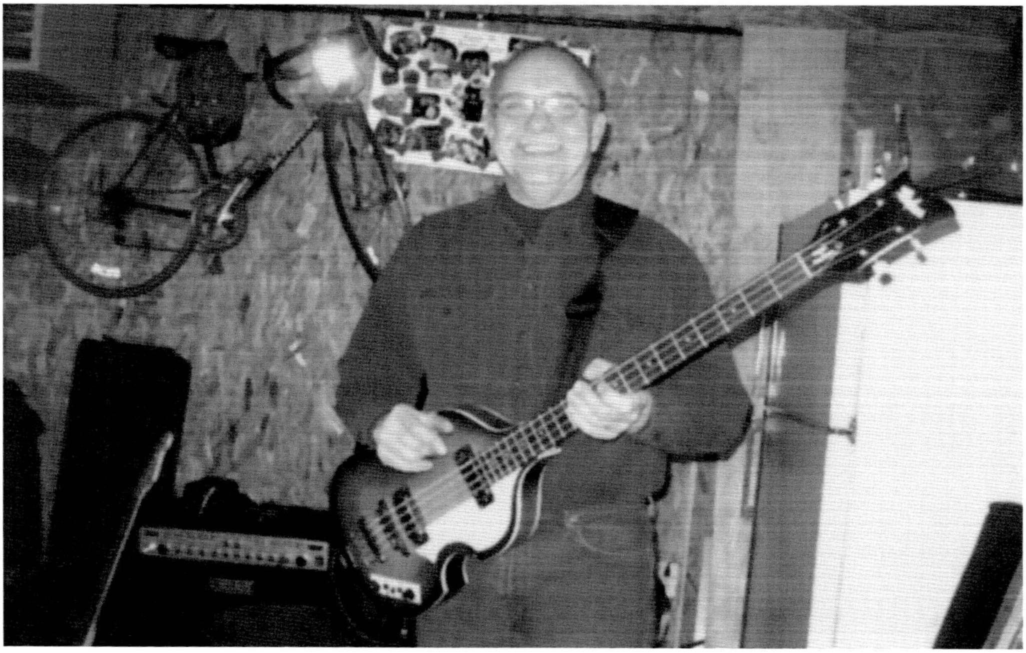

Educators

Education has been an important component of civic life since Cohoes was a small farming village. In fact, Cohoes was one of the first villages in the state to demand an improvement on the system of district schools, and it had a law passed in 1850 establishing free schools. One of the first public schools in Cohoes was the State Yard School on Saratoga Street, in 1835. From that point on, public education expanded to meet the needs of a growing population. The Egberts High School was organized in 1868 and served the community until a new public high school was constructed on Bevan Street in 1921. Parochial schools played a large role in Cohoes until the 1990s. Nearly all of the churches in the city had neighborhood schools. When Catholics began to arrive in the middle and late 19th century, these schools served to keep native languages and cultures relevant. However, the once great and expansive system of parochial education in Cohoes is no more. That being said, Cohoes still retains three neighborhood elementary schools, a junior high school, and a high school. In 2010, a district-wide school renovation program saw additions and renovations to all of the schools in the city. With the many public and private schools that have existed in Cohoes over the generations, many great educators stand out. These men and women devoted their lives to teaching, whether it was through music, on the playing field, or by their incredible example. The individuals in this chapter are just an example of the many devoted educators who have taught their children well.

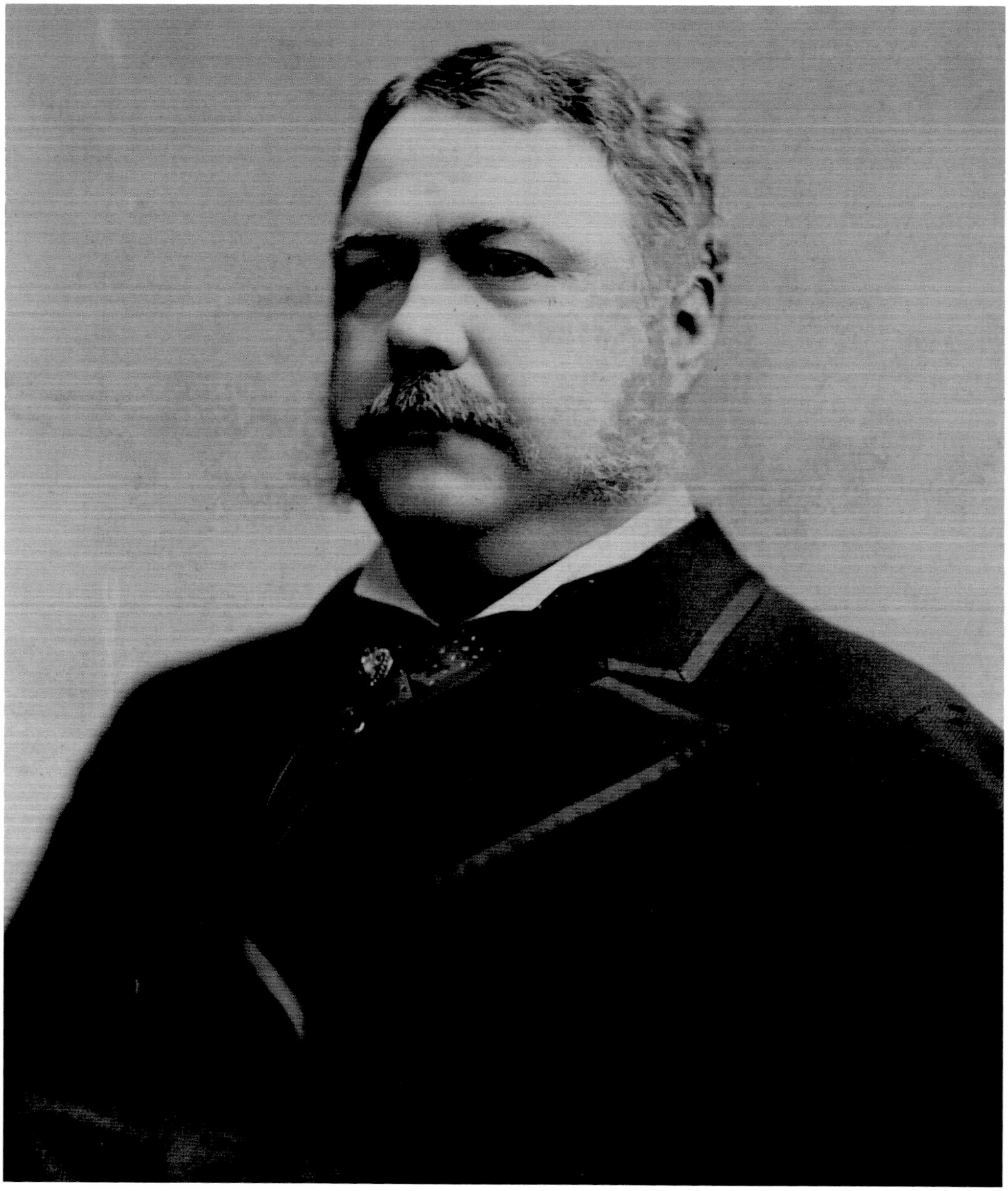

Before becoming the 21st president of the United States upon the assassination of Andrew Garfield in 1881, Chester Arthur served as a principal at the Cohoes Academy for boys from 1852 to 1854. The school was located on the corner of Canvass and Oneida Streets. At the time, the school had a reputation for bad behavior, with several teachers quitting prior to Arthur's arrival. Arthur, a large man at well over six feet tall, did not intimidate his students. Instead, whenever one of the older students acted out, Arthur would make the student spend the entire day among the younger students. The method worked, and much of the bad behavior stopped. In 1854, Arthur left Cohoes to take a position at the New York City law firm of Erastus Culver. (Courtesy of the Library of Congress.)

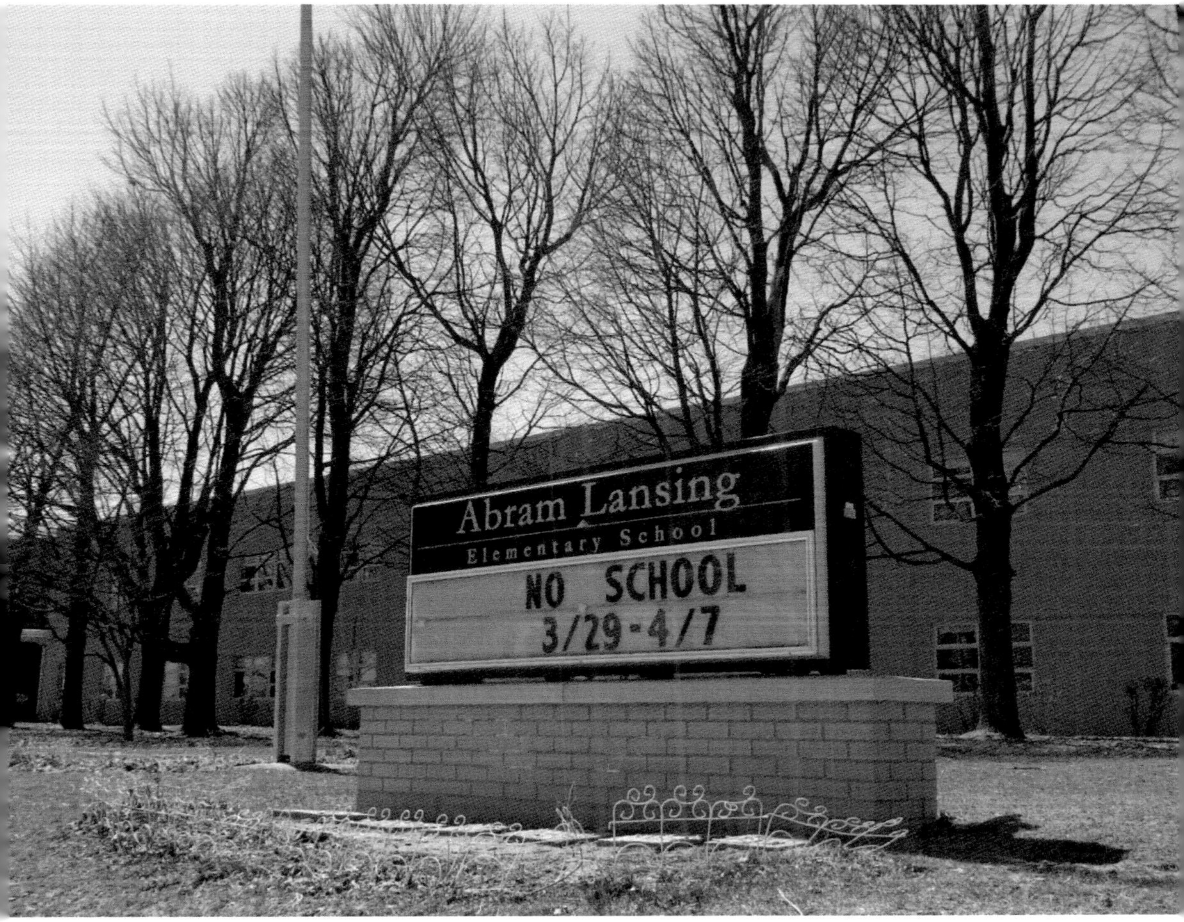

Born in 1861, Abram Lansing was the son of Egbert and Helena Lansing. Educated in Cohoes schools, Lansing went on to Albany Academy and later graduated from Williams College in Williamstown, Massachusetts. He developed a love for sacred music and became a well-regarded organist. Lansing was at the forefront of the many musical organizations of the day, including the Cohoes Philharmonic Society. He was also organist for the Silliman Presbyterian Church and the Presbyterian Church of Albany. In 1917, he was appointed a city school commissioner. He also served as supervisor of music for the schools, and was leader of the Cohoes High School orchestra and glee club. Lansing wrote numerous original scores, ranging from sacred music to polkas, including his award-winning song "I Am the Alpha and Omega." Abram Lansing died in 1928 at the age of 67.

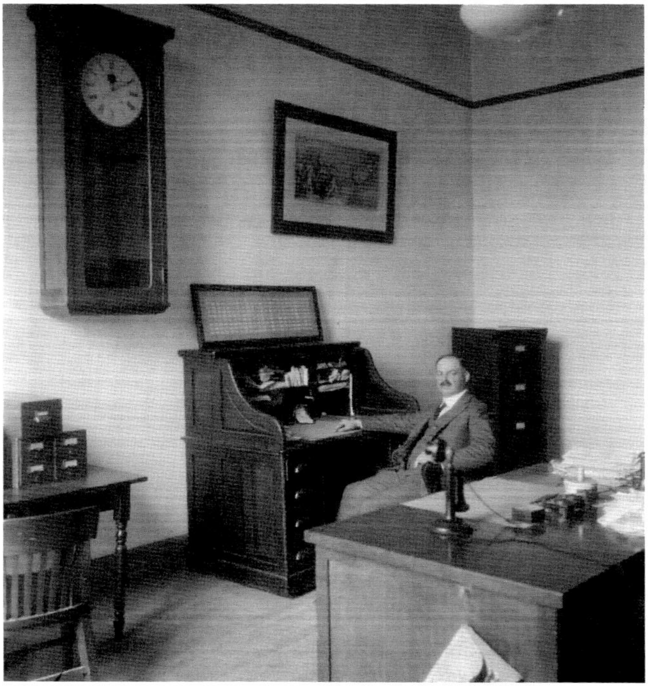

Charles "Pop" Wheeler was a principal in Cohoes for 32 years. He was a graduate of Middlebury College and received his master's degree from Columbia University. He began his career at the former Egberts High School, serving as its principal. In 1921, he became the principal at the new high school on Bevan Street. Wheeler would serve as the principal of Cohoes High School until his retirement in 1946. He was also president of the Cohoes Teachers Association. (Courtesy of the Spindle City Historic Society.)

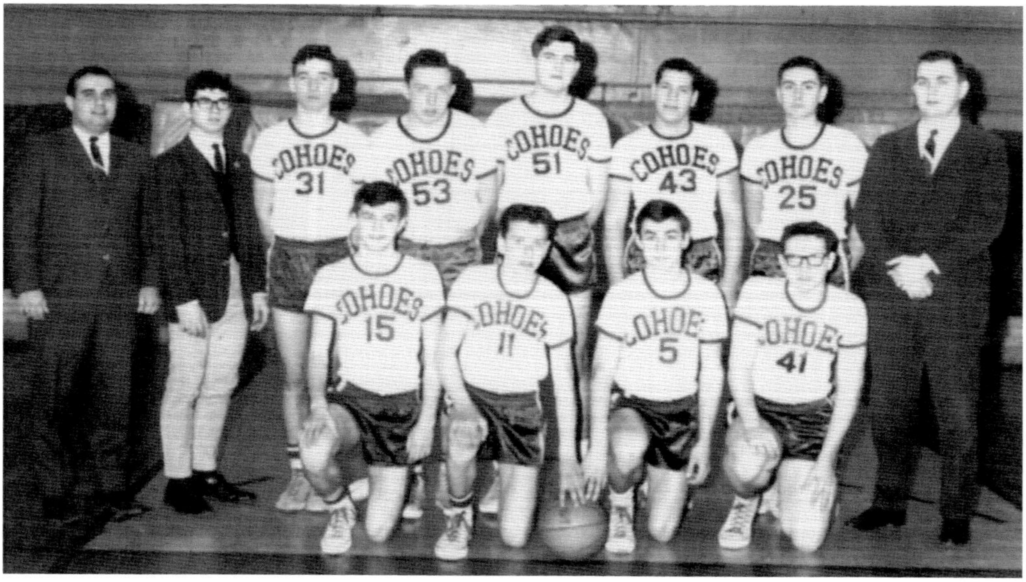

Joe Loudis started his athletic career in 1954 as a member of the Schenectady Little League All-Star Team, which won the Little League World Series. In 1965, he began teaching at Cohoes High and was the varsity basketball coach from 1967 until 1988. He retired briefly before becoming the varsity coach at Mechanicville from 1993 to 1996. A member of the New York State Basketball Hall of Fame, Loudis is one of the most successful coaches in Section II history, with a record 428 wins. Here, Loudis (far left) poses with the 1967 Cohoes junior varsity basketball team.

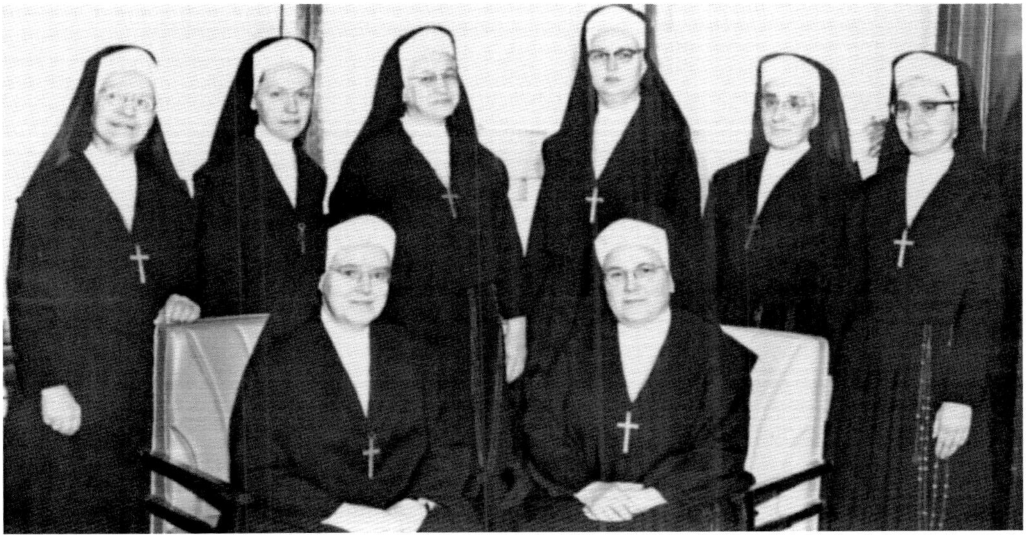

It has often been said that Cohoes was a city of many churches. And with each church came a school. In the case of Catholic schools, they were administered by nuns. In the early days of Catholic education, the schools served as the lifeblood of the parish. They were places where the ethnic language and customs, along with the faith, were instilled in the children of European and Canadian immigrants. However, starting in the 1970s, the parochial schools in the city began to close as the population shifted to the suburbs. As of now, no Catholic school remains in the city of Cohoes. Catholic education as a whole is on the decline throughout the diocese. But for many, fond memories remain of the nuns who dedicated their lives to the education of countless numbers of young Cohoesiers. The above photograph shows the Sisters of St. Ann of the former St. Joseph's Parish in the 1960s. Below, the faculty of St. Agnes School is seen around 1917.

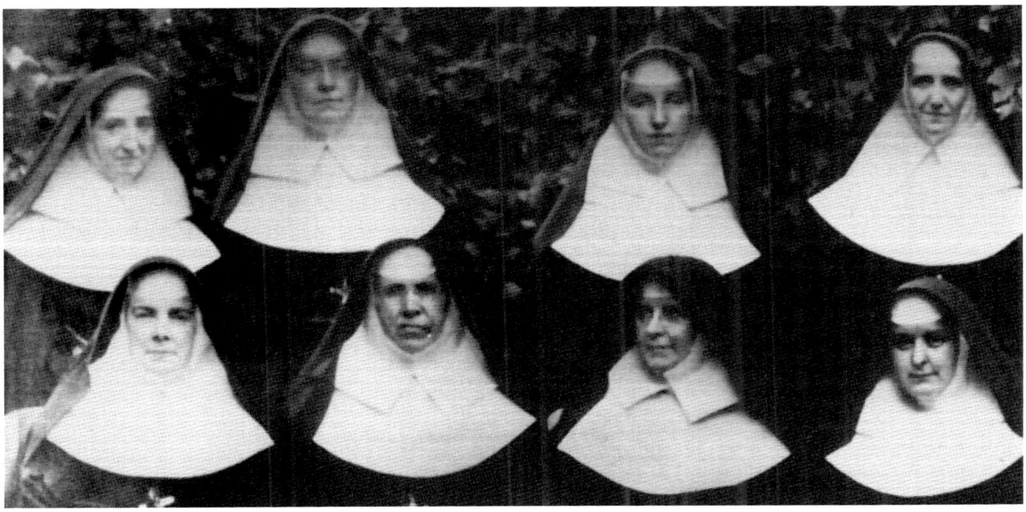

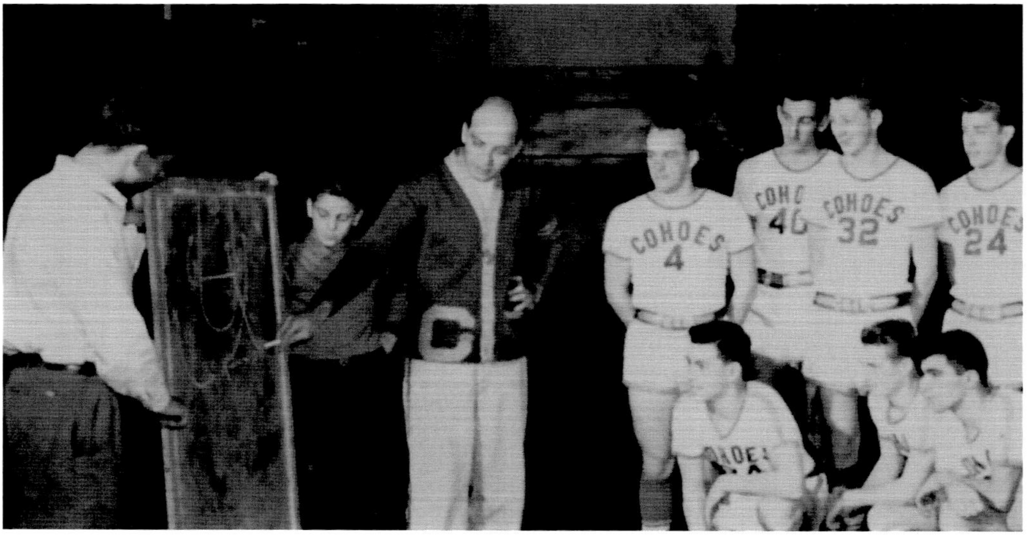

Bob Gullie had a passion and love for children that remained steadfast throughout his life. A graduate of Notre Dame, Gullie began working in education in the early 1950s, with positions in Lansingburgh and in Avril Park, where he served as vice principal of the high school. In 1954, Gullie became the director of athletics for Cohoes schools, serving in that position for six years. He then became the founding executive director for the Lansingburgh Boys and Girls Club, serving in that role until 1966. In 1971, he became executive director of the new Cohoes Community Center (below). For the next 40 years, Gullie devoted himself to the children who came through the center's doors. Gullie died in 2011, but his legacy in Cohoes lives on in all of the lives he touched. Above, Gullie instructs the 1966 Cohoes High basketball team.

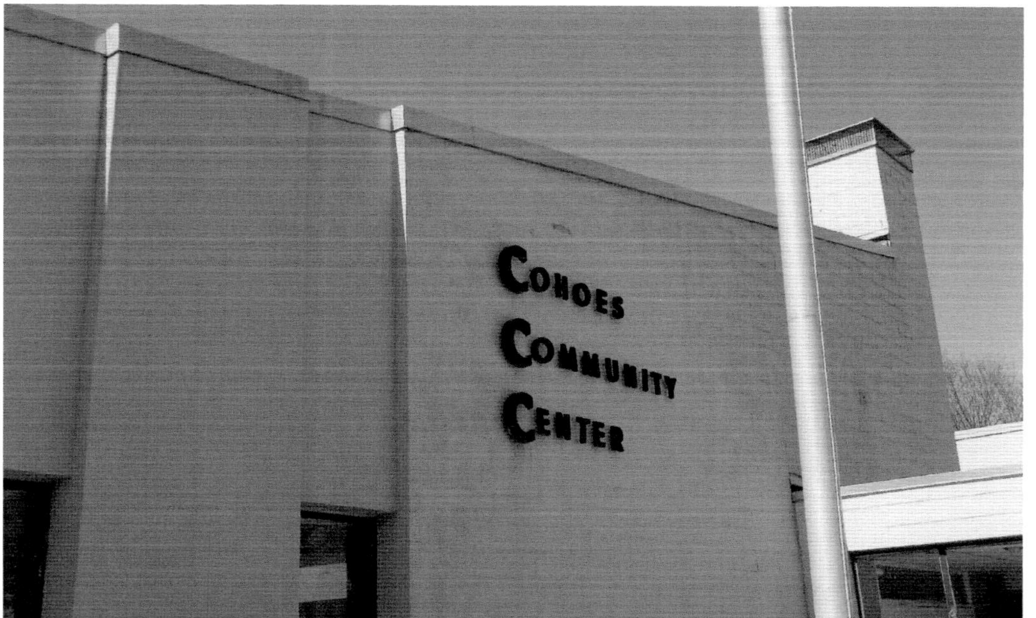

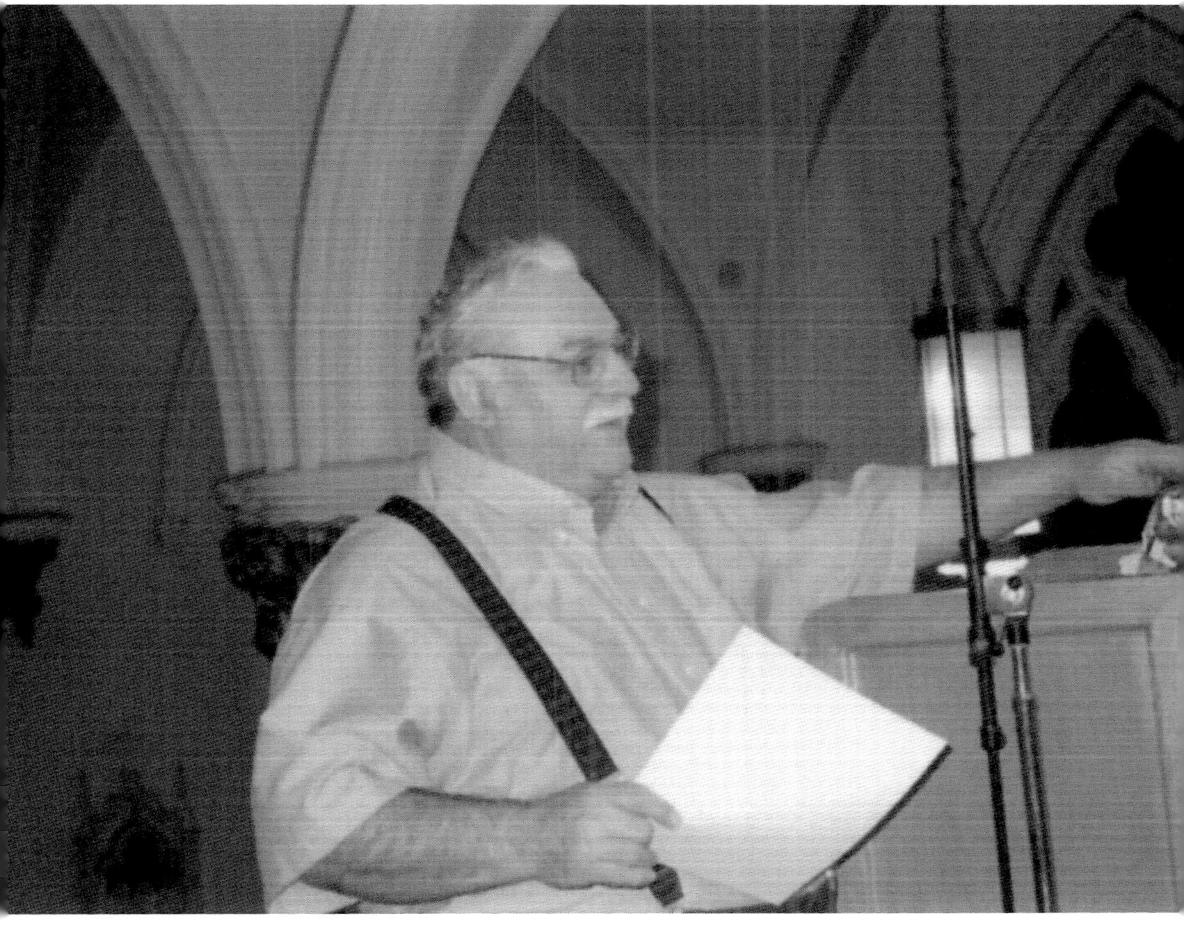

In 1953, Bernard Ouimet, 11, made the trip to Cohoes from Saint-Jacques-le-Mineur, Quebec, sitting in the back of a pickup truck with his father and the family furniture. He brought with him a love for the pipe organ, a love that was introduced to him by his grandmother. Ouimet went on to study music and social studies at the State University at Albany, graduating in 1967. He taught social studies at Cohoes Middle School for 29 years. During that time, he also served as organist for St. Ann's Church in Waterford and for his beloved St. Joseph's Church, the predominant French church in Cohoes, where classical French hymns were commonplace. In 1981, he was instrumental in creating the Franco American Federation, and he has researched and written extensively on the history of the French Canadian population in Cohoes. (Courtesy of Bernard Ouimet.)

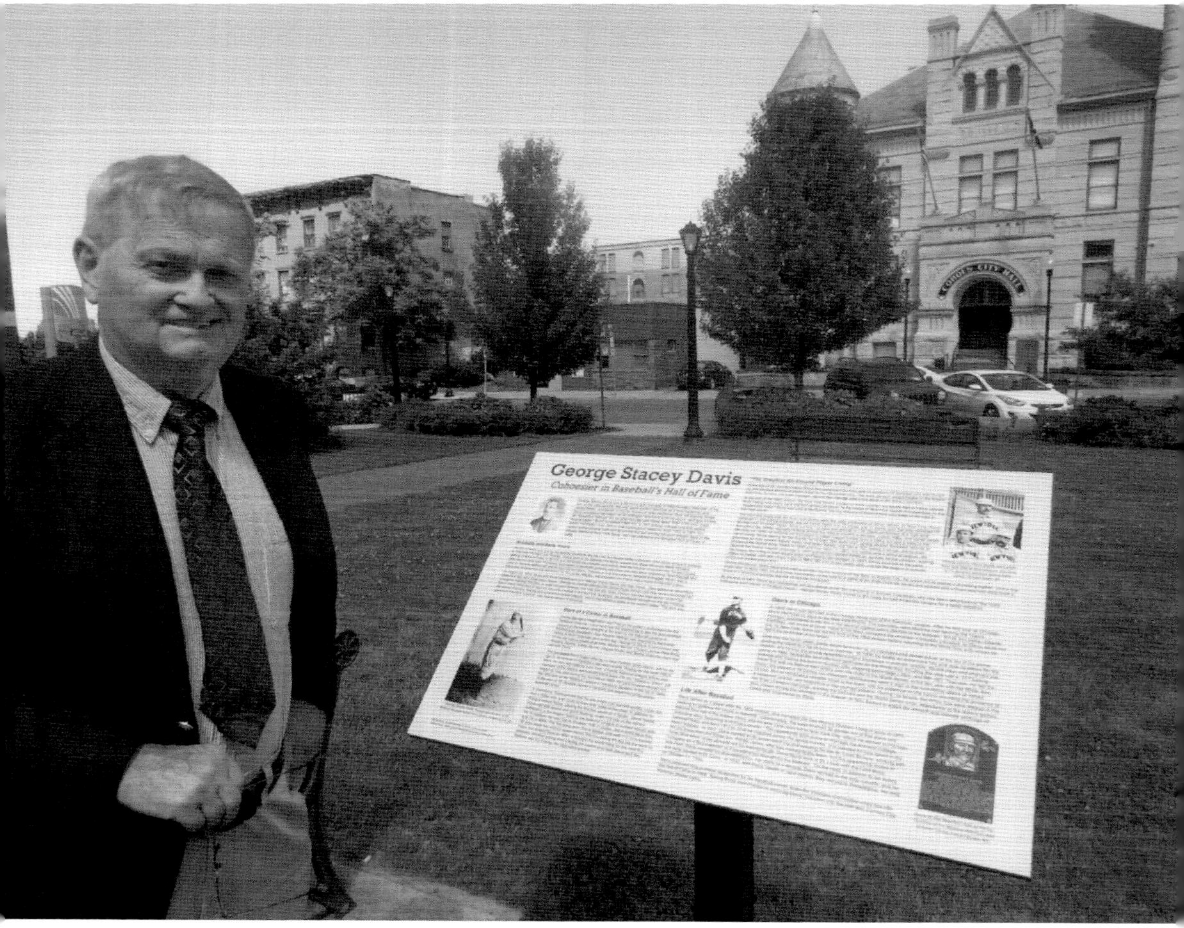

Walt Lipka started in the Cohoes School District in 1963. He taught art for the next 33 years. Although Lipka was always interested in Cohoes history, it was not until 1996, during the controversy surrounding the demolition of the Silliman Church, and upon his retirement from teaching, when history became a driving force in his life. In 1997, Lipka was made city historian by Mayor Bob Signoracci. One of his greatest achievements in this role was discovering a man from Cohoes named George Davis. As it turned out, Davis had been one of the best shortstops in baseball history. Knowing that he deserved greater recognition, Lipka immediately set to work contacting sportswriters and petitioning the National Baseball Hall of Fame in Cooperstown. In 1998, George Stacey Davis was inducted into the hall. It was a proud moment for Lipka and for all of Cohoes.

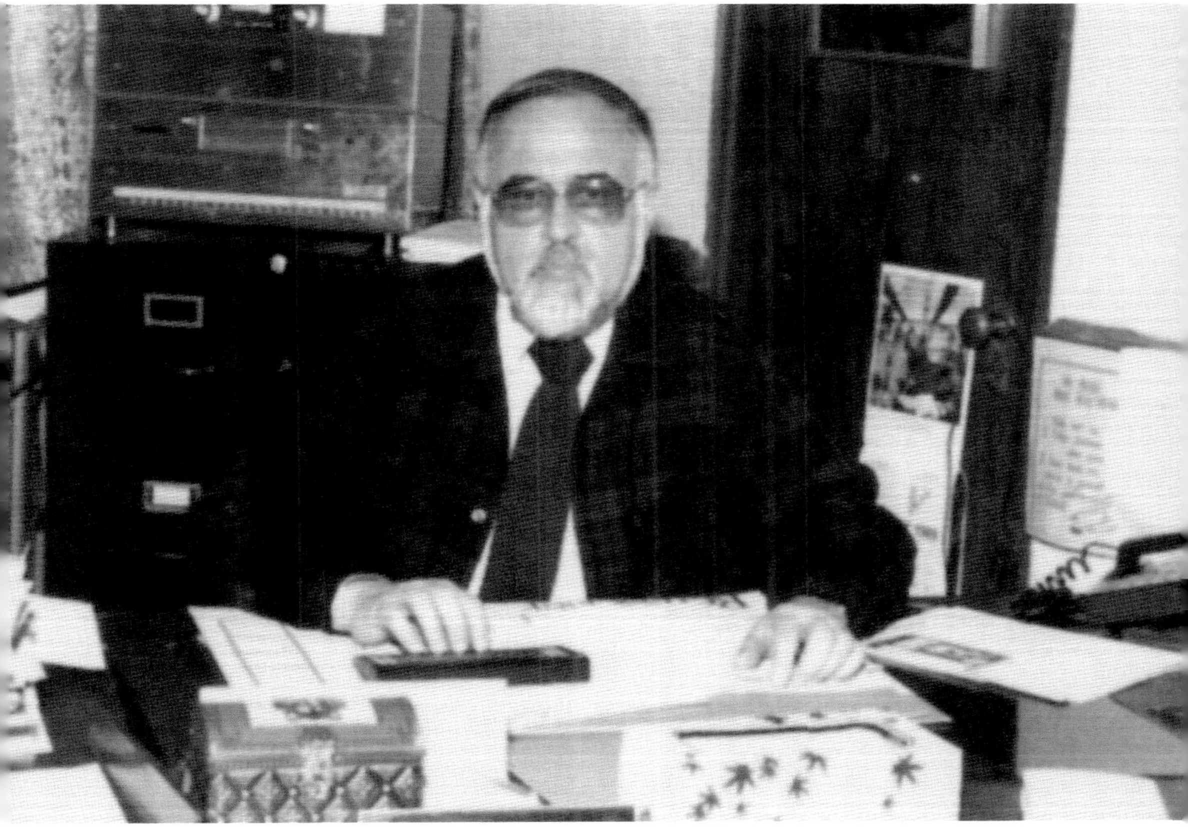

Bob Archambault could walk into a gymnasium filled with hundreds of rambunctious children and silence them in a matter of seconds, simply by raising his hand. That was the respect he commanded of his students. But it was a respect based on love, not fear. Archambault was born in Cohoes and attended St. Agnes School. He then went to the former Vincentian Institute in Albany and to Siena College, where he earned bachelor's and master's degrees. He began teaching social studies at Cohoes Middle School in 1970. A man of great faith, in 1976, he became the first permanent deacon ordained in the Roman Catholic Diocese of Albany. In 1978, he became principal of Van Schaick Elementary School, serving for 12 years until his untimely death in 1990. "Mr. A," as he was known to so many, will not soon be forgotten.

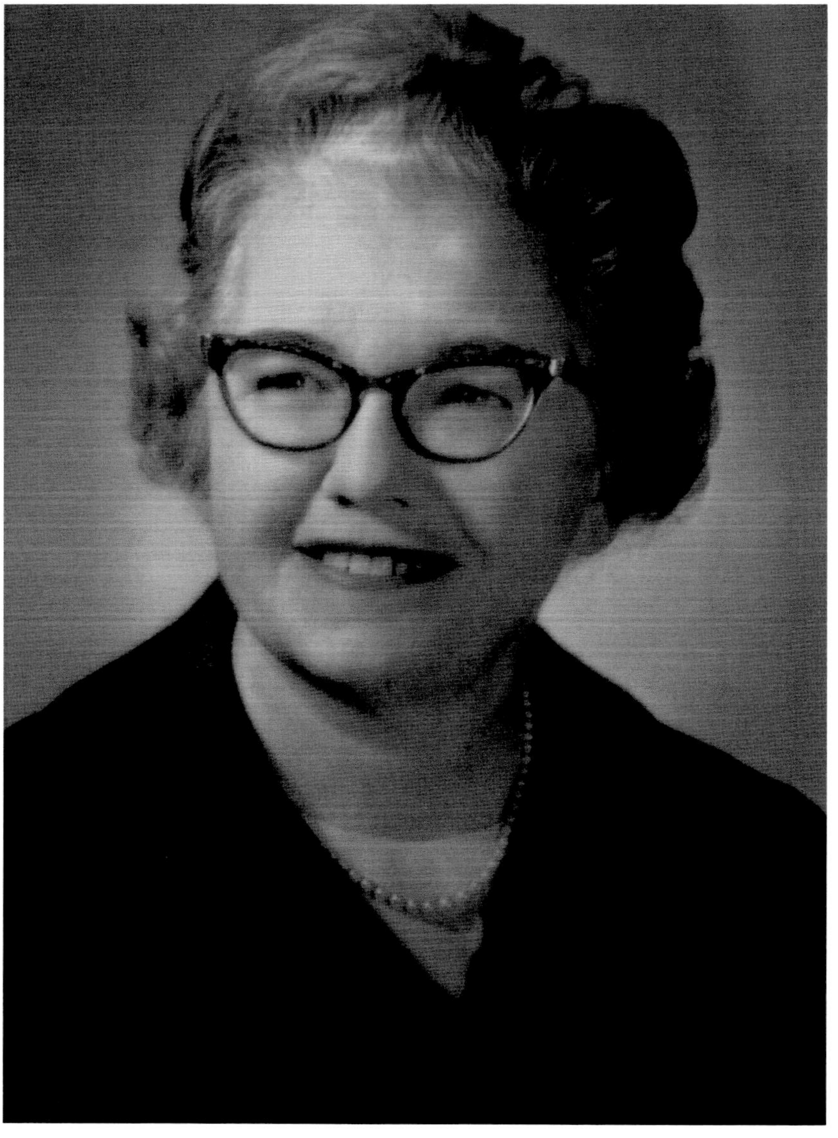

For thousands of students, she was known simply as Ms. Hickey. Stern but extremely caring, Madelon Hickey was a dedicated educator who served in the Cohoes School District for nearly 40 years. A native of Cohoes, Hickey attended the College of St. Rose and SUNY Albany, where she received her master's degree. She began her education career in Cohoes in 1930, teaching third and fourth grades. In 1946, she was named principal of Cohoes High School, where she served for 20 years. As principal, Hickey was known for her no-nonsense approach. But as tough as she could be, she showed immense devotion to her students throughout their academic careers. During the mid-1960s, she was a driving force in the effort to construct a new high school, as the old building had been plagued by overcrowding for many years. In 1966, Hickey was appointed curriculum coordinator for the district, and she served in that capacity until her retirement in 1970. Madelon Hickey died in 1972, but her legacy of leadership and love endures today.

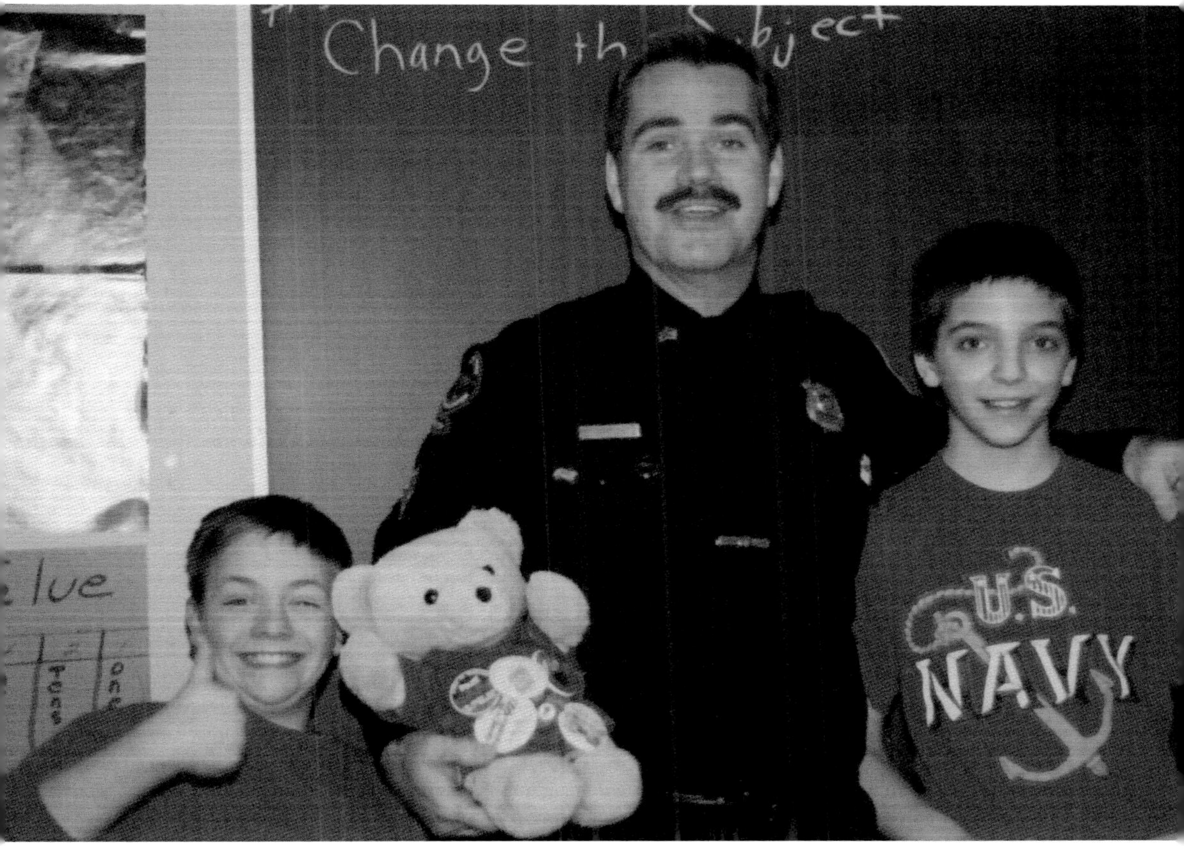

To thousands of Cohoes middle school and high school students, Dave Seguin was known as Sergeant Dave. Seguin joined the Cohoes Police Department in 1978. Always one to stay out of trouble and do the right thing, Seguin thought police work was a good fit. In 1991, he was approached by the chief of police to be part of a new program called DARE (Drug Abuse Resistance Education). Seguin immediately jumped at the opportunity. From the beginning, he began to form bonds of trust with some of the city's most troubled youths. It is hard to estimate just how many kids Seguin helped during the seven years he was stationed in the schools. To this day, Seguin receives messages from individuals who say that if it was not for him, they would never have gotten through school. Those letters are a fitting tribute to a man who always had a smile on his face and was willing to lend a helping hand. (Courtesy of Dave Seguin.)

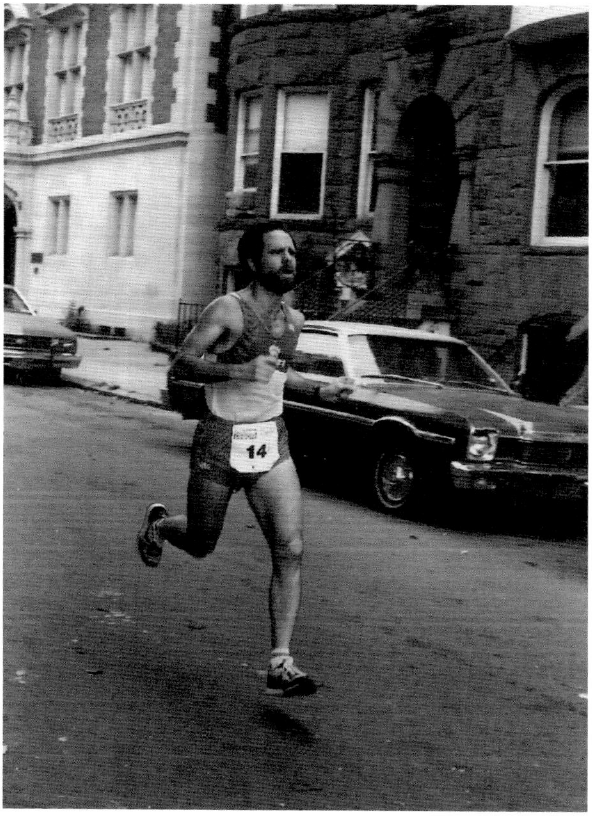

Any runner will tell you that without looking forward, you're not going to get very far. Bill Robinson has spent his entire life doing just that. Robinson grew up in Cohoes, attending Catholic schools and then Christian Brothers Academy in Albany. He graduated from Canisius College in 1968 and entered the Peace Corps in 1969, spending three years in Brazil working with children. In 1972, he went to work for the city, becoming deputy director of human resources. He went on to receive a master's degree in education from the College of St. Rose and spent a year teaching special education at Bethlehem High School. In 1979, he was hired by the New York State Division of Youth, where he spent the remainder of his career. Robinson's passion for running began in high school and continued during college and his time in the Peace Corps. But it was not until his early 40s that Robinson really found his stride. He trained hard every day and became one of the best master's runners in New York state. He won numerous gold medals at the Empire State Games. At local races, he was the man to beat. However, on the afternoon of March 16, 1990, Robinson and a group of other runners were out on their daily afternoon run in downtown Albany. They were within a block of finishing when a man lost control of his vehicle and struck Robinson from behind. He was rushed to Albany Medical Center, where he spent the next seven months. He sustained an injury to his C5 and C6 vertebrate, leaving him paralyzed from the neck down. The weeks and months that followed were extremely difficult for Robinson and his family. But the outpouring of support from the Cohoes community, including assisting the family to retrofit their home, allowed Robinson to begin to feel normal again. Today, Robinson is still active in the Hudson Mohawk Roadrunners Club and serves on the board of the Center for the Disabled. He is optimistic that, one day, injuries like his will be cured. Robinson has been an inspiration to countless individuals who for one reason or another had lost hope. Bill Robinson never lost hope, and he still looks forward. (Courtesy of the Hudson Mohawk Roadrunners Club.)

Civic Leaders

No city, town, or village can be successful without civic engagement and participation on the part of its citizens. It is at the very root of what it means to live in a democratic republic. Civic participation comes in many shapes and forms. There have been those who have devoted themselves to better government, the arts, medicine, public health, and overall quality of life in the community. Some have been leaders, while others have gone largely unnoticed. But all have made impacts on Cohoes that are almost impossible to measure, as their work has touched countless numbers of people. Today, civics is a lost art form. Many people in the hustle and bustle of modern life find it difficult to devote time to their communities. And, sadly, the physical and social environment of suburban life makes it difficult for residents to know their neighbors, let alone become involved in the community. Civic institutions like the Elks and Knights of Columbus have seen declining memberships. City council meetings are sparsely attended. But Cohoes remains a place where civic participation is a constant. It remains a place where people continue to devote themselves to the betterment of the community. Through civic groups like Kiwanis and the Rotary, to the Adopt-a-Park program and neighborhood watch, Cohoesiers continue to move their city forward. The individuals profiled in this chapter displayed a civic commitment to Cohoes that has come to define their lives. They are those to whom current citizens look for inspiration and guidance, and they will inspire future generations.

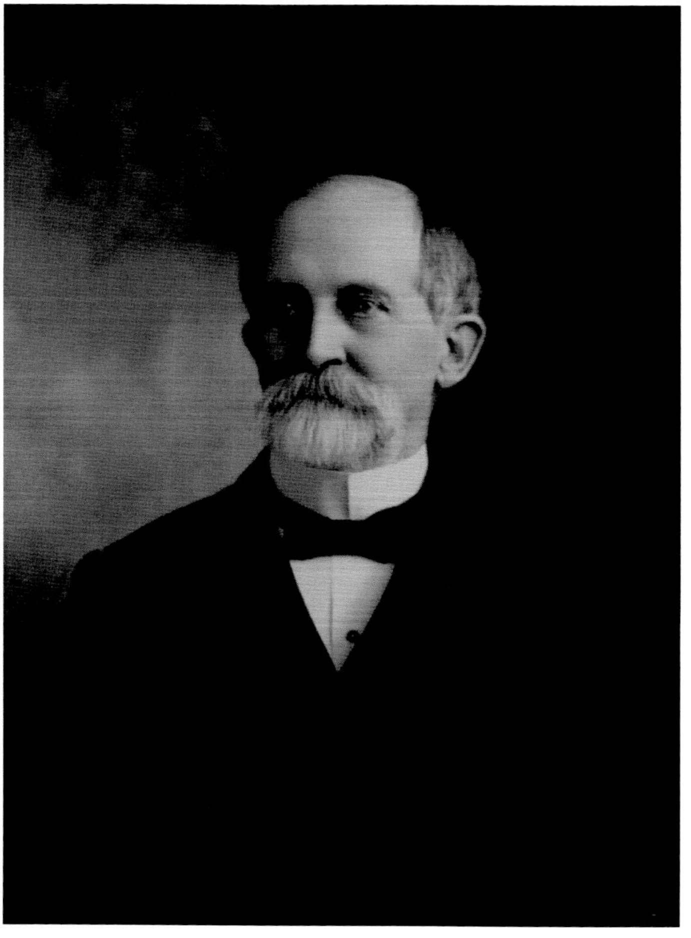

Horace Silliman was, without question, one of the city's greatest civic leaders. He was born in 1825, the only one of six children to live into adulthood. He was a graduate of the Albany Academy and went on to Union College in Schenectady. He also received an honorary degree from Hamilton College in Clinton, New York. Upon graduating from Union, Silliman opened a pharmacy on Remsen Street. In 1849, he and business partner Stephen Miller established a city newspaper, the *Cohoes Cataract*, and Silliman served as publisher until 1851. Silliman also became involved with the burgeoning textile industry in the city. He invested in several companies, including the Harmony Company, which, by the 1860s, gave Silliman a hefty dividend. He would use much of that wealth to better the lives of the people of Cohoes. He became active in relief for the poor and, during the Civil War, was involved with returning soldiers' relief efforts. He worked to establish the Cohoes Hospital and helped improve the water system. One of his greatest gifts to the city was the construction in 1896 of Silliman Memorial Presbyterian Church, a massive Romanesque Revival structure on Mohawk Street that he built in memory of his parents, Levi and Clarissa. Silliman's reach extended beyond Cohoes. In 1901, he donated $10,000 to start the Silliman Institute, a small elementary school in Dumaguete City, Philippines. In 1938, the school became Silliman University, which now has over 9,000 students. At the dedication of Cohoes City Hall in 1896, Silliman told those assembled to "cultivate a spirit of patriotism toward your city, make sacrifices for it and have the courage to support the good and antagonize the bad." Silliman died in May 1910 at the age of 84. (Courtesy of the Hamilton College Library.)

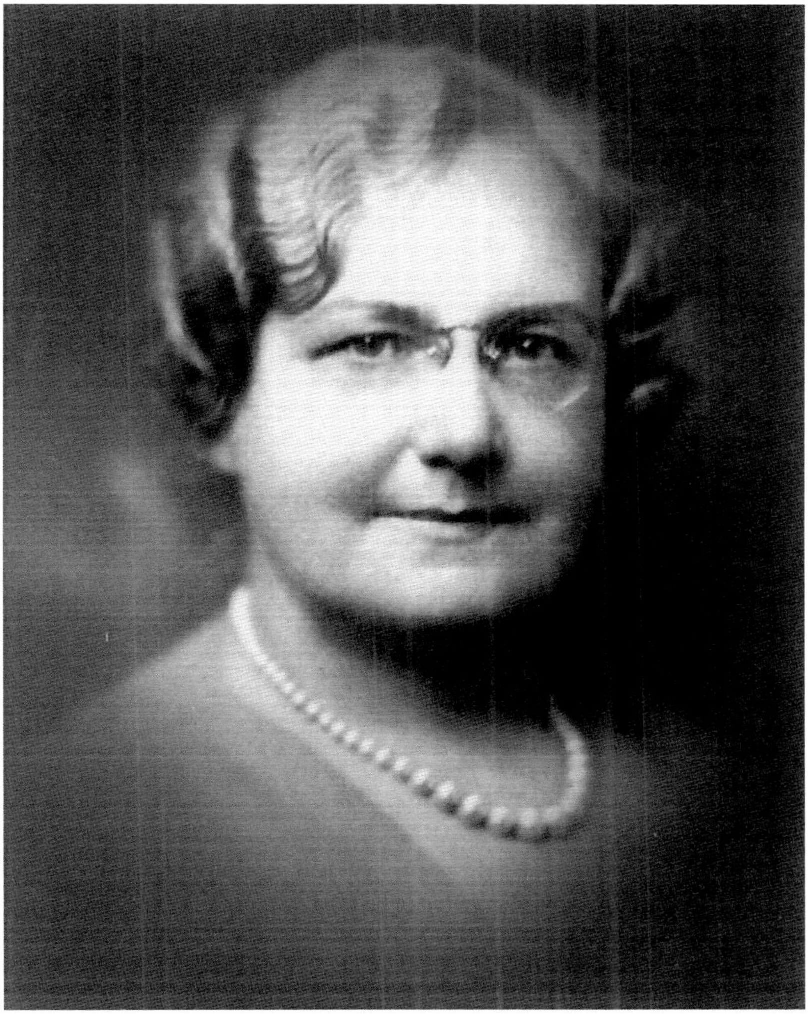

Born in 1877, Grace Reavy would shatter many glass ceilings over the course of her life. She attended St. Bernard's Academy and later went on to explore her talents in music, entering the New England Conservatory in Boston, where she became a pianist. She then took over the family funeral home upon the death of her father, Frank, in 1905. But it was not in the world of business or even music that Reavy would leave her biggest mark. During the early part of the 20th century, Cohoes was not immune to the problems vexing urban America, primarily, public health and overall quality-of-life issues. Reavy founded the Women's Municipal Welfare League, which established the city's first public playgrounds in 1913. She also worked to fight tuberculosis and infantile paralysis. In 1919, she was appointed city comptroller, making her the first woman in New York state appointed to a municipal public office. She later became city treasurer and Albany County commissioner of elections, then quickly moved on to become deputy secretary of state under Gov. Franklin Roosevelt. In 1937, Gov. Herbert Lehman appointed Reavy to the New York State Civil Service Commission, and she later became its president. During the remainder of her public life, Reavy worked with Eleanor Roosevelt on women's rights issues, specifically, advancing the role of women in business. Reavy died in 1959 and was buried from the Reavy family funeral home on Remsen Street. (Courtesy of John and Jackie Reavy.)

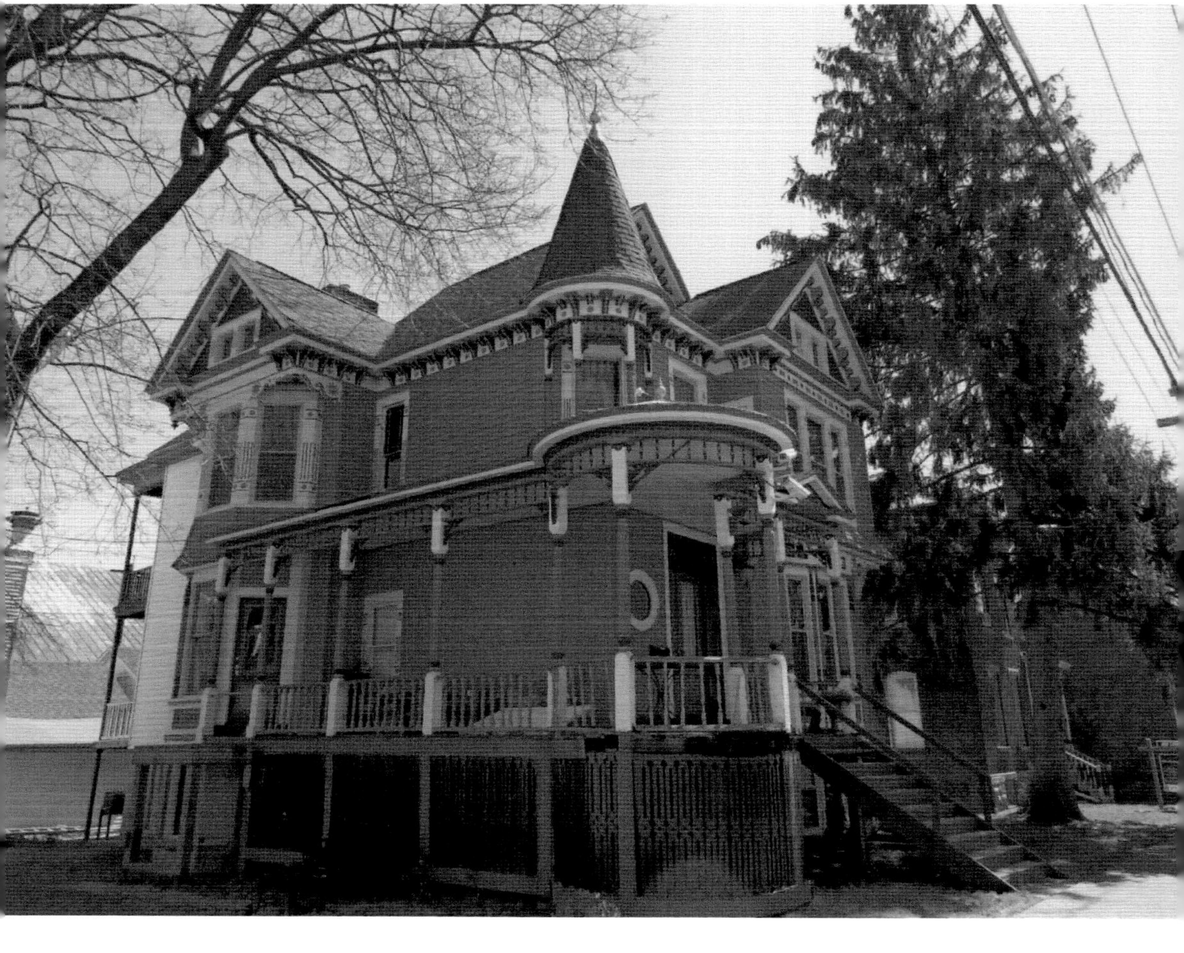

G. Upton Peltier was one of the most respected doctors in Cohoes during the latter part of the 19th century. Born in Quebec in 1848, Peltier received his medical degree from McGill University in Montreal in 1873. He immigrated to Cohoes soon after and established a medical practice on White Street. As a French-speaking doctor, Peltier had no shortage of patients, as the French population of Cohoes was beginning to spike around this time. In 1895, Peltier moved himself and his family into a new house on Congress Street (shown here) and saw patients in the basement. He also served on the staff of Cohoes Hospital. Peltier died in 1916, and is buried in Saint Joseph's Cemetery in Waterford, New York.

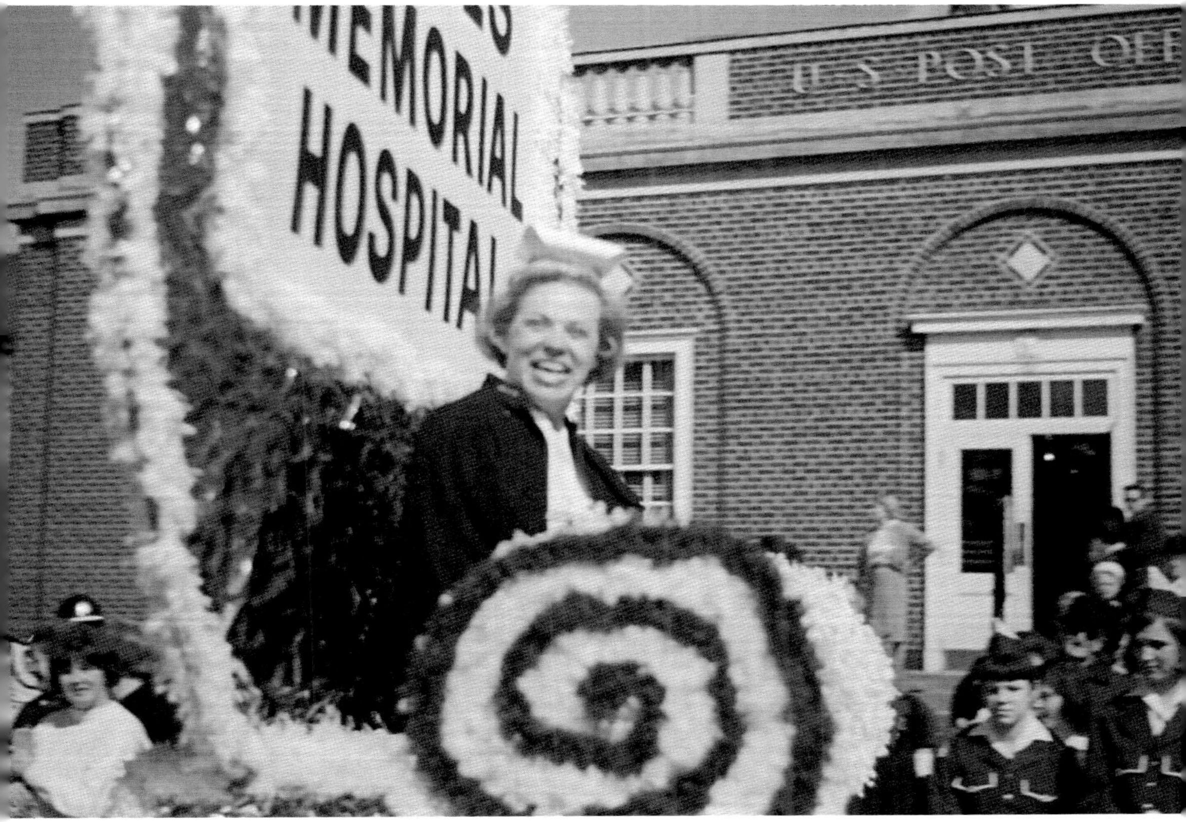

For nearly 70 years, Eunice Antonucci has played an active role in the civic affairs of Cohoes. Antonucci started her career as a nurse, working in the former Cohoes Hospital and eventually becoming director of nursing. During the 1970s and early 1980s, she served as director of human services for the city of Cohoes and was instrumental in the creation of Residential Opportunities Incorporated, an extremely successful organization that deals with the needs of developmentally disabled adults. From 1982 until 2008, Antonucci owned and operated the legendary Smith's Restaurant on Remsen Street with her daughter Margaret Kehn. Today, Eunice remains active in the business community and with many nonprofit organizations, including the Cohoes Music Hall, Choose Cohoes, and Holy Trinity Parish. (Courtesy of Paul Van Buskirk.)

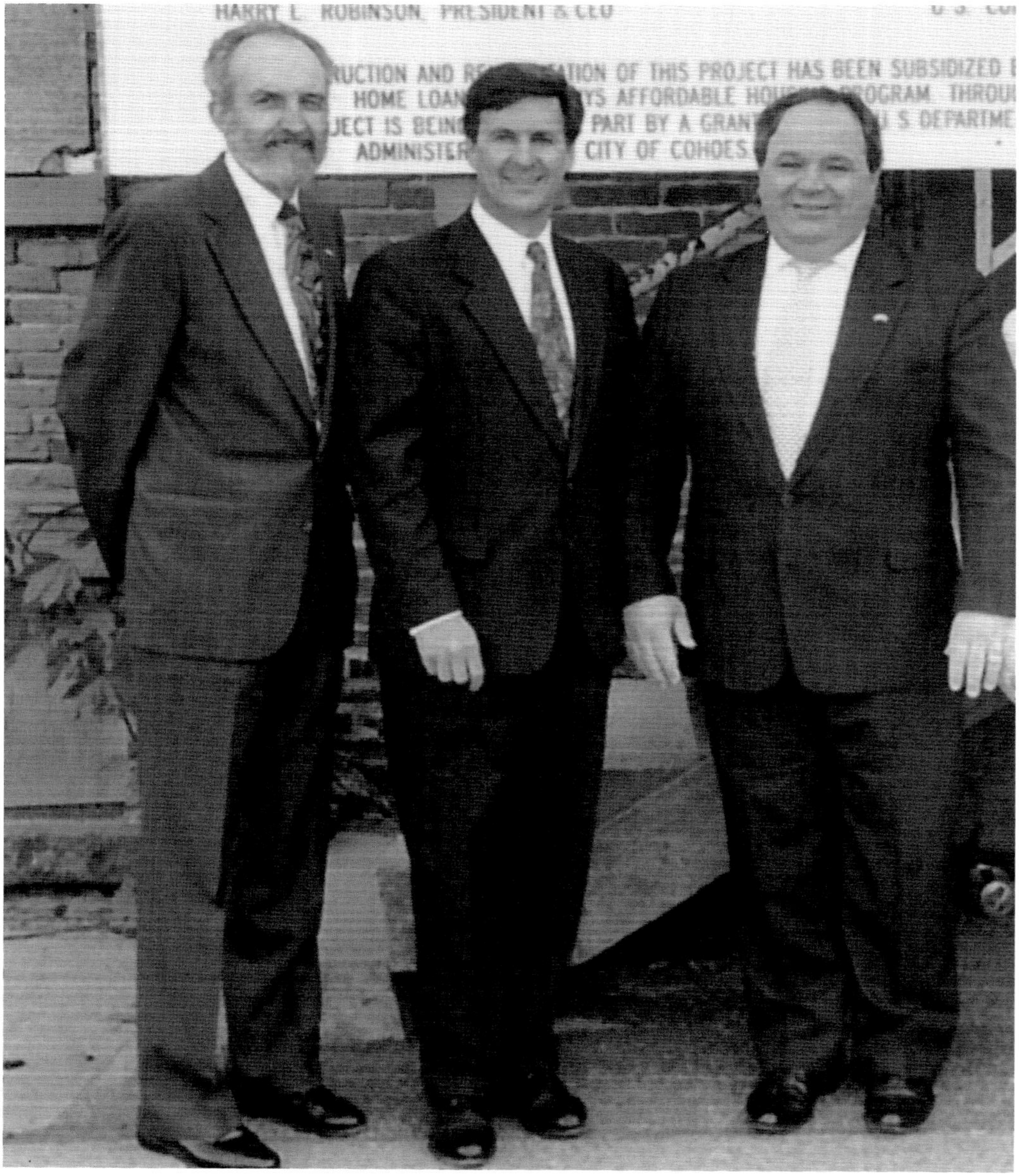

It could be said that Harry Robinson has one of the best jobs in the world. As chairman of the Cohoes Savings Foundation, Robinson has overseen the distribution of nearly $1.8 million over the last 12 years to various nonprofit and charitable organizations. The money has primarily stayed in the Capital Region and has gone to such groups as the Cohoes Community Center, Cohoes Music Hall, and the Center for the Disabled. The foundation was established soon after the sale of the Cohoes Savings Bank, where Robinson served as president for 11 years during the 1990s. Robinson, the first chairman of the Albany County Airport Authority, was instrumental in the reconstruction of the terminal in the mid-1990s. In this photograph, Robinson (left) poses with former mayor Bob Signoracci (right) and an unidentified person. (Courtesy of Bob Signoracci.)

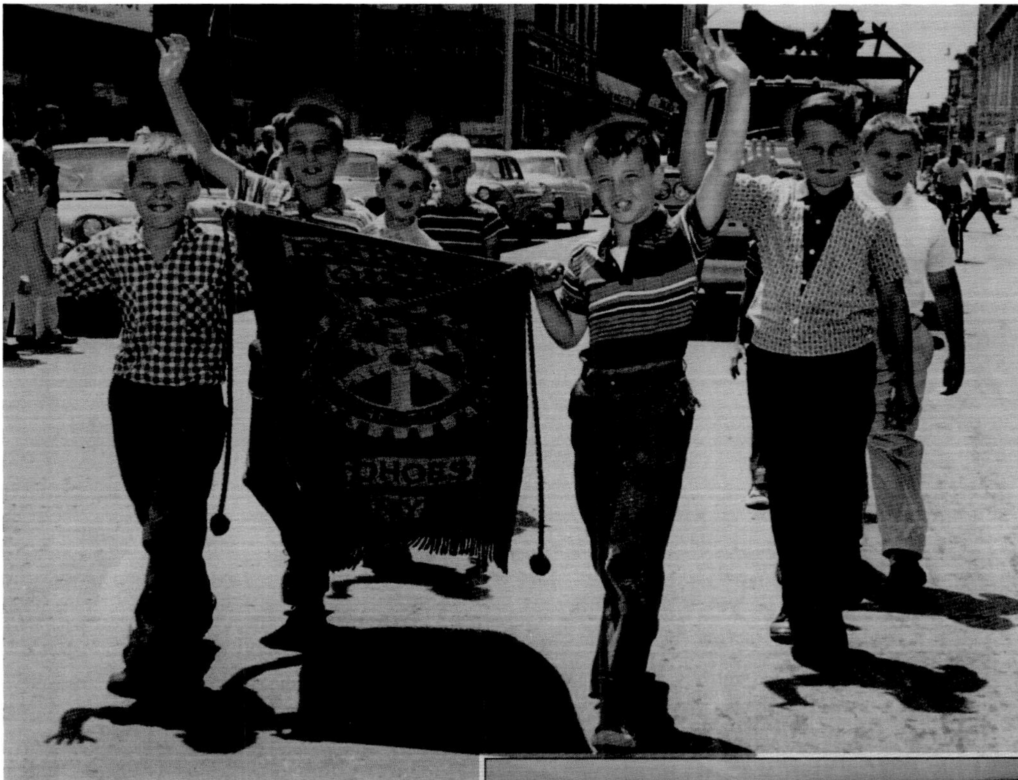

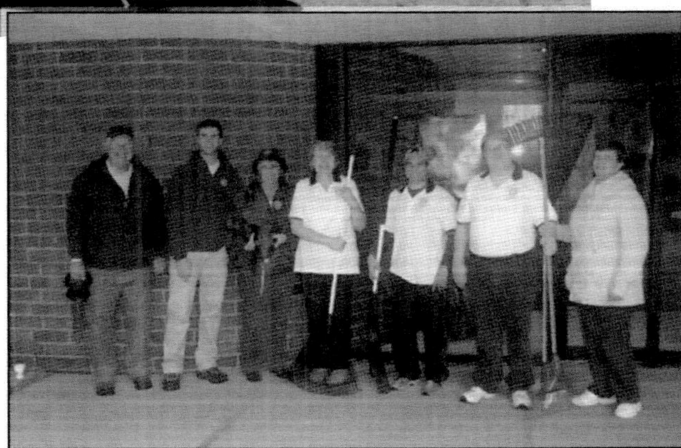

"Service above self" is the motto of the Rotary International, which has hundreds of thousands of members in 150 countries. The Cohoes Rotary, formed in 1927, was organized by Edward Doyle. For over 80 years, the Rotary has been dedicated to the betterment of Cohoes and its people. Currently, the club sponsors an annual scholarship to a graduating senior at Cohoes High School. Its fundraising activities include an annual Cohoes ornament sale, with proceeds going to benefit such organizations as the Cohoes Public Library, Salvation Army, and the Cohoes Community Center. The club also has adopted Cayuga Plaza as part of the city's beautification program. In the above photograph, children carry the Rotary banner in a parade down Remsen Street in the late 1950s. Members of the Cohoes Rotary participate in a cleanup at the Cohoes Senior Center (inset). (Above, courtesy of Tom Bessette; inset, courtesy of Ed Tremblay.)

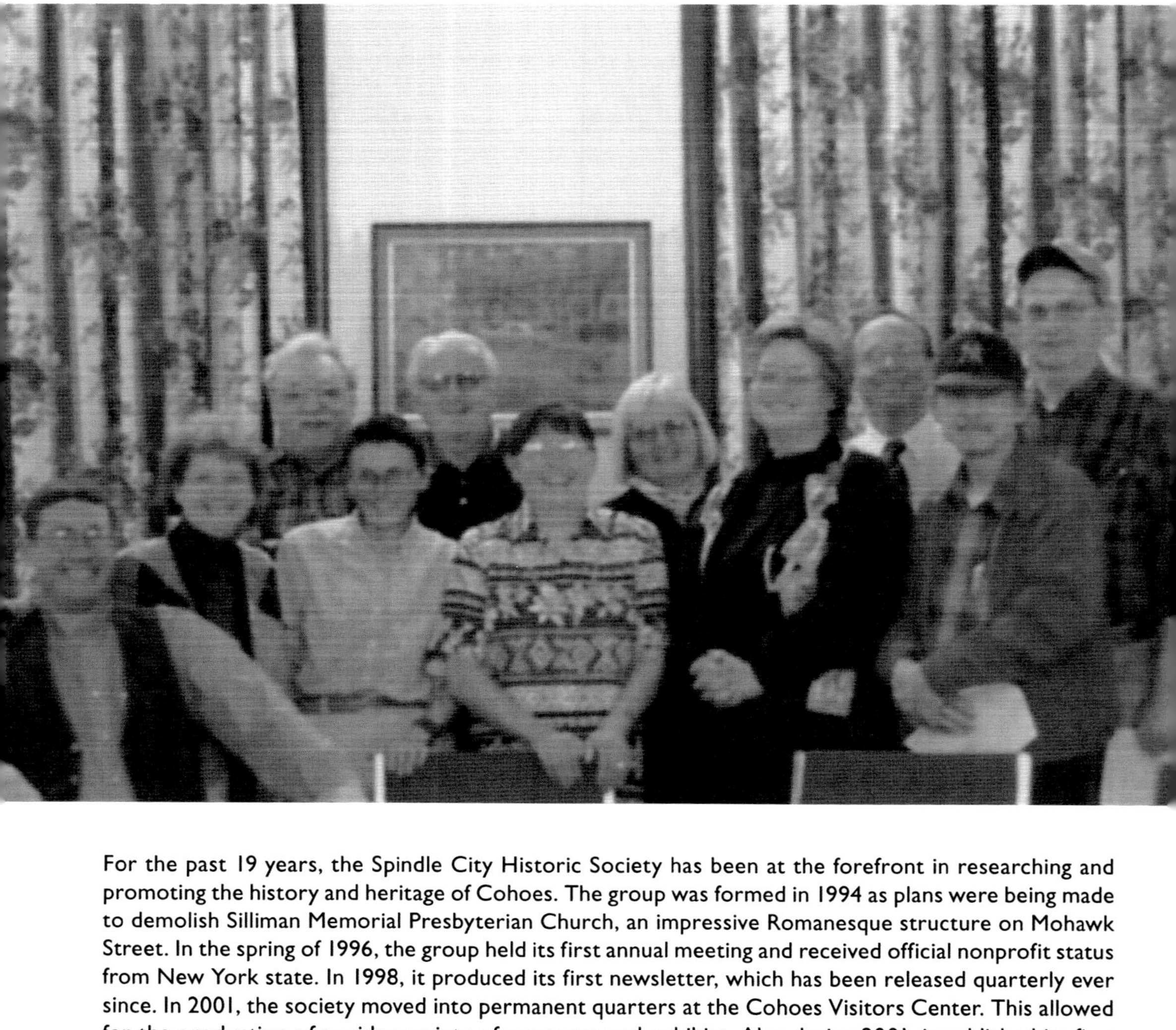

For the past 19 years, the Spindle City Historic Society has been at the forefront in researching and promoting the history and heritage of Cohoes. The group was formed in 1994 as plans were being made to demolish Silliman Memorial Presbyterian Church, an impressive Romanesque structure on Mohawk Street. In the spring of 1996, the group held its first annual meeting and received official nonprofit status from New York state. In 1998, it produced its first newsletter, which has been released quarterly ever since. In 2001, the society moved into permanent quarters at the Cohoes Visitors Center. This allowed for the production of a wider variety of programs and exhibits. Also during 2001, it published its first book, *Cohoes*, a pictorial history of the city. In 2006, a second book, *Cohoes Revisited*, was published. In 2004, the society spearheaded an effort to memorialize Horace Silliman on the site of the former Silliman Church by creating a public park. Today, the Spindle City Historic Society remains as active and dedicated as ever in promoting the history of Cohoes. Pictured here from left to right are Paul Dunleavy, Linda Christopher, Bernie Ouimet, Daniele Cherniak, Walter Cherniak, June Cherniak, Mary De Rose, Donna Riley, Tor Shekerjian, Dennis Rivage, and Walter Lipka. (Courtesy of the Spindle City Historic Society.)

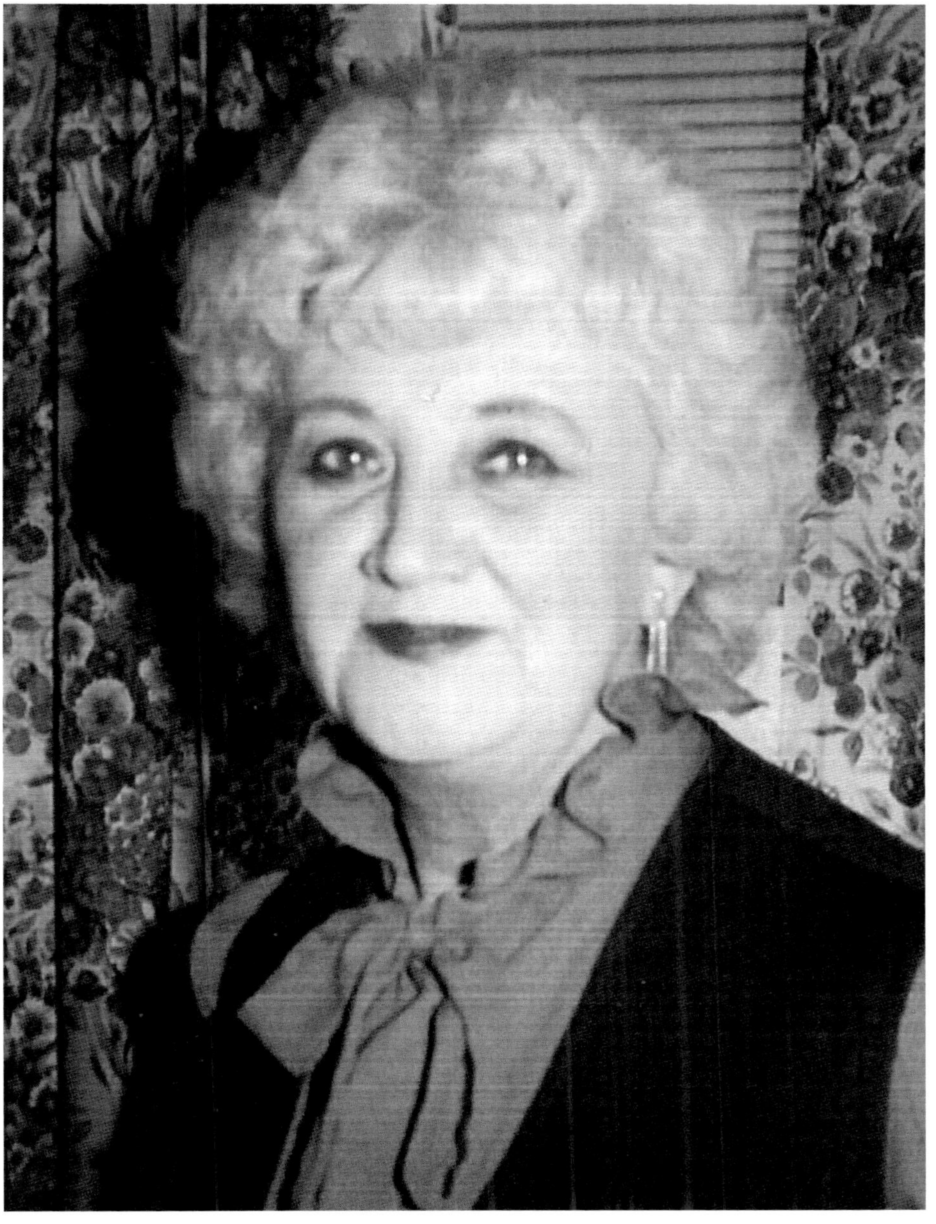

In July 1976, Ruth Vore wrote what would become the unofficial theme song for the city of Cohoes. Born and raised in Cohoes, Vore was very active in the community, particularly with the arts. She worked for many years at the Cohoes Music Hall and served as its director. She also taught religion at the former St. James Church. Her song, *I Love Cohoes*, is a lasting tribute to a life dedicated to family and community. "I love my hometown, I love Cohoes. I love the spot where the Mohawk flows! I love the people whose spirit glows! I love my hometown, I love Cohoes! With God's help and guidance we bravely carry on. I'll sing of her praises till life and breath are gone. I love the memories of days of yore, of our dear loved ones who have gone before. I love my hometown, I love Cohoes!" (Courtesy of Dane Vore.)

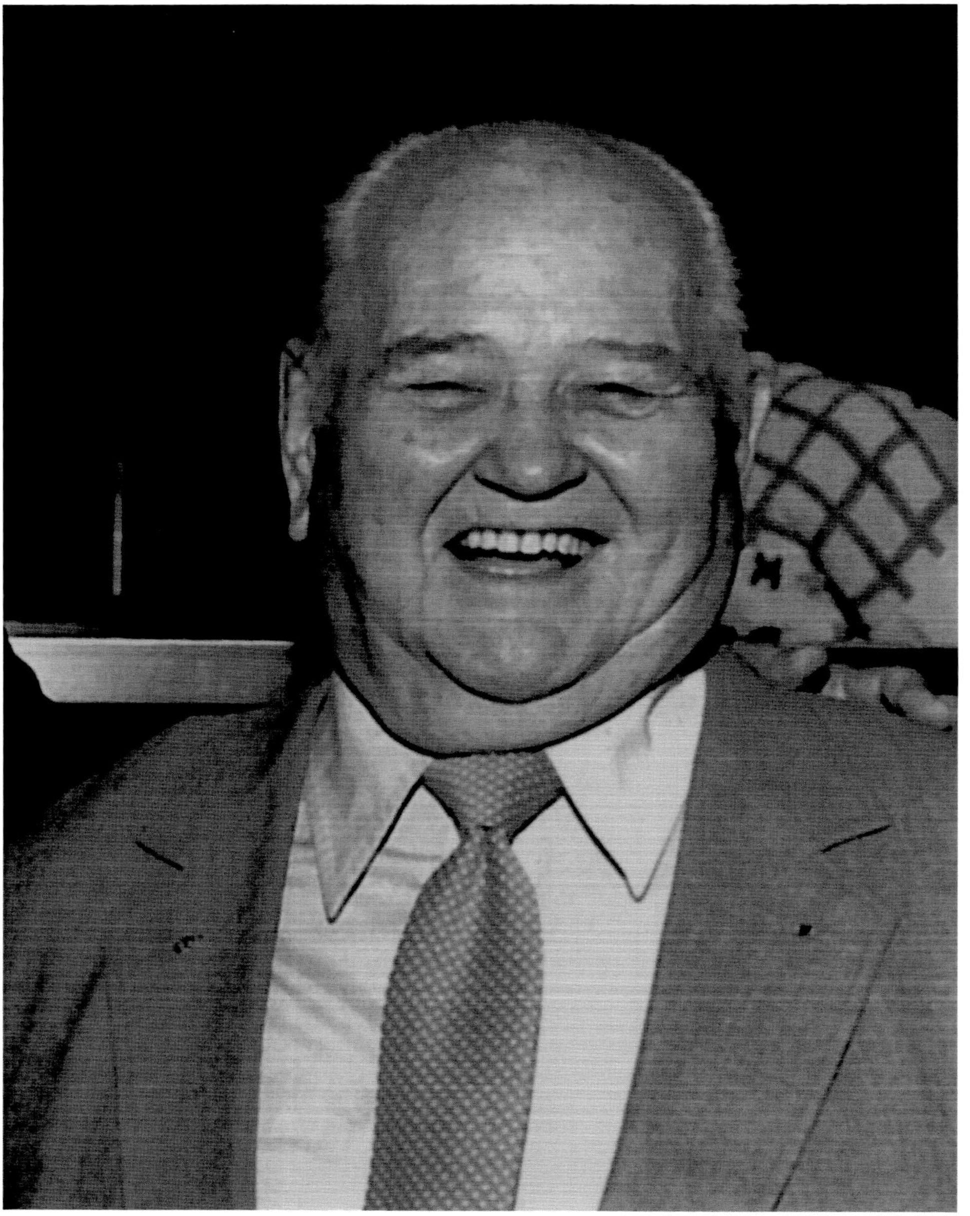

Dubbed "Mr. Cohoes," Ken Green contributed to the community in a variety of ways. He served for 30 years at the Cohoes Post Office, where he was known as a regular welcome wagon for new residents. He then served as director of the Cohoes Tool Library, an innovative program for its time. Prior to the days of Home Depot, Green would be the go-to person for advice on home repair and maintenance. Green also had a passion for music, and he is most famous for singing the city's theme song, *I Love Cohoes*, written by Ruth Vore. In his later years, Green was a member of the Silver Tops and served as a cook at civic functions throughout the city. Ken Green was a man who truly loved his hometown, he loved Cohoes. (Courtesy of Theresa Thibodeau.)

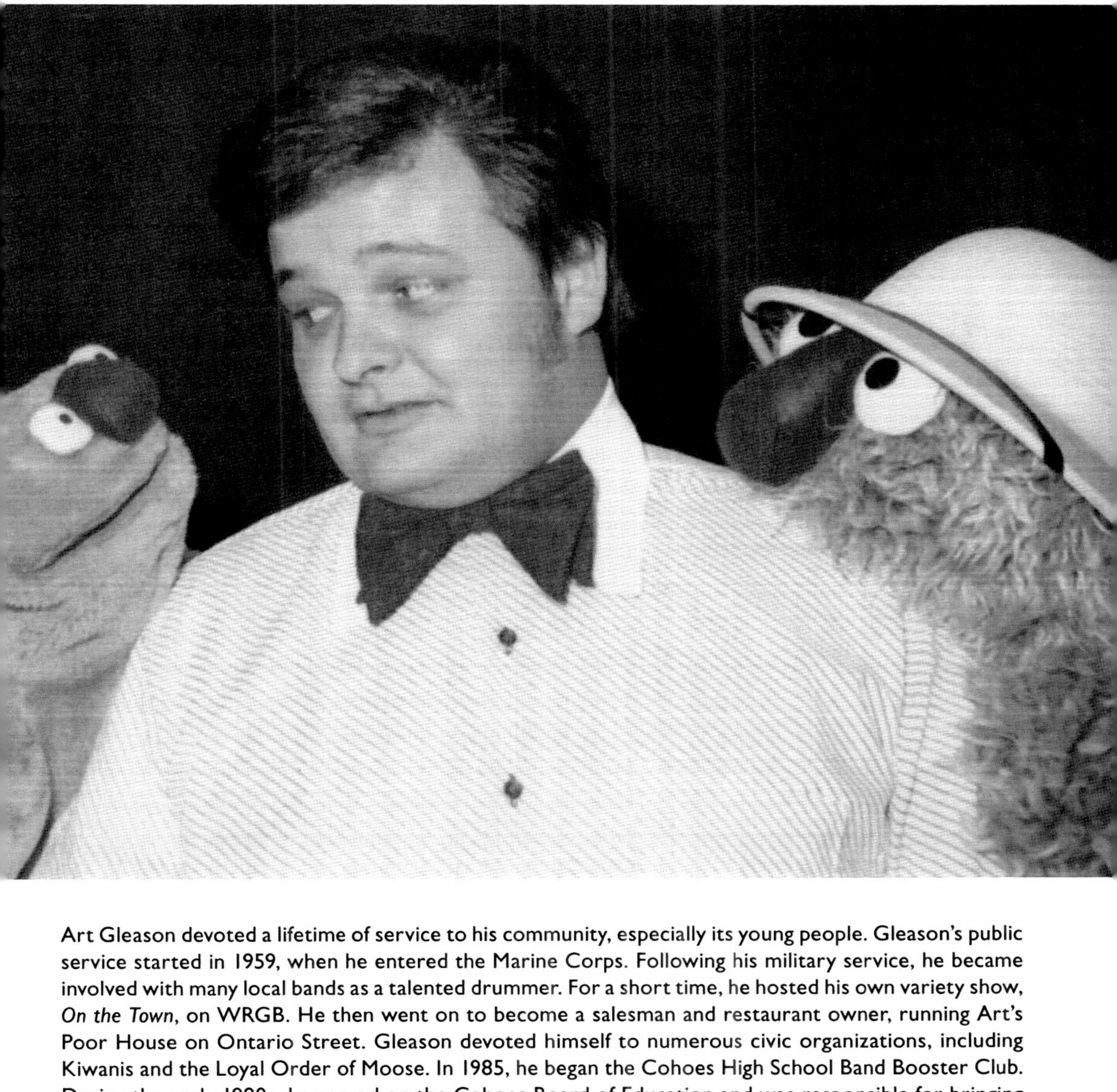

Art Gleason devoted a lifetime of service to his community, especially its young people. Gleason's public service started in 1959, when he entered the Marine Corps. Following his military service, he became involved with many local bands as a talented drummer. For a short time, he hosted his own variety show, *On the Town*, on WRGB. He then went on to become a salesman and restaurant owner, running Art's Poor House on Ontario Street. Gleason devoted himself to numerous civic organizations, including Kiwanis and the Loyal Order of Moose. In 1985, he began the Cohoes High School Band Booster Club. During the early 1990s, he served on the Cohoes Board of Education and was responsible for bringing drug-free zones to Cohoes schools. Throughout his life, he touched the lives of numerous young people going through rough times. Through that devotion, his legacy lives on. Gleason is seen here on his show, *On the Town*. (Courtesy of the Gleason family.)

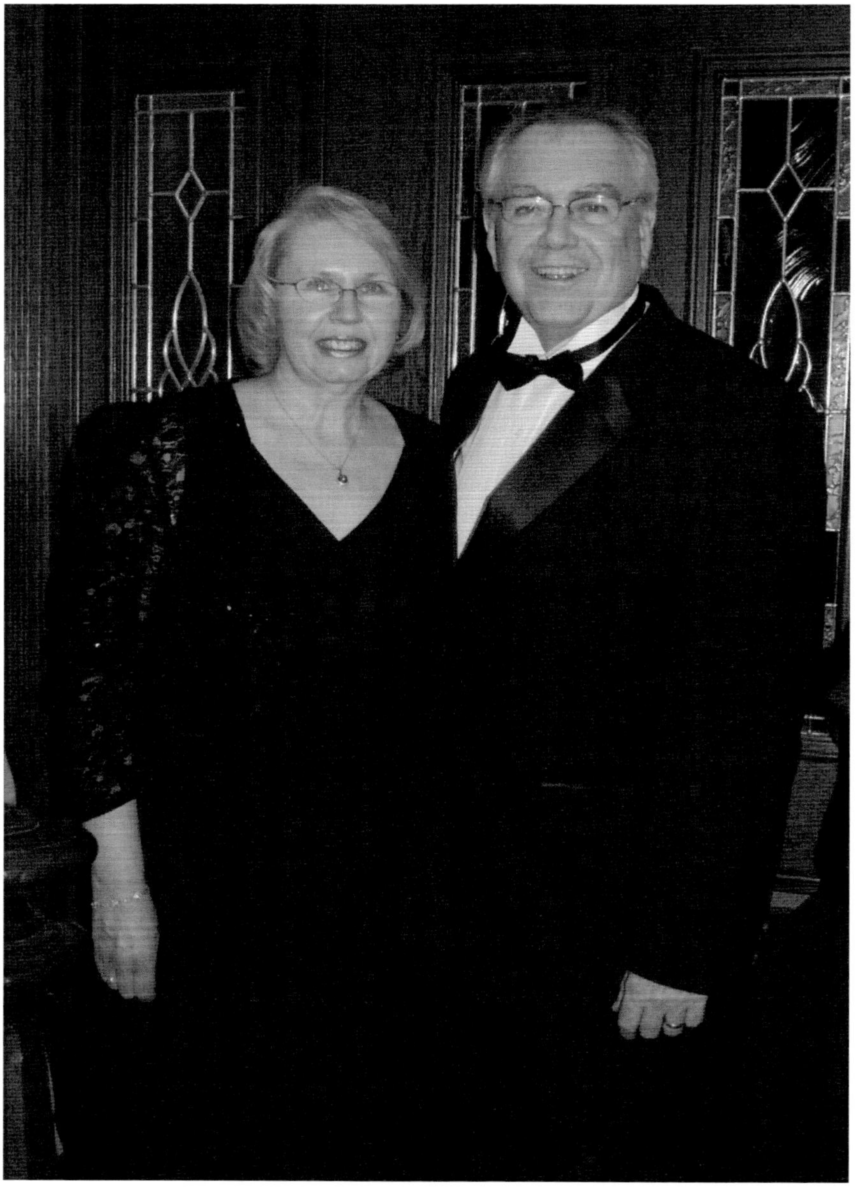

Born and raised in Cohoes, Ed and Linda Tremblay can trace their roots in the community back generations. They were high school sweethearts and married in 1975. Ed went on to a career in banking, and Linda entered the world of public relations. Once their children became involved with school activities, Ed and Linda made it a point to become involved as well. This grew into civic leadership that has spanned the last several decades. They have been instrumental in the success of a variety of civic groups, including the Rotary, Kiwanis, the Cohoes Caretakers, the Cohoes Chamber of Commerce, and Choose Cohoes. For the last nine years, Ed has been the city's director of community development and has played a key role in the resurgence and revitalization of Cohoes. The Tremblays continue to lead and inspire future generations to become involved with their community. (Courtesy of Kelly Tremblay Brady.)

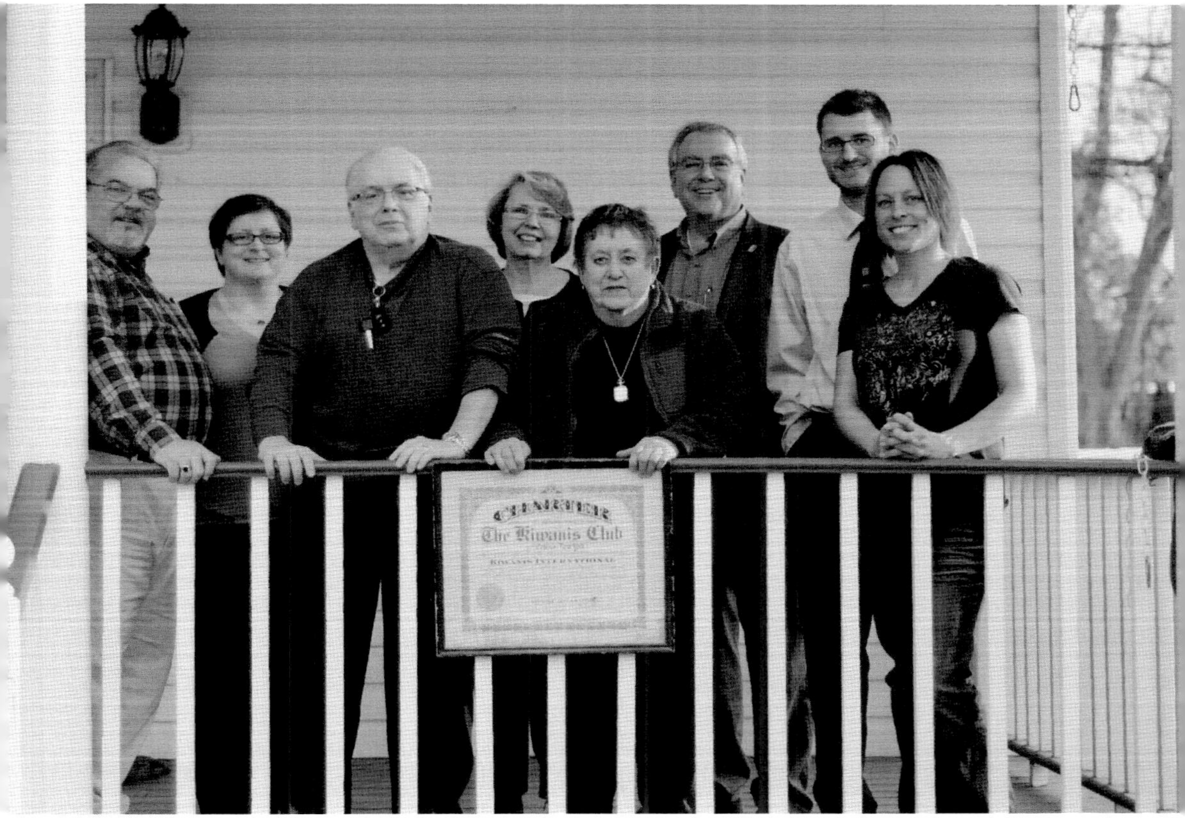

Kiwanis International was founded in 1915 in Detroit, Michigan, with a mission to serve the community. The Cohoes Kiwanis was chartered in 1947 and has played a vital role in community service ever since. The Cohoes organization has been primarily dedicated to serving the youth of Cohoes. And while the Cohoes club has always been small, its impact has been large. Since the late 1980s, Kiwanis has sponsored an annual fall festival, bringing the city's youth and families together. The organization also assists with the annual Halloween parade and provides scholarships. Today, the Kiwanis continues its commitment to the community and looks to sustain its mission into the future. Pictured here from left to right are Bob Austin, Theresa Thibodeau, Mike Brooks, Linda Tremblay, Myrtle Scott, Ed Tremblay, Christopher Nolin, and Jill Havens. (Courtesy of Teigan Powell.)

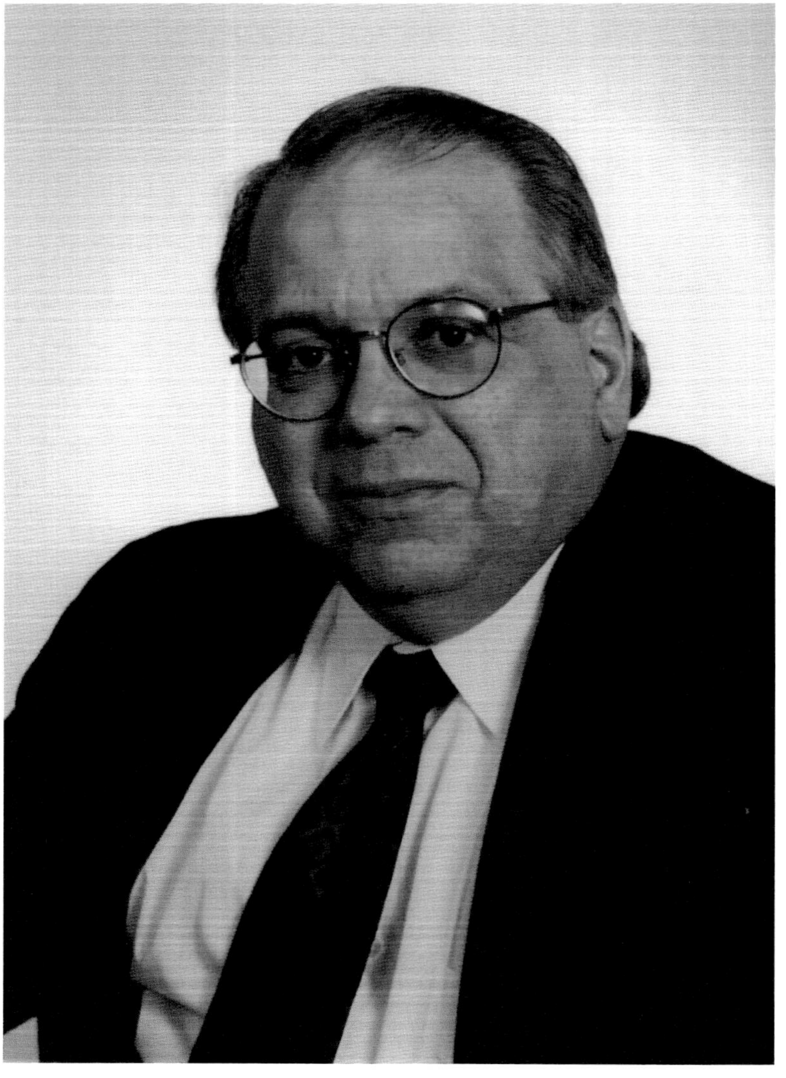

Originally from Baltimore, Mike Brooks moved to Cohoes at age 12 upon the death of his father. He and his mother, Jeannette, settled into a house on Bridge Avenue on Van Schaick Island. It was here that Brooks got to experience such neighborhood institutions as Frank's Store and Little Nick's. This experience formed an unwavering commitment to his community. Brooks worked at the *Troy Record* and the Bendix Company in Green Island before spending 30 years with NYNEX, retiring in 1996. He was then appointed to head the Cohoes Housing Authority, a job he absolutely loved. But in 1999, Brooks resigned from the authority in order to make a run for mayor. He was the man with the plan, but he lost the Democratic primary to John McDonald. In the mid-1990s, he cofounded the Cohoes Caretakers, a civic group dedicated to the betterment of Cohoes and its people. He has served and continues to serve in numerous civic organizations, including the Cohoes Kiwanis, the Cohoes Rotary, the Cohoes Senior Center, and the Business Council of Cohoes. He is cofounder and president of the Cohoes Youth Boxing Club. For Brooks, his most significant achievement was working to bring the Vietnam War Healing Wall, a half-scale replica of the National Vietnam Wall Memorial, to Lansing Park. (Courtesy of Mike Brooks.)

A People of Faith

Cohoes has been described as "the city of many churches," an apt title considering the church steeples dominating the skyline. Ever since Native Americans inhabited the area, faith has played an important and primary role in Cohoes. When the Dutch settled in the area in the late 17th and early 18th centuries, they brought with them Christianity in the form of Dutch Reformed Protestantism. The first church built north of Albany was the Reformed Church of the Boght, constructed in 1781. In 1837, the Dutch Reformed Church of Cohoes was established by Dutch, English, and Scottish families. The English organized St. John's Episcopal Church in 1831, and in 1839, the First Baptist Church was organized, primarily by mill workers. During the middle to latter part of the 19th century, Cohoes saw a large influx of Irish, French Canadian, Italian, Polish, and Russian immigrants. Each ethnic group organized its own Catholic parish. For the Irish, it was St. Bernard's, organized in 1847, and, later, St. Patrick's Church in the Orchard neighborhood and St. Agnes Church at the top of Harmony Hill. The French constructed three churches in the city from the 1860s to the 1890s: St. Joseph's downtown, Sacred Heart on Van Schaick Island, and St. Maries on the Hill. The Italian population built St. Rita's on Lansing Street, and the Polish built St. Michael's on Simmons Island. Eastern Rite Catholics organized St. Nicholas Church on Saratoga Street and St. Peter and St. Paul on Ontario Street. These churches were the center of civic, cultural, and ethnic life in the city well into the 20th century. However, by the early 1990s, with the Catholic population shifting to the suburbs and the increasing shortage of priests, many of the parishes found it difficult to sustain their vibrancy. Today, only two Catholic parishes remain in the city. The church buildings themselves, however, still stand as city landmarks, and many have been reclaimed by Protestant churches, which are now thriving. Good Ground Family Church, which occupies the former St. Agnes Church, has centered itself around youth. Heritage Baptist Church, which occupies St. Rita's, continues to grow as it offers a simple gospel-centered message. This chapter highlights individuals who have built up and continue to sustain the steeples of Cohoes.

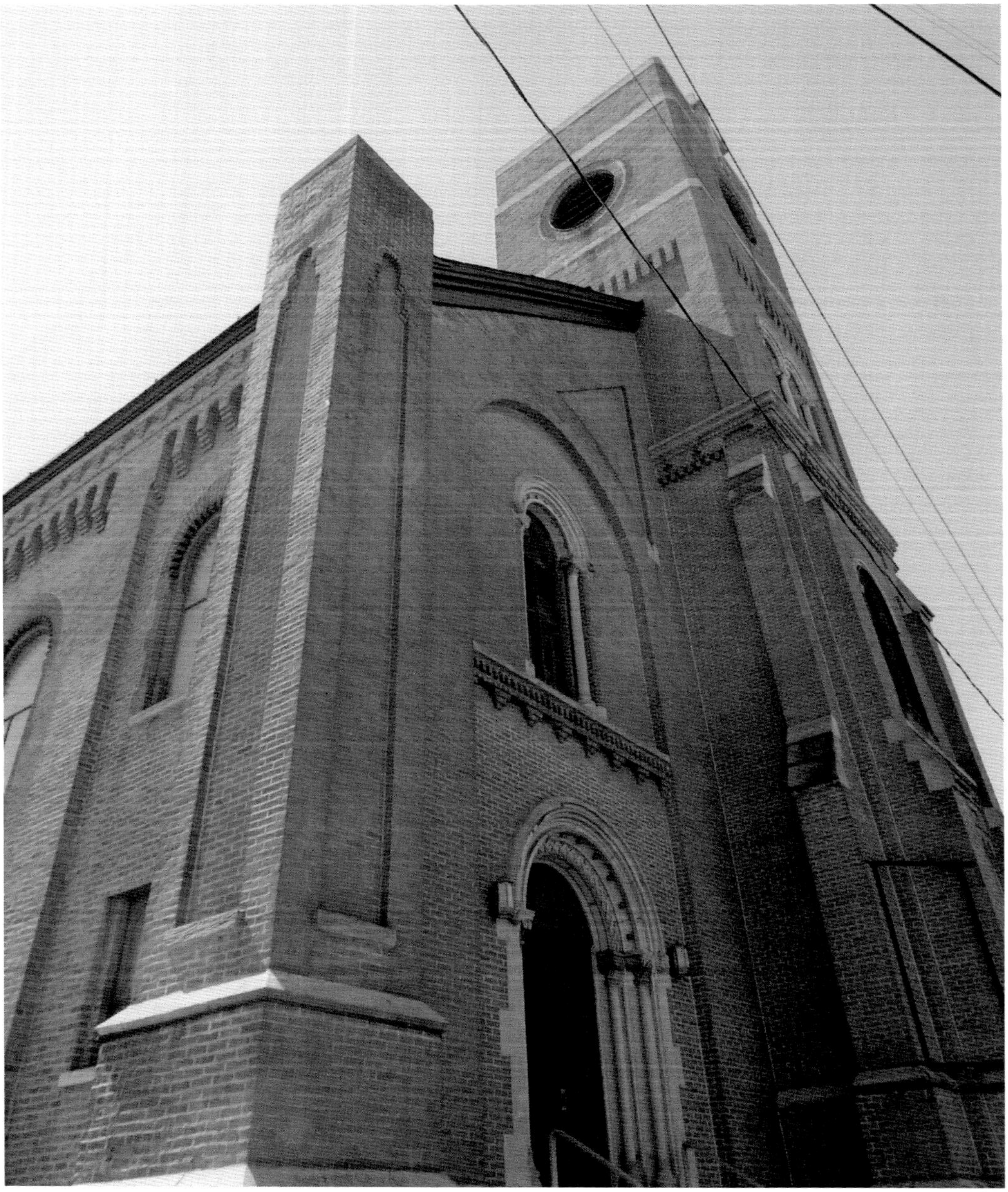

Bernard Van Reeth was the first Catholic priest to set foot in Cohoes. He was educated at the Cistercian Abbey of St. Bernard in Belgium and had done missionary work in England before coming to the United States. The first Catholic mass in the city of Cohoes was celebrated in the spring of 1847 in a private home at 213 Remsen Street. The first parish was named for St. Bernard, and regular services were held at a carpenter shop on Remsen Street below Howard Street. In November of the same year, the cornerstone for the first Catholic church building in Cohoes was laid by Van Reeth and Bishop John McCloskey on land donated by the Harmony Company, on the site of the former Keveny Academy. Van Reeth returned to Belgium in 1853. Shown here is the former St. Bernard's Roman Catholic Church.

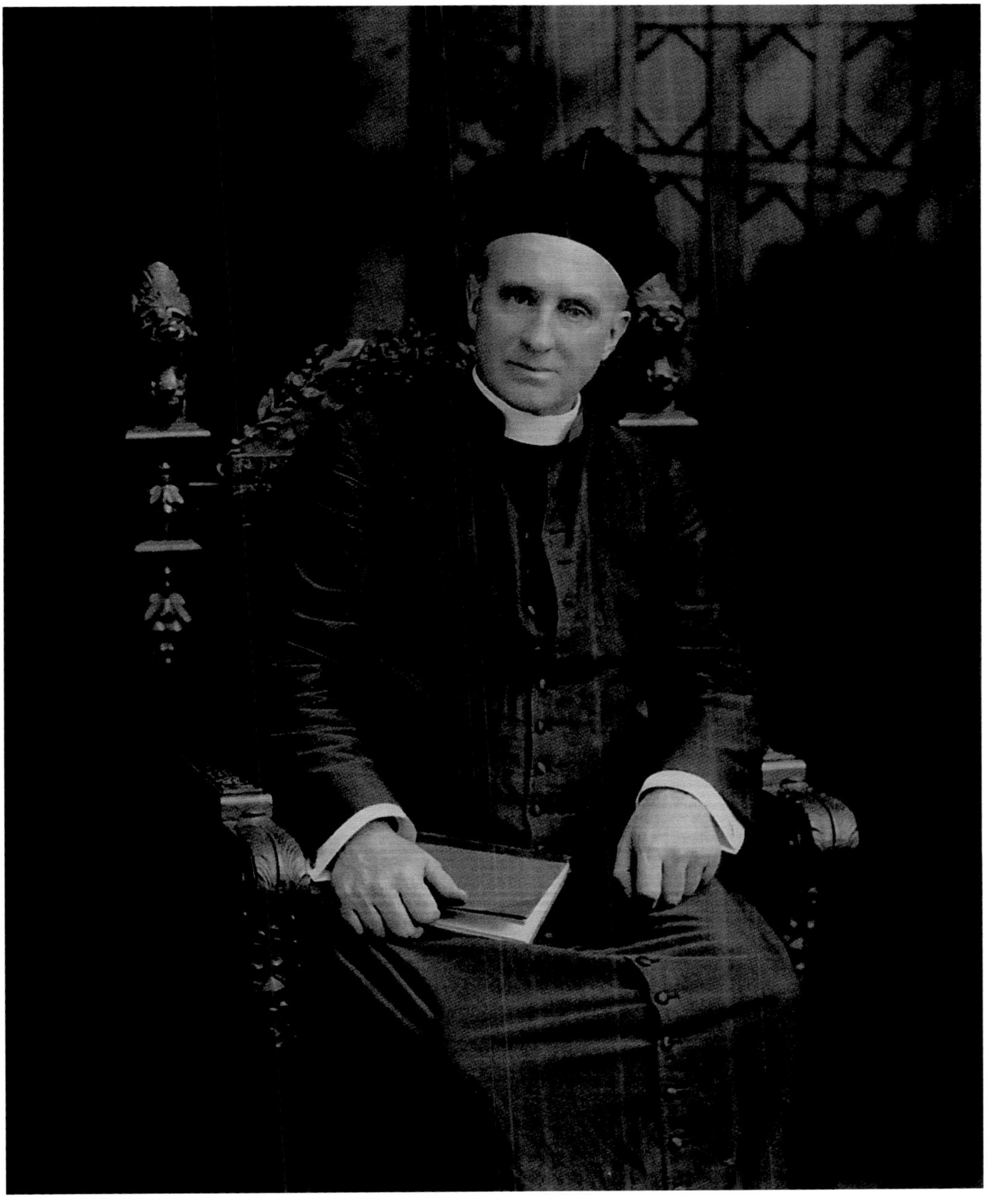

Thomas Keveny was ordained a priest on October 5, 1873, in St. Bernard's Church. He spent the next 51 years of his life at St. Bernard's, starting as an assistant pastor to his uncle, Rev. Thomas Keveny, and becoming pastor upon the death of his uncle in 1882. In 1895, he was named an irremovable rector and, in 1904, was elevated to the title of monsignor. In 1923, upon the occasion of his 50 years in the priesthood, the church was redecorated, with a new floor installed, and the church debt was paid off. Monsignor Keveny died the following year and was buried in Calvary Cemetery in Cohoes. In February 1931, a new parish school was dedicated, named Keveny Memorial Academy. (Courtesy Cohoes Public Library.)

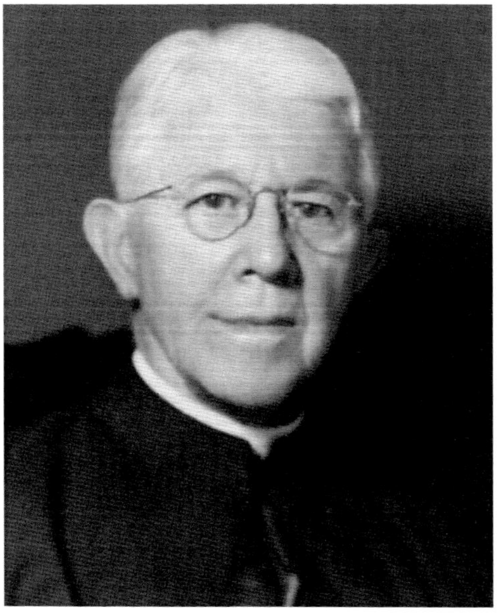

Joseph Franklin was ordained a priest on December 17, 1910, by Bishop Thomas Burke. He served as an assistant pastor at several area churches until becoming pastor of St. Agnes Church in Cohoes in November 1921. In 1955, he was elevated to the rank of monsignor by Pope Pius XII. Franklin was known for standing on the corner near the school, asking students who passed, "Have you said your stations today?" Msgr. Franklin served St. Agnes Parish for 38 years, until his death in December 1959. He was recalled in the parish newsletter of that year as "our pastor, our mentor and our friend. No timid penitent ever failed to receive help and courage during a talk with Fr. Franklin, surely, God blessed three generations in our parish when he whispered to the boy Joe Franklin, come, follow me." The photograph below shows the former St. Agnes Roman Catholic Church.

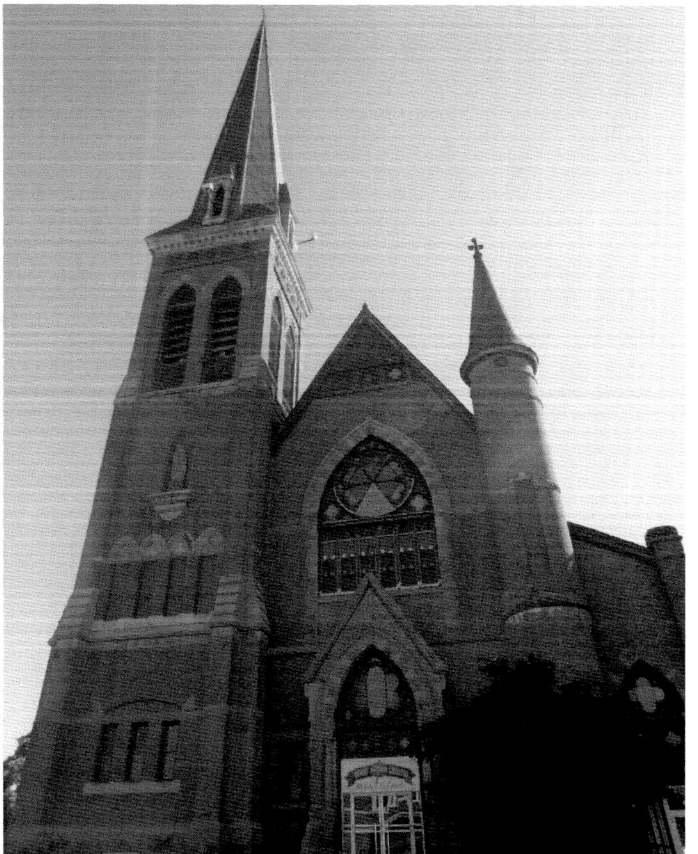

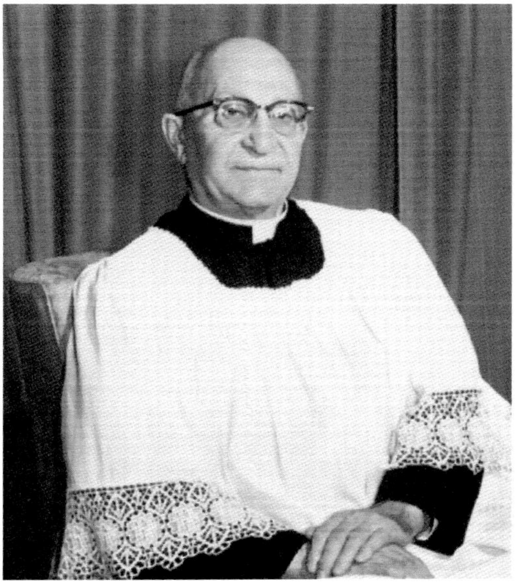

Father Robitaille spent the majority of his priestly life in Cohoes. He arrived in June 1924, shortly after he was ordained. He was pastor of St. Joseph's Church on Congress Street from 1951 to 1970, and he continued to celebrate mass until his death in 1977. He was well known for his devotion to the sick of Cohoes, making frequent visits to the Cohoes Hospital. Pictured below is the former St. Joseph's Roman Catholic Church.

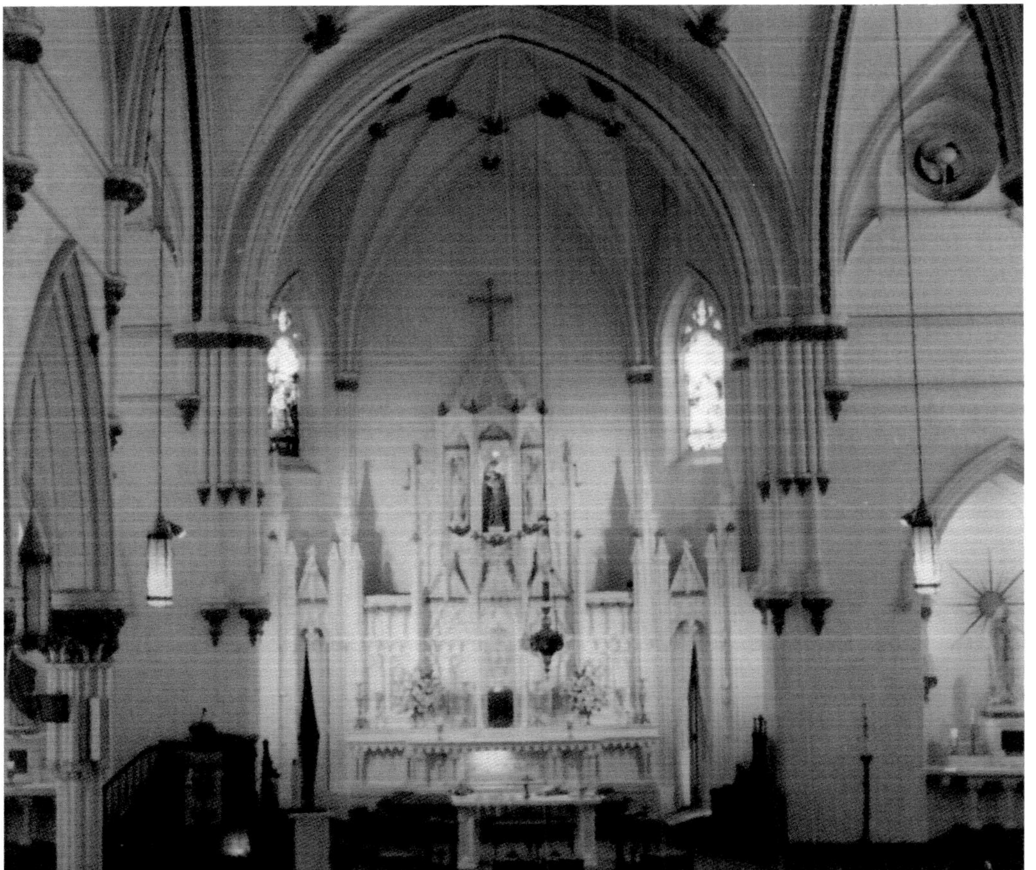

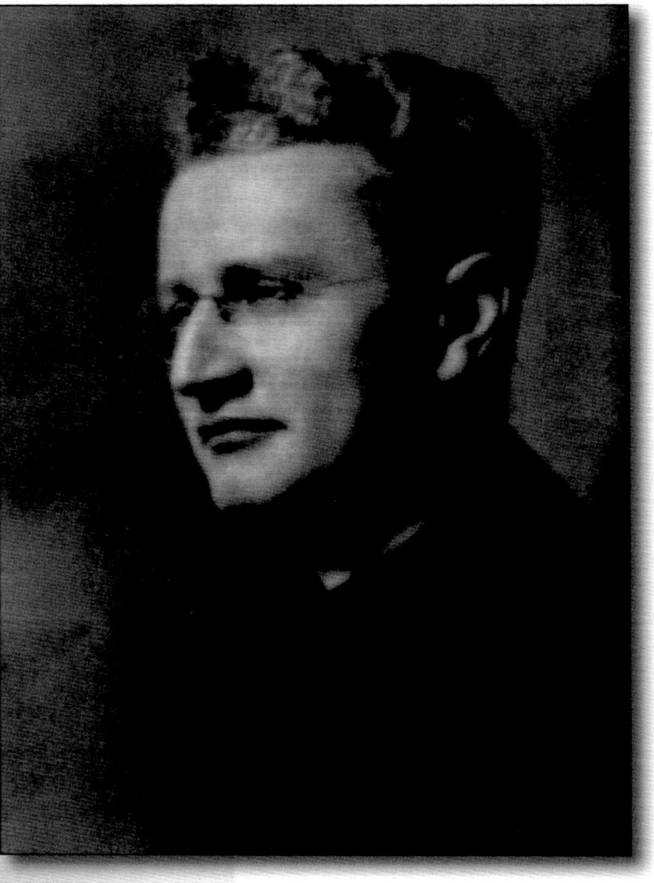

Father Kavanaugh was pastor of St. Patrick's Catholic Church on North Mohawk Street during the 1950s. St. Patrick's, located in the Orchard section of the city, served the Irish population in that area. Reverend Kavanaugh was most known for establishing a new school building, which is said to have created a cohesive parish community. Sadly, the school closed in 1970, and the church closed in 1975. The former St. Patrick's Roman Catholic Church is seen below. (Courtesy of Sue Baird.)

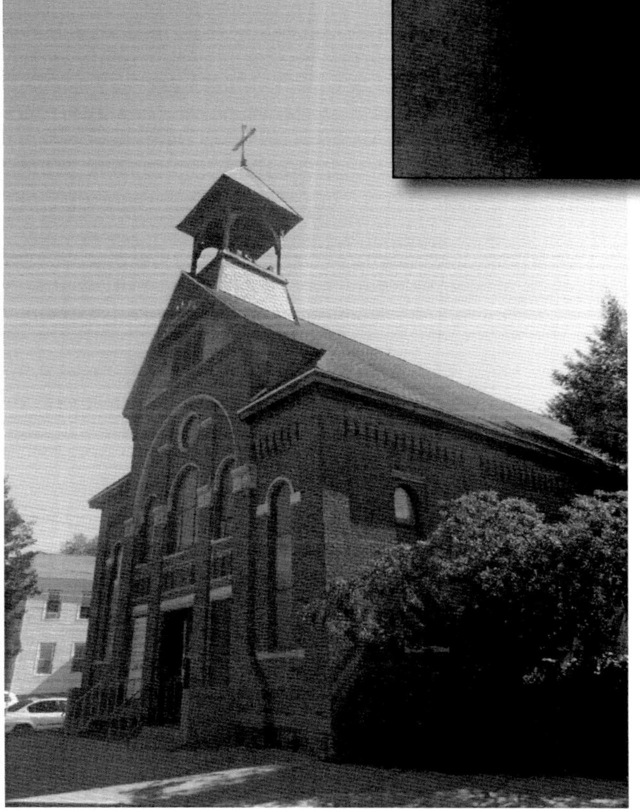

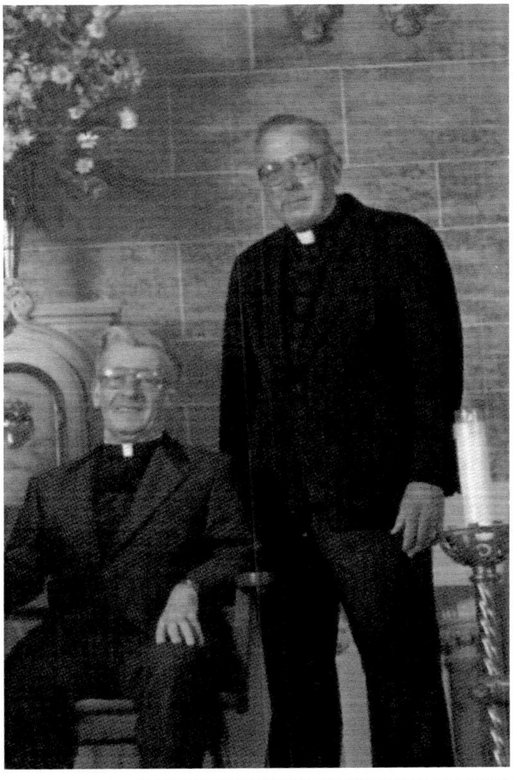

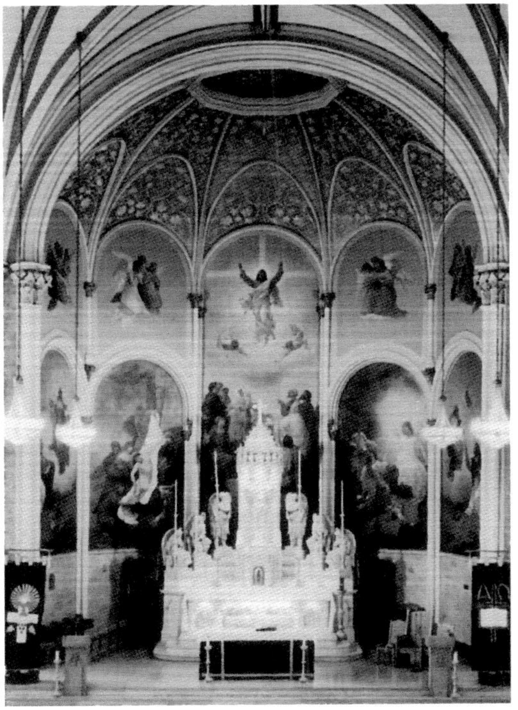

Lawrence McTavey, who retired as pastor of St. Bernard's Church (below) in 2007, never imagined that his tenure would stretch 35 years. McTavey, originally from South Troy, started his career as a Catholic school principal in Albany. He was assigned to St. Bernard's in 1972. During his pastorate, the parish grew by nearly 50 percent. However, that was not enough to save the parish from closure by the Albany Roman Catholic Diocese in 2009. In 2012, an outdoor mass was held at the Cohoes Falls, celebrating the Catholic heritage of the city. In giving the homily, McTavey stated, "If we are to preserve our heritage of faith, we must be strong, willing to sacrifice and ready to show the courage our ancestors maintained as they met the problems and the opposition of their day. We must embellish that strong faith and heritage for our children and their children." In the above photograph, Reverend McTavey (right) poses with Rev. Mark Touchette.

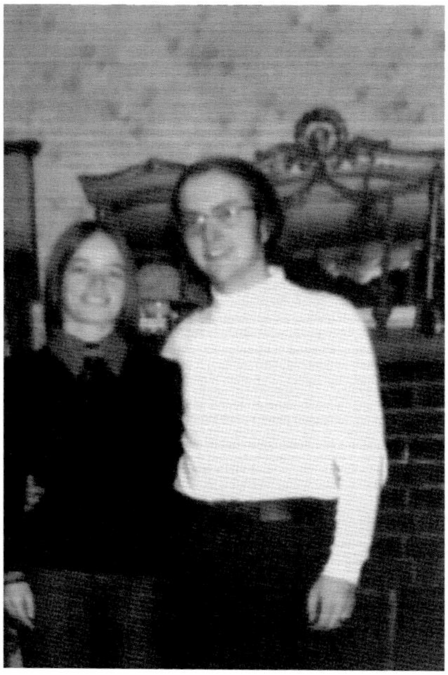

Nick was pursuing a career in law, and Terrie was studying for a career in medicine. However, they found themselves turning away from their chosen career paths, entering Princeton Theological Seminary. Nick and Terrie both received the call during the early 1970s. The couple met at a retreat in 1974, and they were married one year later. As they moved closer to graduation, they looked for a church that would accept them as a husband-and-wife team. They settled on an old stone church in the picturesque town of Lake Luzerne, New York, but Nick received a call from Cohoes that would forever change their lives. After spending just one hour with the congregation of the United Church of Cohoes on Mohawk Street, the Tebordos became aware that this was where God had called them to be. They graduated from seminary the morning of June 1, 1977, and started their new positions in Cohoes that afternoon. For the next 26 years, pastors Nick and Terrie Tebordo poured out their hearts and souls to the church and the community. Terrie created a thriving youth program and proved to have a great empathy for the sick. Nick's passion to share the ministry of Christ in word and deed attracted more people and families to the church. However, tragedy struck in 2003, when Terrie passed away suddenly while on vacation. The weeks and months that followed would prove challenging. As Nick and his family grieved, an entire congregation was also grieving. But, one day at a time, with the faith that God was always with them, Nick and the congregation carried on doing God's work. Today, the United Church of Cohoes is thriving. Since 2009, it has served a free dinner every Saturday night, feeding thousands of people. The historic church itself, built in 1860 as the Dutch Reformed Church of Cohoes, has seen extensive renovations. A new program, "Heart of the City Ministry," will partner the United Church with First Presbyterian Church in Watervliet in what could become a regional ministry. While recent polls show that people are becoming less religious, Reverend Nick is confident that the area is primed for revival and renewal. After 36 years in ministry, Nick Tebordo is as passionate about the gospel message as he ever was. (Courtesy of Rev. Nick Tebordo.)

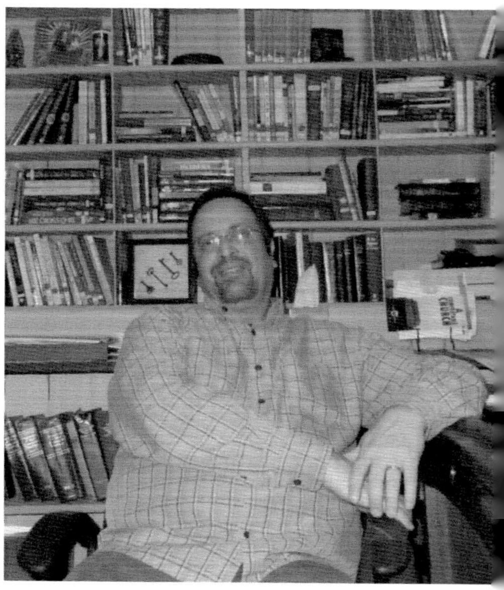

For Rick Colquhoun, it all started during a dream. It seemed that God was calling Colquhoun to the church in a very big way. Colquhoun entered Bible College after high school and then Fuller Theological Seminary in Pasadena, California. In 1998, he came to the Capital Region and started the Vineyard Church in Latham. But Colquhoun was determined to establish a church in an urban area, and Cohoes seemed the perfect location. He settled on a small storefront on White Street and began to reach out to the surrounding downtown neighborhood. In 2009, the congregation bought the former First Methodist Church on Remsen Street (opposite page). In 2011, the exterior of the church was renovated, including the historic bell tower. Small but powerful, the Vineyard Church plays an important role in reaching out to the less fortunate and the unchurched in the downtown area. Anyone who walks through its doors is likely to hear the church's simple yet poignant motto, "Can I pray for you right now?"

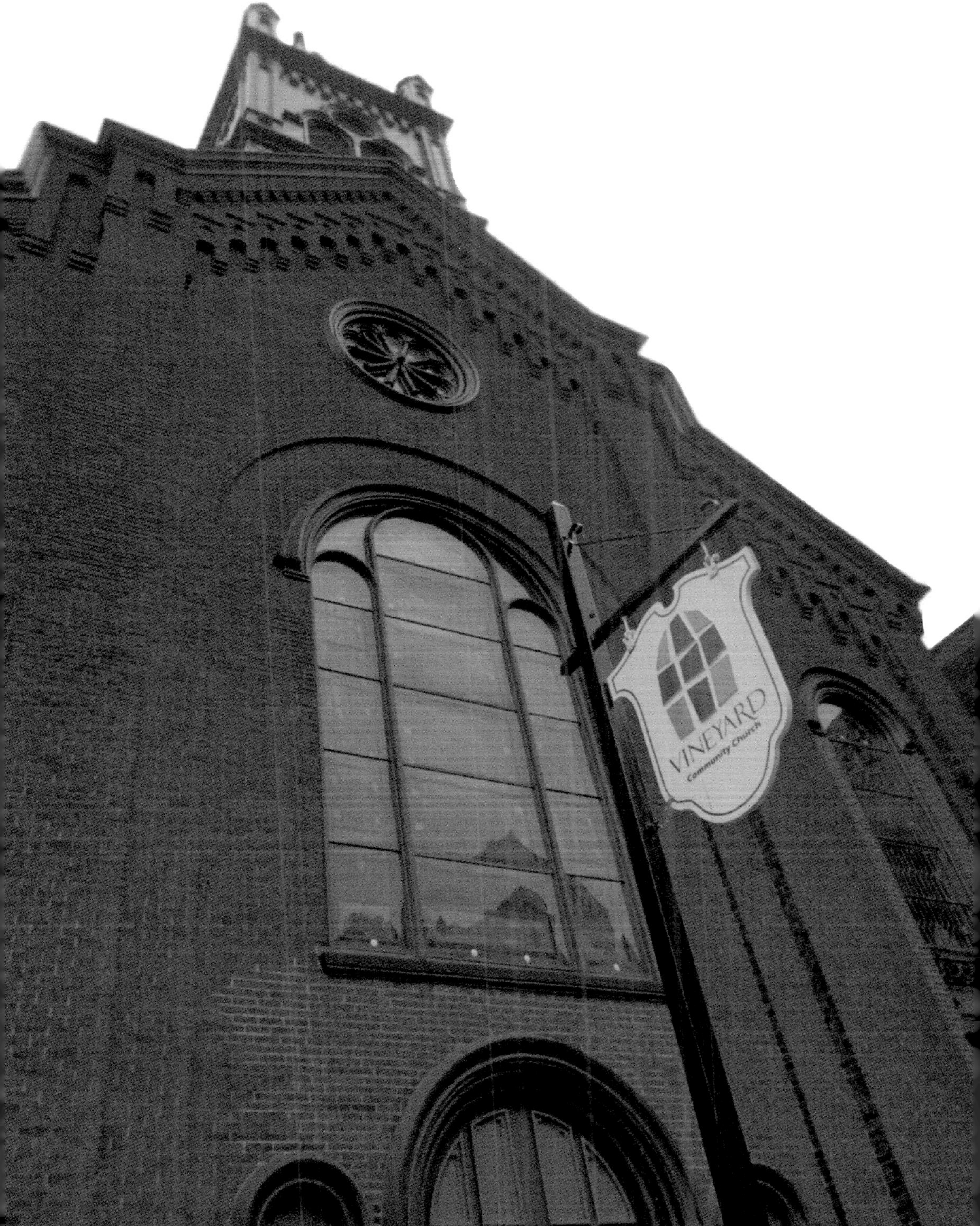
VINEYARD
Community Church

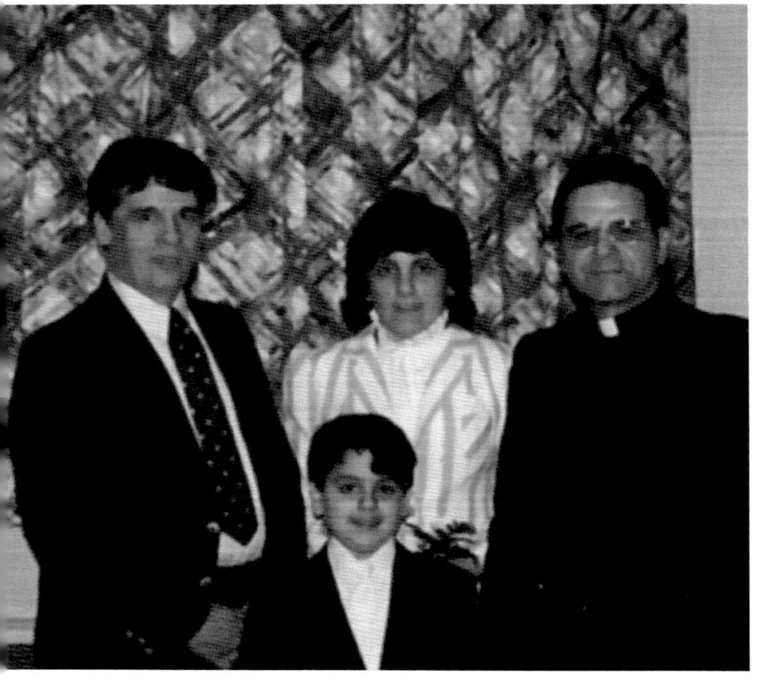

Mario Pacini was born in Rome, Italy, on January 20, 1940. He entered the Society of the Catholic Apostolate in September 1957 and was ordained a priest in St. John Lateran Basilica in Rome on March 26, 1966. Pacini was sent to the United States and served in several parishes in the New York City metropolitan area. In 1978, he was appointed pastor of St. Rita–Sacred Heart Parish in Cohoes. The following year, he received his doctorate in sacred theology from the Pontifical Lateran University. Father Mario quickly became a beloved figure in the parish and throughout the city. He became the chaplain for the police and fire departments and joined the New York National Guard. He enjoyed life to the fullest, and his warm and jovial personality left its mark on the many people he touched over the years. Simply put, Pacini loved people, and people loved him. Father Mario died in 1995 after suffering from a brief illness. He was just 55 years old. His memory will certainly live on in the hearts and minds of those who had the opportunity to know him. Pictured above are, from left to right, Anthony Koniowka Jr., Darlene Koniowka, Randy Koniowka (front), and Father Mario. (Below, courtesy of Kathy Duval Beattie.)

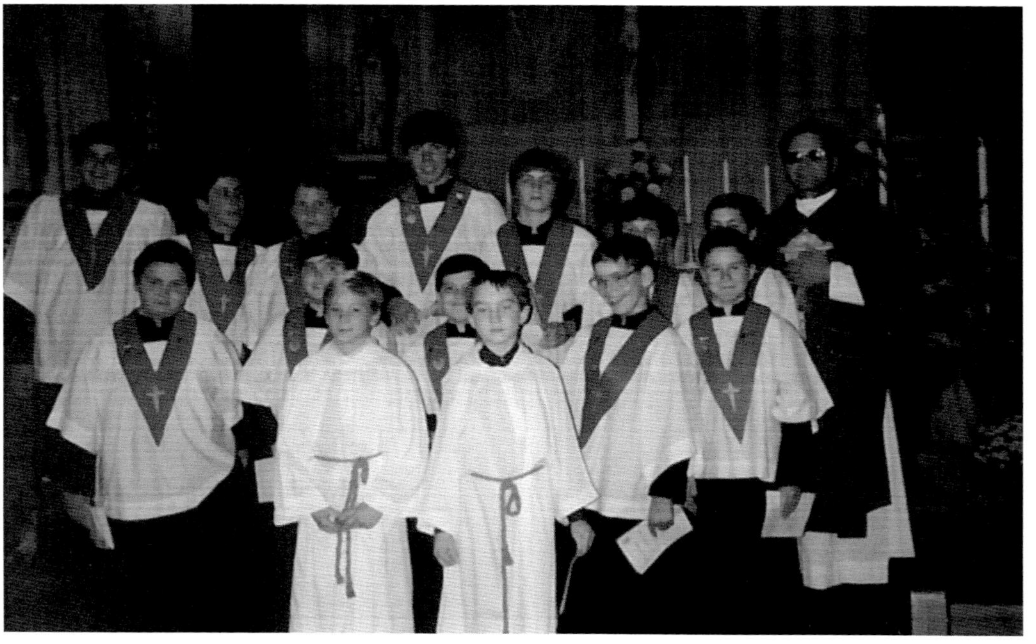

Small Business Owners

Small business is the lifeblood of any community, and Cohoes is certainly no exception. Being a city of neighborhoods, Cohoes has been witness to hundreds of small family-owned businesses over its long and storied history. These businesses often defined the neighborhoods they were in, serving as landmarks. It is here that many Cohoesiers made their livings and sought employment. Many of the first small businesses developed when the Erie Canal was completed in 1825. Cohoes, being at the junction of both the Erie and Champlain Canals, saw a heavy amount of boat traffic. Service businesses catering to the canal boaters sprang up in and around the Juncta, which is where Dyke Avenue is now. Later in the 19th century, Remsen Street would develop as the main commercial street. The rise of major industry toward the latter part of the 19th century saw an increase in commercial enterprise in the majority of neighborhoods. In simple economic terms, these were the "spinoff" businesses. Until the automobile age, and even for many decades after, the neighborhoods of Cohoes were self-sustaining, with grocery stores, taverns, barbershops, and restaurants. This was a time when people had a real civic identity. The tavern owner, the restaurant owner, and the barber all took immense pride in their work, especially the Italian, Irish, Polish, and French Canadian immigrants who made up the neighborhoods of Cohoes in the 20th century. Even when the textile industry was a shadow of its former self, the neighborhoods and downtown business district of Cohoes were thriving. But beginning in the late 1980s and early 1990s, the retail expansion in the suburbs, along with the increase of automobile usage, saw many of these neighborhood institutions close their doors. Downtown lost much of its former vibrancy. Today, however, new small businesses are opening their doors, and a number of family-owned businesses that have been in Cohoes for generations are still going strong. This chapter highlights some of the legendary businesses that are now just fond memories, those that are still going, and new businesses destined to serve Cohoes for generations to come.

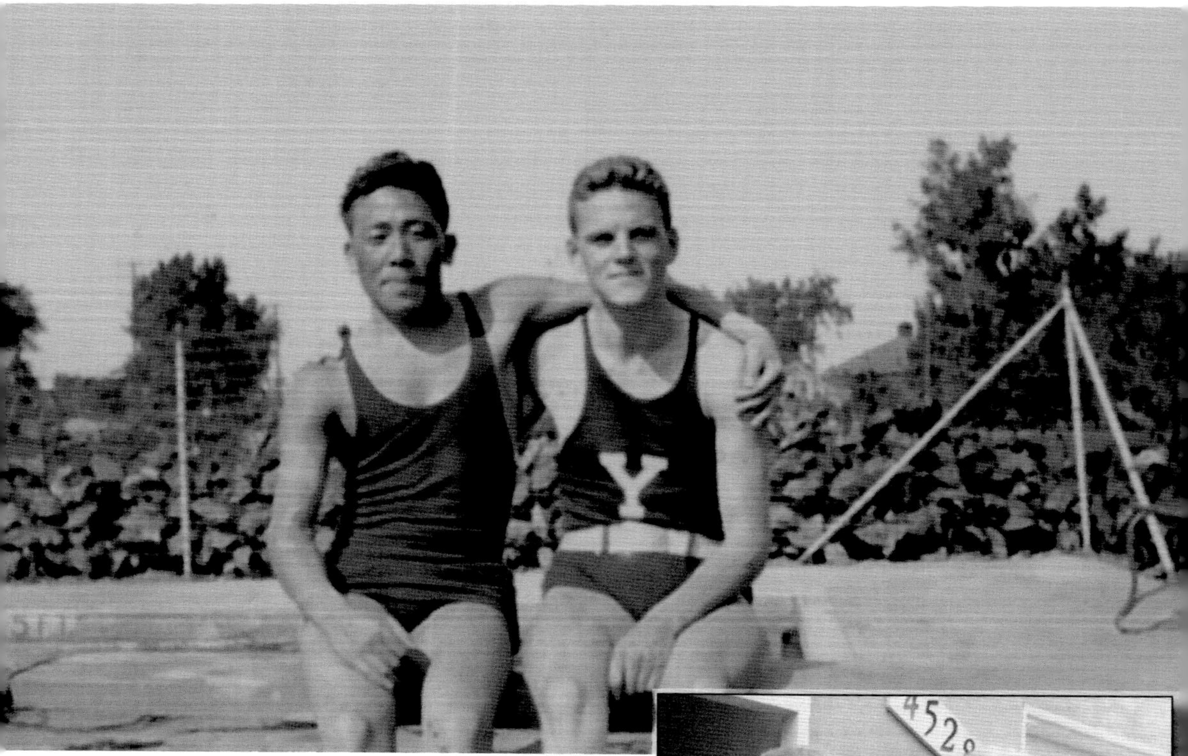

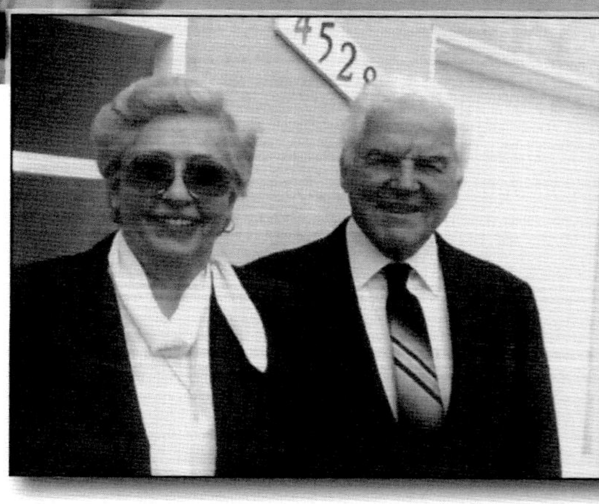

For a kid growing up in Cohoes during the middle part of the 20th century, chances were good that many a day was spent at Carlson's. Located on Bridge Avenue near the old Champlain Canal, Carlson's was a year-round attraction bringing together the youth of the entire city. In the summer, it was a popular swimming hole; in the winter, there was ice-skating, bonfires, and dancing. Carlson's was started in 1917 by Iver Carlson, a Swedish immigrant. In 1950, he sold the business to his son, E. Iver Carlson, who, with his wife, Doris, operated the establishment for another 24 years. The task of filling the large pool became problematic during the early 1970s, when the Champlain Canal was filled in. Filling the pool through others means proved too costly, and Carlson was forced to close the facility. In 1977, his daughter Linda opened the Sassy Swede Restaurant in the elegant family home built by Iver Carlson in the 1930s. While Carlson's is long gone, its memory is alive and well. In the above photograph, E. Iver Carlson (right) poses with an unidentified person in the 1930s. Shown in the inset are Doris and Iver Carlson. (Courtesy of the Plowman family.)

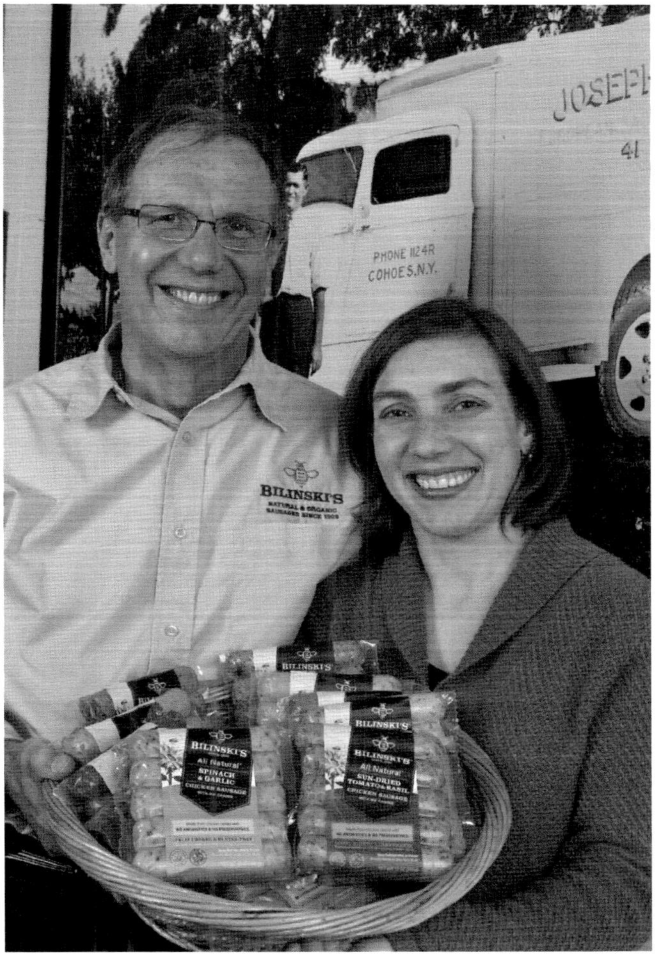

In 1924, Joseph Bilinski, a Ukrainian immigrant, started making traditional sausage and beef products from his home on Lark Street, selling them door-to-door. For the next 60-plus years, the Bilinski family operated the Lark Street business and created a brand known for its high quality. In 1983, the company was bought by Steve and Cathie Schonwetter, who have transformed Bilinski's into a nationally known brand famous for its healthy organic chicken products. They decided to keep the Bilinski name and managed to continue the tradition of quality while totally reinventing the company. In the late 1980s, they started to produce organic chicken sausages. Slow to catch on, the product is now a national sensation. While the days of bologna and liverwurst may be over, the commitment to quality remains. Shown at right are Steve Schonwetter and his daughter, Stacie Schonwetter-Waters. (Courtesy of the Schonwetter family.)

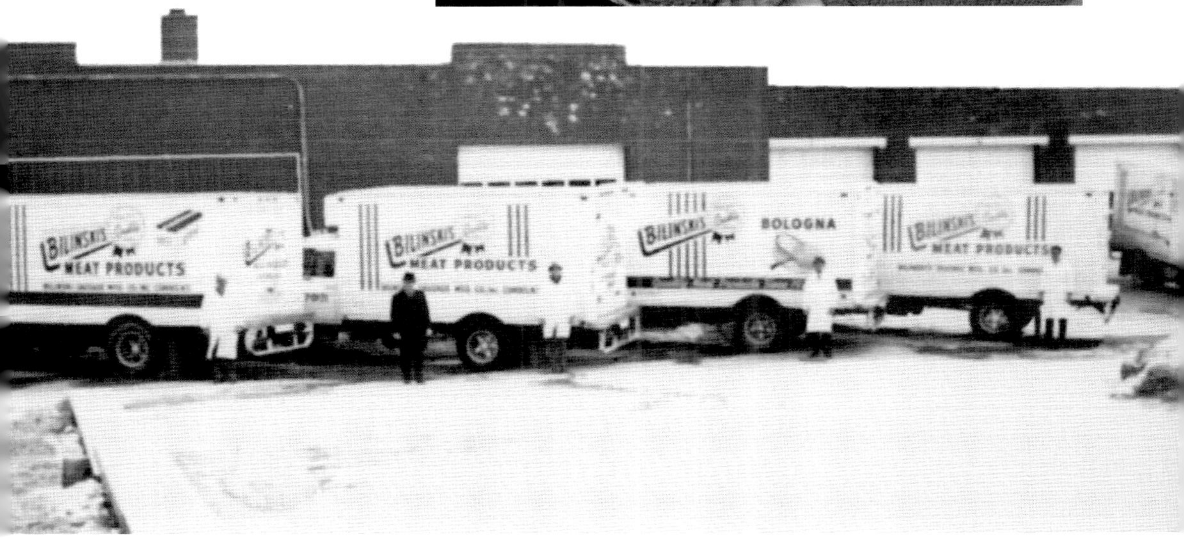

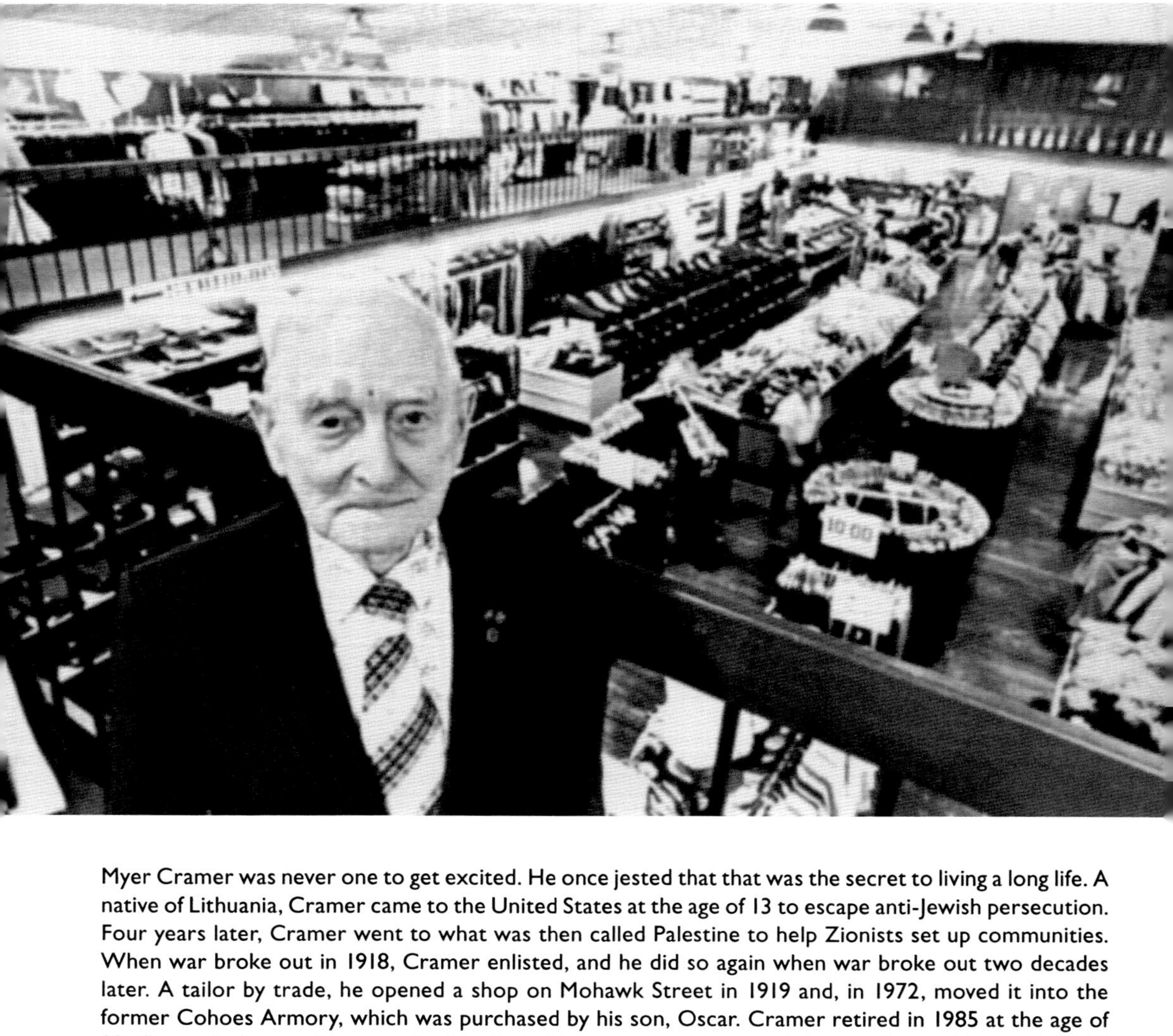

Myer Cramer was never one to get excited. He once jested that that was the secret to living a long life. A native of Lithuania, Cramer came to the United States at the age of 13 to escape anti-Jewish persecution. Four years later, Cramer went to what was then called Palestine to help Zionists set up communities. When war broke out in 1918, Cramer enlisted, and he did so again when war broke out two decades later. A tailor by trade, he opened a shop on Mohawk Street in 1919 and, in 1972, moved it into the former Cohoes Armory, which was purchased by his son, Oscar. Cramer retired in 1985 at the age of 92. Cramer's Armory became a landmark clothing store in Cohoes until it moved out of the city in 1997. In 2001, it went out of business entirely. (Courtesy of the Spindle City Historic Society.)

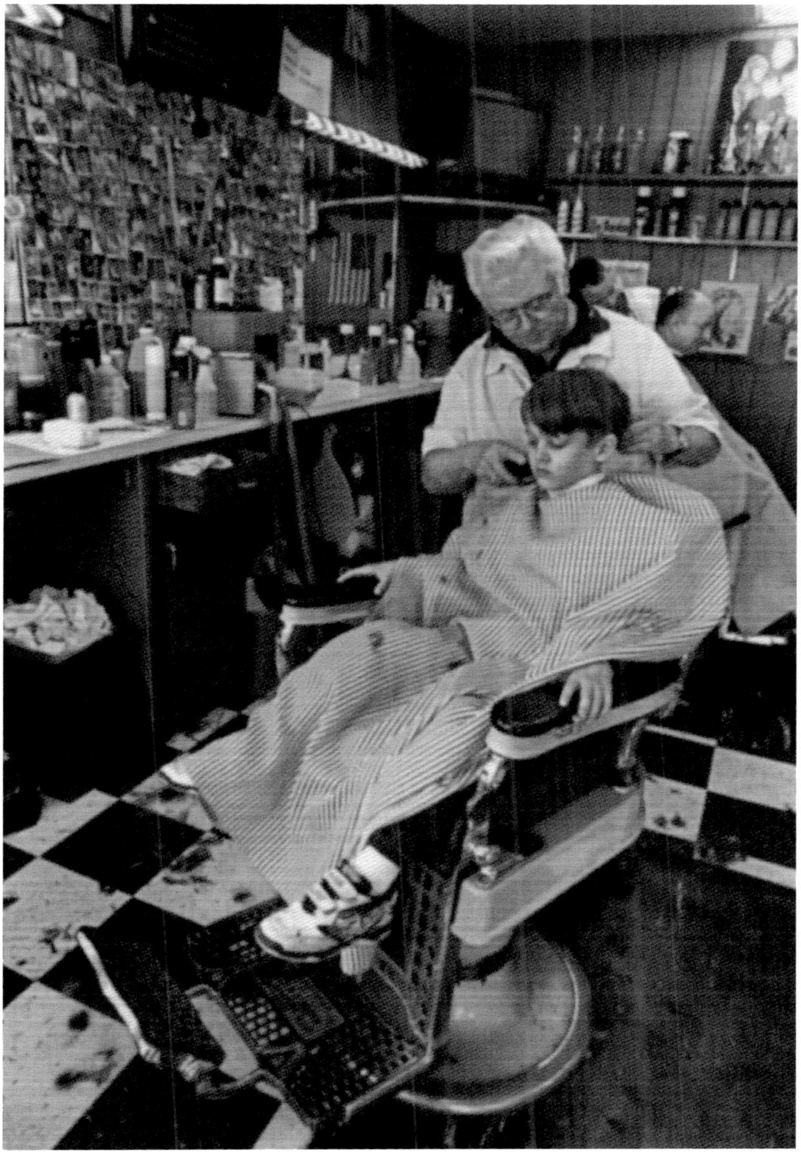

When Bernie Heroux began cutting hair in Cohoes, the cost for a cut was 25¢. Over the decades, while the price of a haircut changed, Heroux remained a fixture in the community he loved. A veteran of World War II, Heroux took the advice of his mother and became a barber. He opened his first shop on Van Schaick Island in 1948, but quickly moved to the corner of Remsen and Ontario Streets, where he was an indelible fixture in the heart of downtown for nearly 64 years. Inside the shop was a cavalcade of ephemera. There were plaques, steins, and, most famously, the box of pens. The walls were adorned with pictures of clients, past and present, mostly children who received their first haircut from Heroux (this author included). He passed away several months following his retirement in 2010, leaving behind thousands of customers. They were, as Heroux put it, much more than customers; they were friends. (Courtesy of Tom Bessette.)

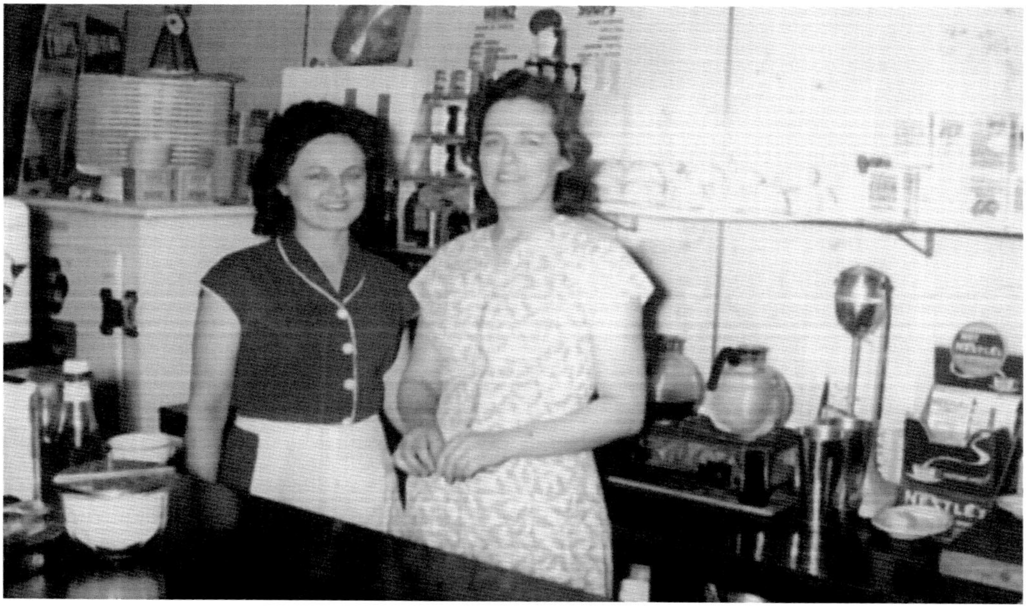

Since 1948, Bill's Diner has been a landmark eatery on Simmons Island, serving up classic American fare. The diner started out as a small grocery store operated by Bill and Tess Linen. During the early 1950s, upon the inquiry of a hungry passerby in search of a sandwich, the grocery store became a restaurant. Bill's is still going strong 65 years later, and it is still operated by the Linen family. It is a place where family and friends gather for good food, good company, and one of the best fish frys in town. Shown above are Tess Linen (left) and her sister Kate Decicco. Posing below are, from left to right, Danise (Linen) Stevens (holding Brenton Stevens), Dan Linen, Donna Linen (holding Brently Stevens), and Tim Linen. (Above, courtesy of the Linen family.)

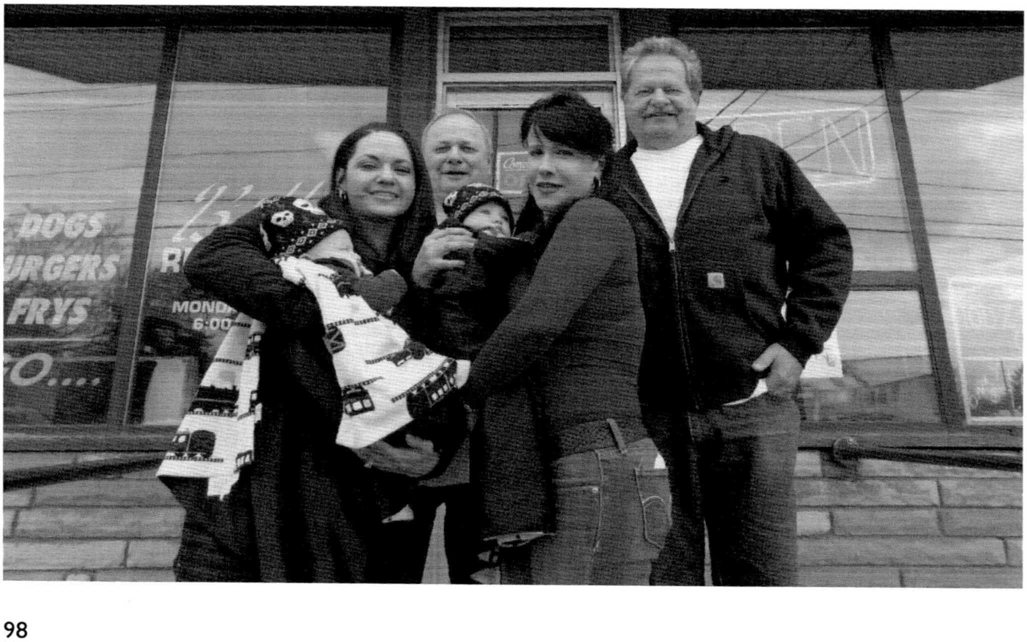

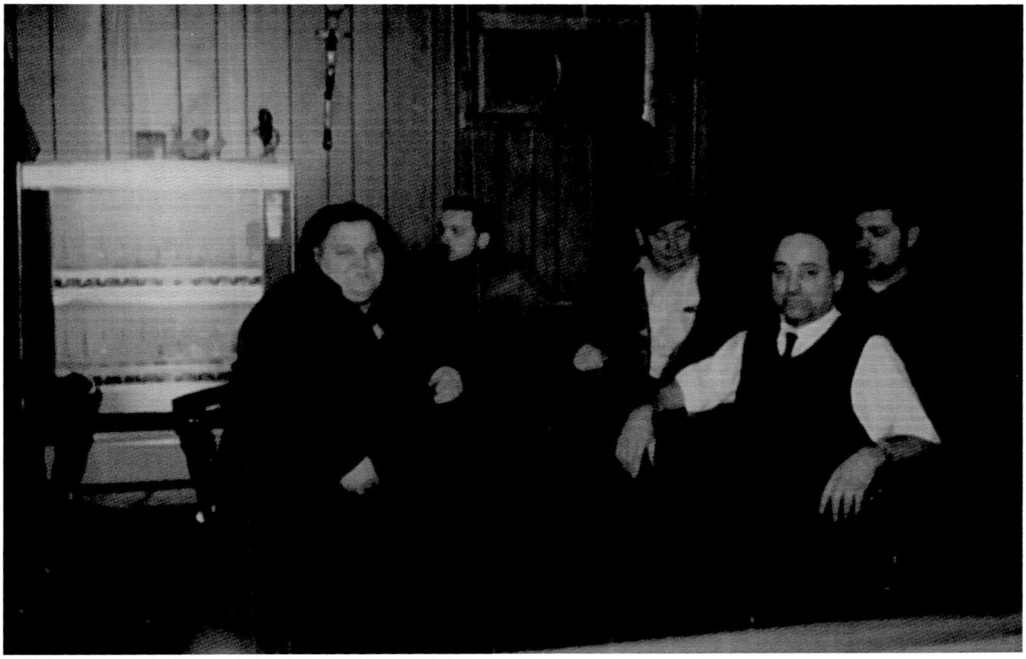

Located on Bridge Avenue, Little Nicks was a tavern and restaurant started in the 1930s by Nicholas DiSisto, an Italian immigrant. During the 1950s, it was operated by his son Augustus and his wife, Mary, who was known for her amazing meatball sandwiches. During the 1980s and 1990s, the business saw a third generation of DiSistos, with Gus's sons Anthony and Tom taking active roles. It remained in the family until the mid-1990s. Pictured from left to right are Mary DiSisto, David DiSisto, Len Sunkes, Gus DiSisto, and Tom DiSisto. (Courtesy of Pam McGrath.)

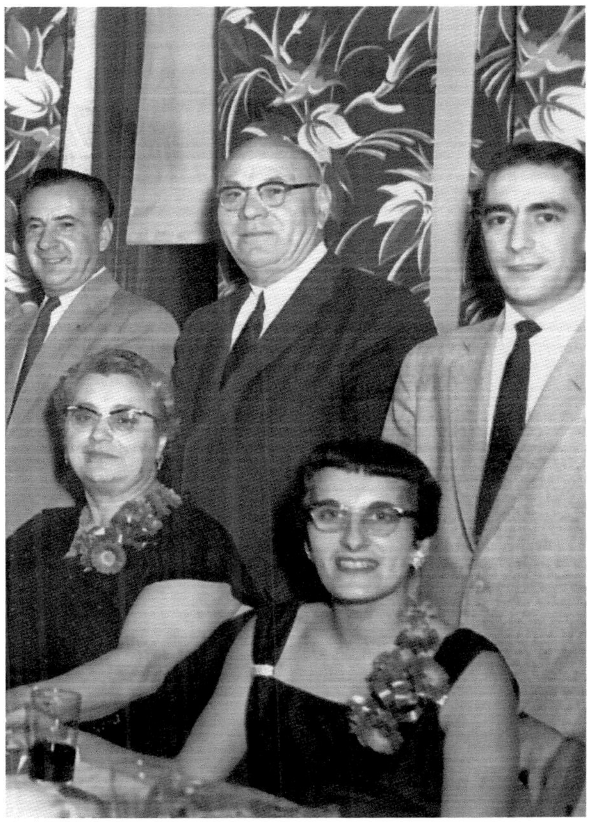

Raffaele Signoracci came to America when he was just eight years old. In 1939, he opened Ralph's Tavern on Ontario Street. Signoracci was not only self-taught, but self-made. He became a neighborhood leader and was heavily involved in Democratic politics. Often referred to as "the boss," Signoracci was known to help anyone in need and asked for nothing in return. Ralph's Tavern remained in the Signoracci family until it was sold in 1989. Raffaele Signoracci is seen here, standing at center. (Courtesy of Mary Donlon.)

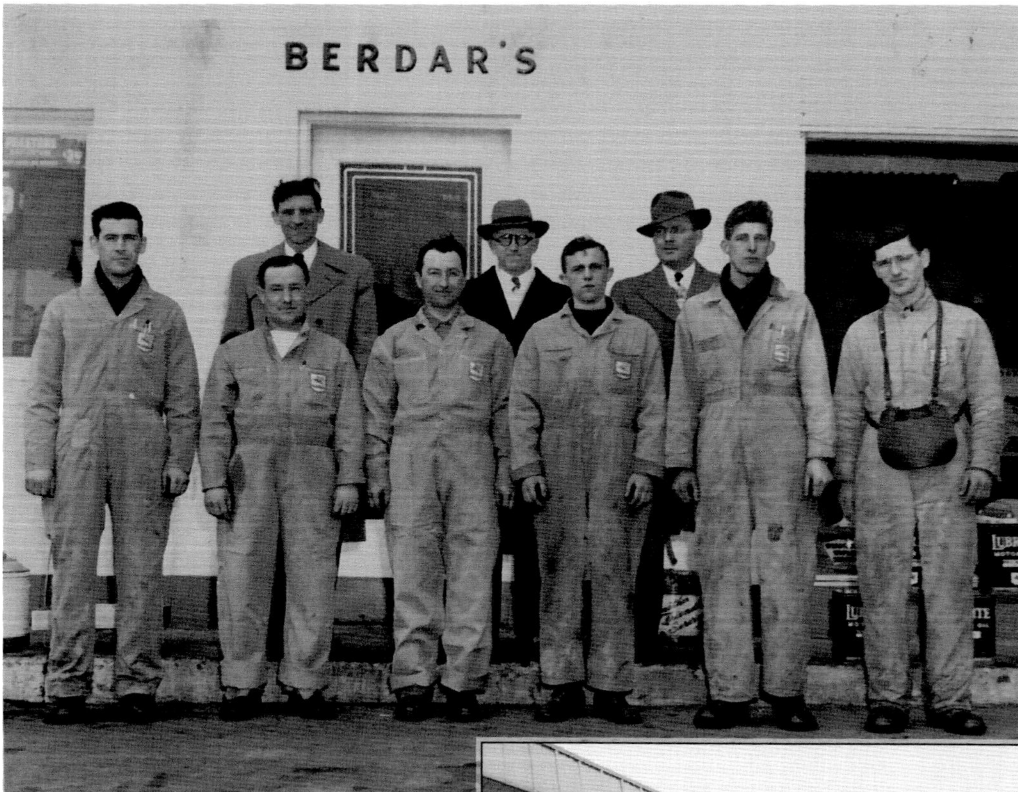

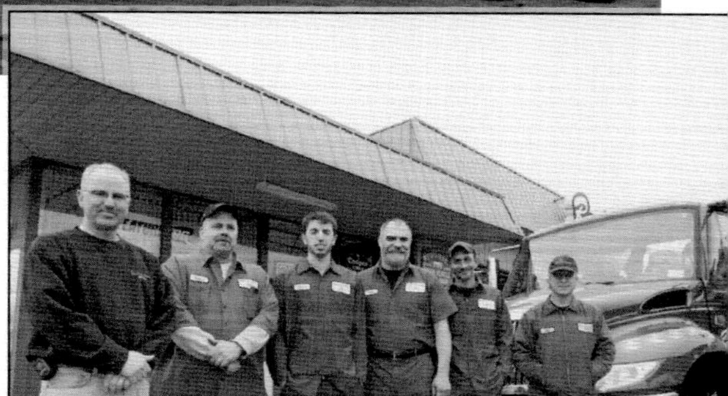

Anthony Berdar came to the United States from Poland in 1904. In 1929, as the automobile age was beginning to take shape, he started a service station on Saratoga Street. Berdar's would go on to serve the motorists of Cohoes for generations. In the late 1960s, Anthony's son Joe took over operations, along with Joe's wife, Rita. In 1997, Joe handed the reins over to his son Dave, who currently runs the business. Berdar's continues to serve the automotive needs of Cohoes and the Capital Region, 74 years after Anthony Berdar started the business. Shown in the c. 1950 photograph above are, from left to right, (first row) Don McLaughlin, Peter Hytko, Bill Fuzz, Tim Powers, Bill Burns, and Joe Berdar; (second row) Anthony Berdar Jr., Anthony Berdar, and Ed Spinaci. Inset, Dave Berdar (left) poses with the current automotive team at Berdar's. (Above, courtesy of Dave Berdar.)

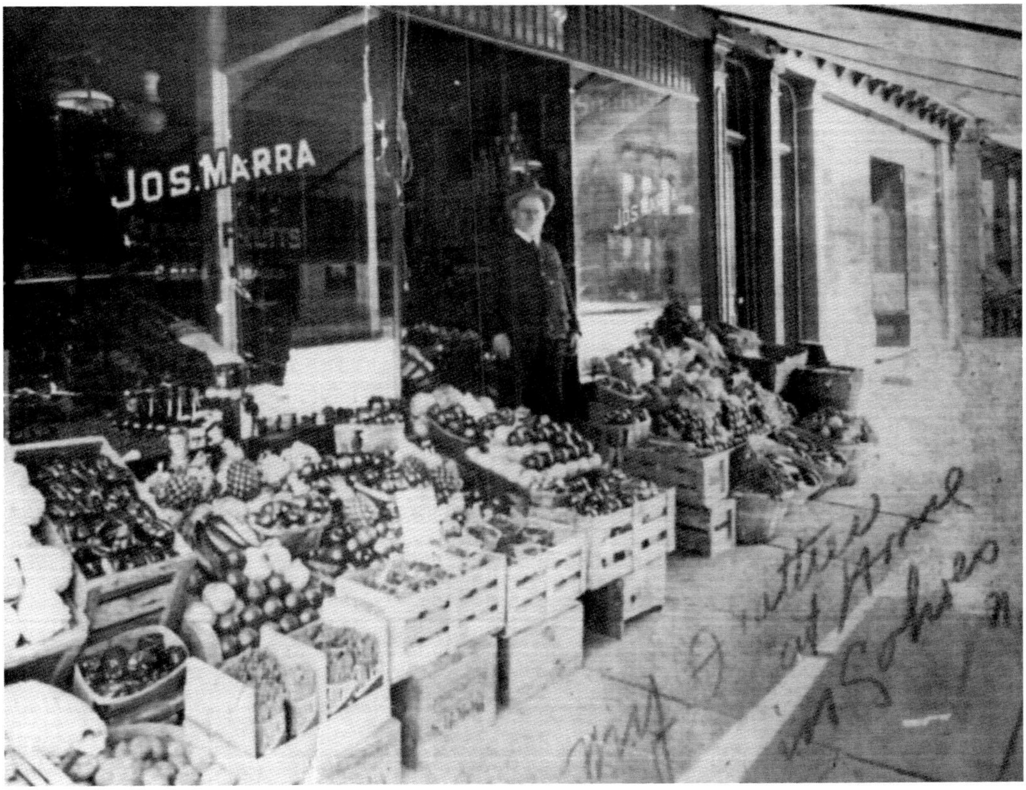

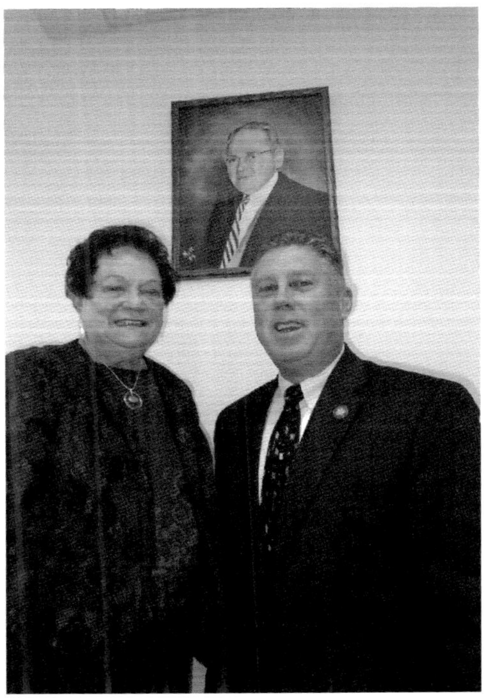

For well over 100 years, the Marra family has been a prominent fixture in the Cohoes business community. In 1885, Joseph Marra (above), an Italian immigrant, started a fruit and vegetable stand downtown. In 1931, his son, James V. Marra, opened a pharmacy on Remsen Street. James Marra ran the business for 40 years, until his death in 1971. His daughter Barbara, who began working in the pharmacy at the age of eight opening doors for customers, took over operations. In May 1988, the pharmacy was destroyed by a fire that consumed an entire downtown block. Determined to remain part of the community, Marra's was rebuilt and, in 2011, celebrated its 80th anniversary. Despite competition from large chain retailers and mail-order pharmacies, Marra's endures. This is due to the company's commitment to James Marra's mission: provide personal service, accuracy, and efficiency, all from the heart. At right, Barbara McDonald poses with her son, former mayor and current assemblyman and pharmacist John T. McDonald III. (Above, courtesy of Barbara McDonald.)

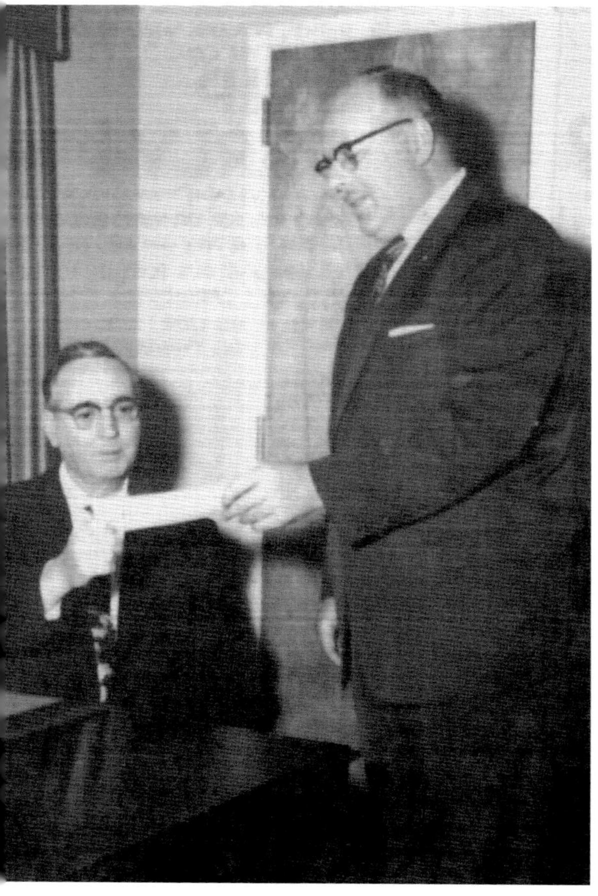

For over 100 years, the Dufresne family has been providing funeral services in the city of Cohoes and the surrounding area. In 1909, Arthur Dufresne (on the right) opened a small funeral home on the corner of Heart and Main Streets. In 1925, he expanded his operations and moved to a facility on Mann Avenue. In 1949, he expanded again, moving to 216 Columbia Street, where the home operates today. Upon his death in 1967, his son Arthur E. Dufresne took over operations. In 1972, Arthur's brother David became the manager. In 1991, David's son Mark joined the family business and began to modernize the facility, adding a computer system. Today, the Dufresne Funeral Home continues the tradition started by Arthur Dufresne of "service to all." (Left, courtesy of Mark Dufresne.)

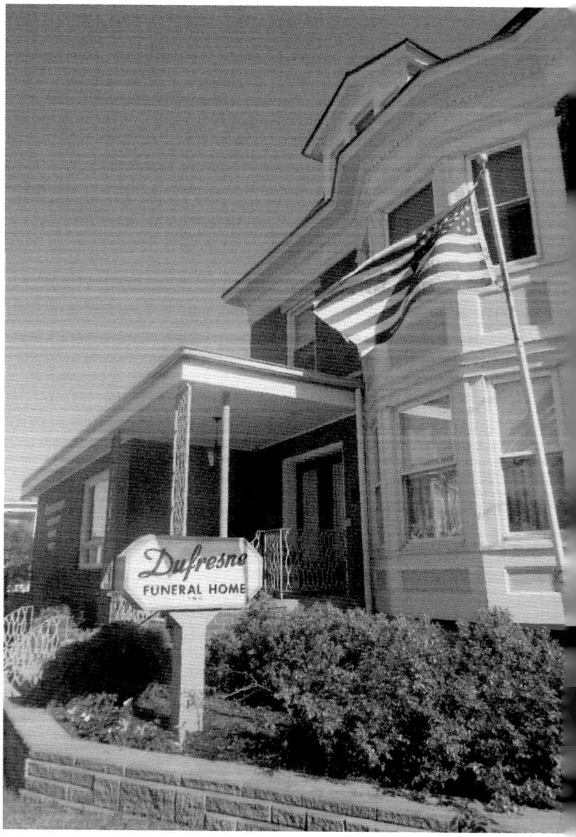

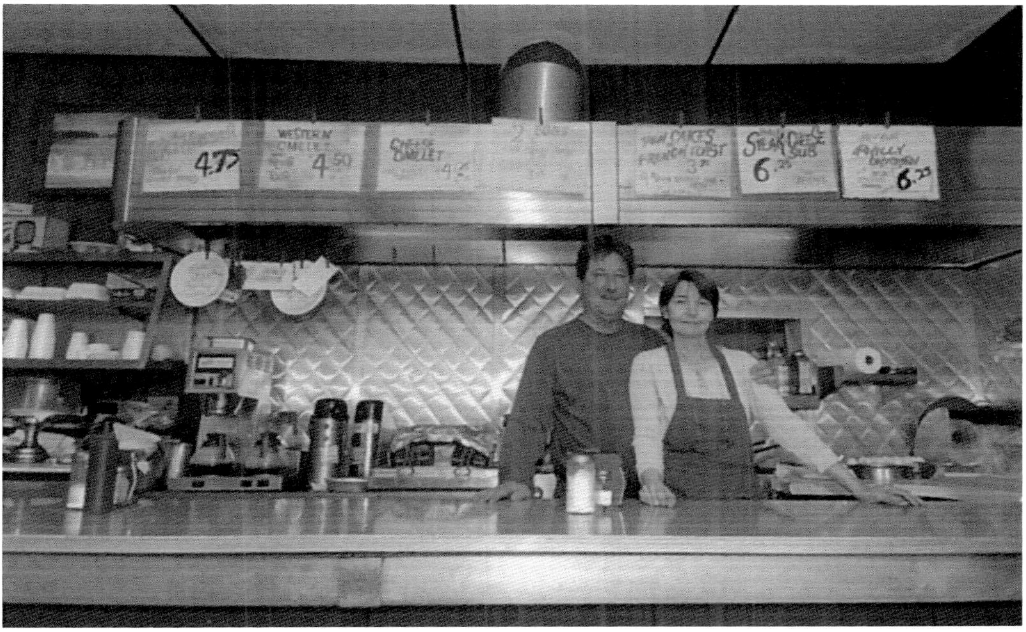

John and Jackie Reavy have owned and operated Uncle John's Diner on Ontario Street since 1995. The diner itself has been around since the 1920s and has changed little since its early days. Inside, the walls are adorned with photographs of days gone by, as John and Jackie are lovers of Cohoes history. At the counter, patrons enjoy simple classic American breakfast fare and coffee that's just plain coffee. Conversation runs the gamut, from history and local politics to international relations and everything in between. But more than anything else, Uncle John's is a refuge from the complex and often chaotic modern world. Its intimate setting breeds real human interaction, something the digital age has all but stripped from society. Quite simply, Uncle John's is a place where small-town life is at its absolute best. (Above, courtesy of Lee Webb.)

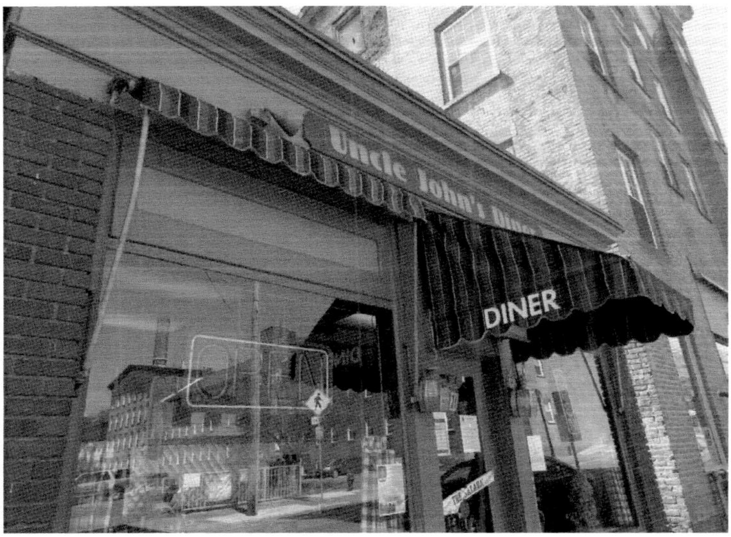

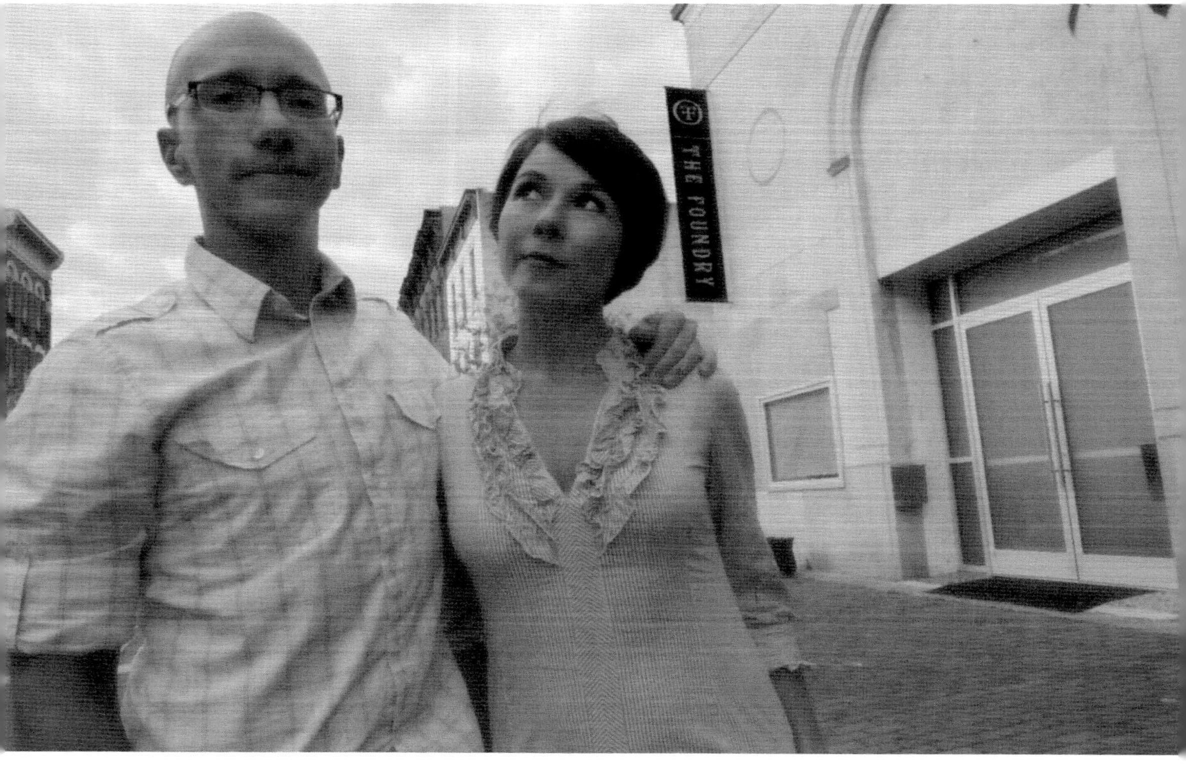

Over the last several years, downtown Cohoes has taken on a new identity as a place for the creative class. The arrival of art galleries, cafés, yoga studios, and specialty stores has brought a renewed vibrancy to Remsen Street. At the heart of this transformation have been Jesse and Alana Matulis and the Foundry for Art, Design and Culture. The two artists met in 2003 and moved to Cohoes shortly thereafter. They were both seeking their own creative live/work space and began looking at locations across the Capital Region. After looking at nearly 80 buildings, they decided to purchase the structure on the corner of Remsen and Newcomb Streets. Built in 1931 for the Mechanic Savings Bank, the building was most known for housing the former Timpane's Jewelers. After Timpane's closed in the early 1990s, the building saw a variety of uses but had remained vacant for several years prior to 2005. The condition of the building prompted friends and family to think that Alana and Jesse were absolutely crazy for taking on such a project. But the two were undaunted and began to renovate the building, including the removal of some nine tons of debris from the outer building in the rear. They were able to secure grants from the city of Cohoes, which was very welcoming of the project. They transformed the second floor of the building into a remarkable modern living space and designed the first floor as gallery and event space. However, in 2009, the economy went into a deep recession, and financing dried up. It was uncertain if the project would be completed. But a $50,000 award from Pepsi allowed the Matulis team to finish the first floor, including the installation of state-of-the-art lighting and sound. In 2011, the Foundry opened its doors and, since then, has welcomed thousands of visitors from all over the world to downtown Cohoes. To say the Foundry is just an art gallery would be a gross understatement. It is a place where art is promoted for its value in society. It is a place where the work of the creative class is cultivated and advanced, for it has been dubbed the "chamber of commerce for the creative class." For the Matulises, the texture of the neighborhood has kept them grounded and has given them more compassion for the plight of those less fortunate. The Foundry is a place where joy is experienced and hope is given. (Courtesy of Jesse and Alana Matulis.)

American Heros

Since the American war for independence, Cohoesiers have been answering the call of duty and fighting to defend freedom and liberty, both on the homefront and around the world. The American Revolution saw men from the Cohoes area serve in the Northern Department of the Continental Army. Many from Cohoes fought in the Battle of Saratoga, which was the turning point of the war. Cohoes has also been host to many national military heroes, including George Washington himself, who is said to have made at least two visits to the Van Schaick Mansion. The mansion, on Van Schaick Island, served as a military headquarters during the Revolution and the War of 1812. When the Civil War broke out in 1861, Cohoesiers immediately rallied behind the Union cause. In the wars that followed, sons and daughters of Cohoes would continue to answer the call, both abroad and at home. From World Wars I and II, Korea, Vietnam, the Gulf, and the War on Terror, Cohoesiers have continued to answer the call of duty. The individuals in this chapter are a sample of the many brave Americans who have served their country.

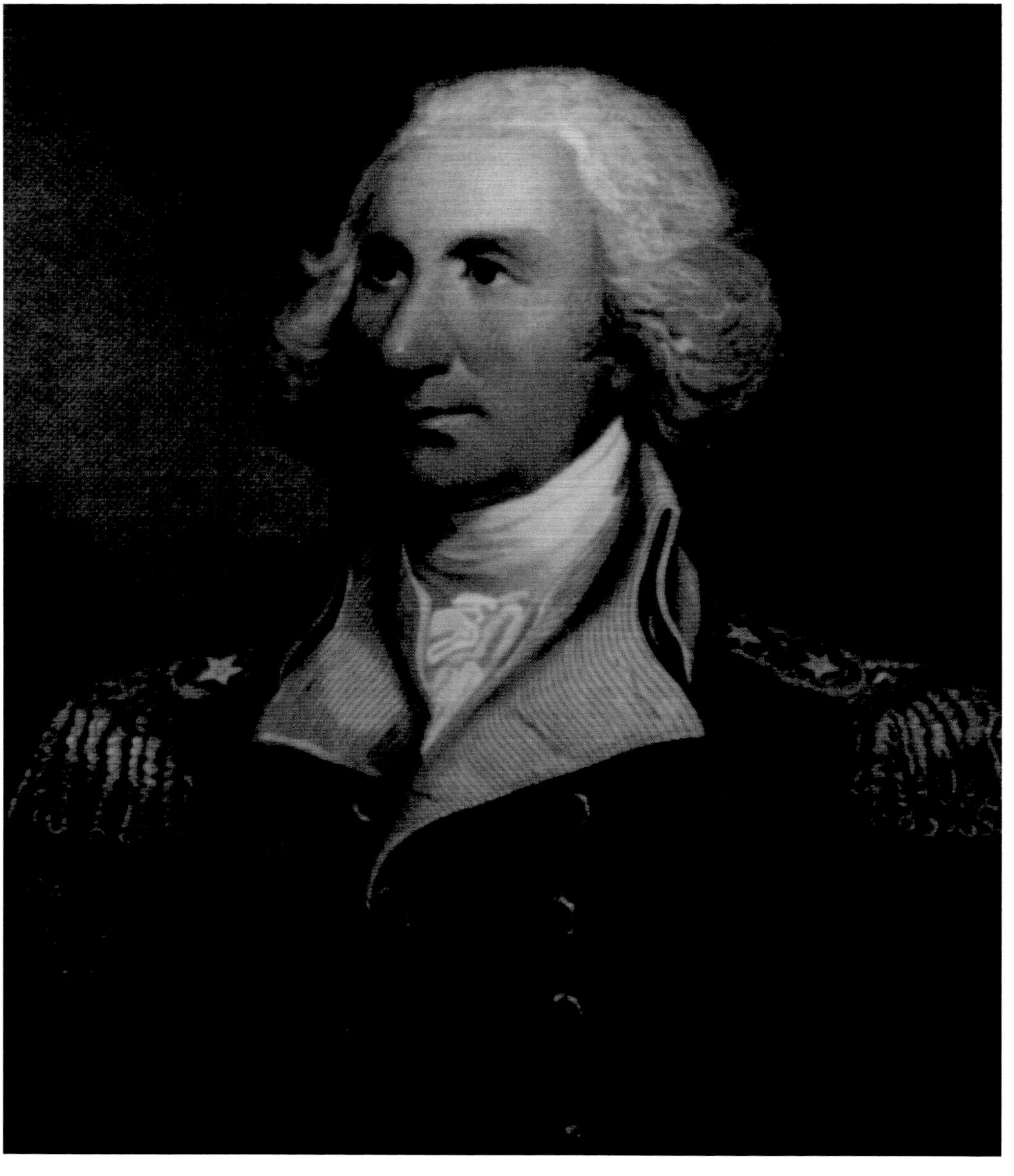

In August 1777, Philip Schuyler, commander of the Northern Department of the Continental Army, arrived on Van Schaick Island with between 5,000 and 7,000 bruised and battered Colonial soldiers. They were being followed by the British and anticipated a major battle at Cohoes at the mouth of the Mohawk River. In preparation for the invasion, Schulyer ordered the construction of a line of fortifications on Peebles Island to slow the British march to Albany. However, shortly after his arrival on Van Schaick Island, Schuyler was ordered to turn over his command to Gen. Horatio Gates, who then accused Schuyler of dereliction of duty for failing to halt the advancing British. In 1779 Schuyler was exonerated, but he resigned from the Army the same year. He went on to a prominent career in politics, serving as a New York state senator and member of Congress. (Courtesy of the Library of Congress.)

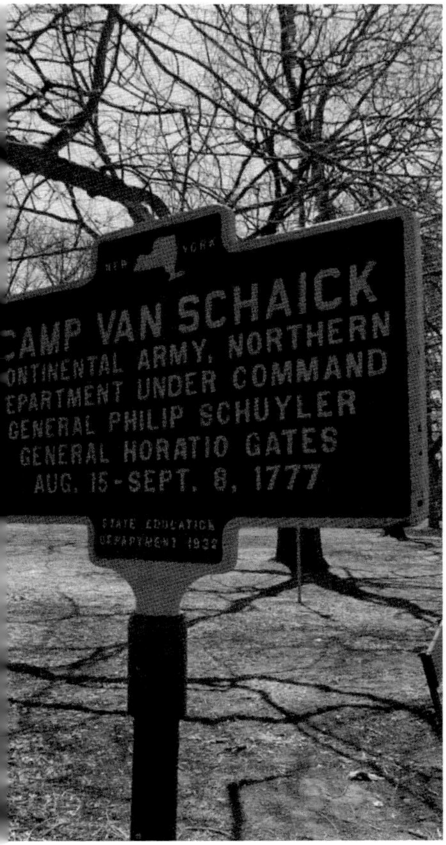

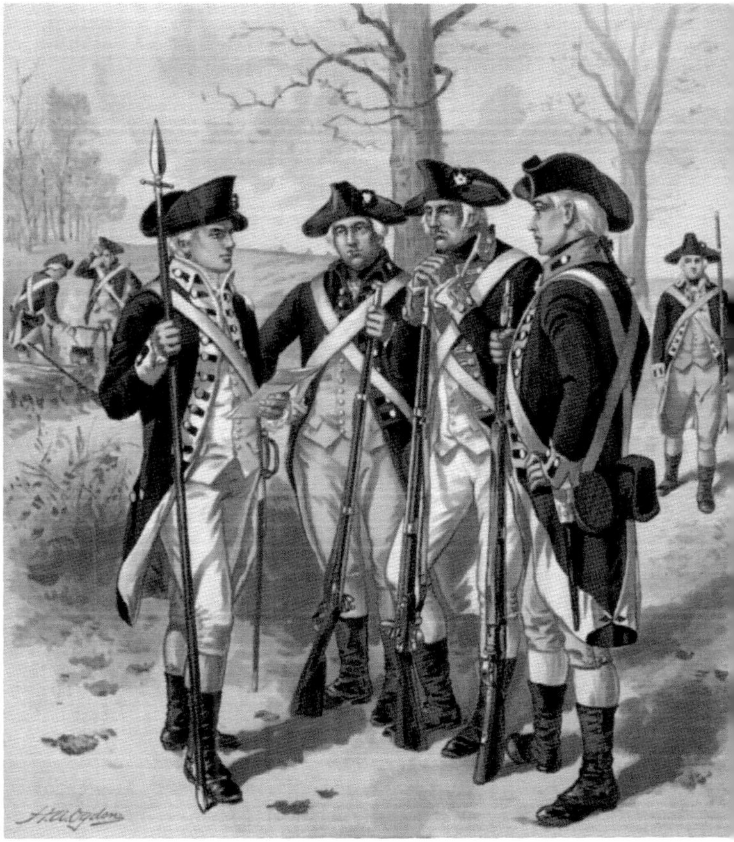

On August 18, 1777, a beleaguered regiment of Continental soldiers reached Van Schaick Island, having been in retreat from the British. Several thousand soldiers, many suffering from sickness and exhaustion, made camp on the great lawn of the Van Schaick Mansion. Panic and dismay began to spread throughout the island and surrounding area as the British regulars, led by Gen. John Burgoyne, were headed south to capture Albany and the islands at the mouth of the Mohawk. The Army, however, would not sit and wait for what would have been the "Battle of Cohoes." On September 9, the Army moved north to Stillwater and then to Saratoga, under the command of Gen. Horatio Gates. It was the Colonials from Cohoes, fighting in Saratoga, who achieved the turning point in the war for independence. The 1897 Henry Ogden painting on the right is *Infantry, the Continental Army.* (Courtesy of the Library of Congress.)

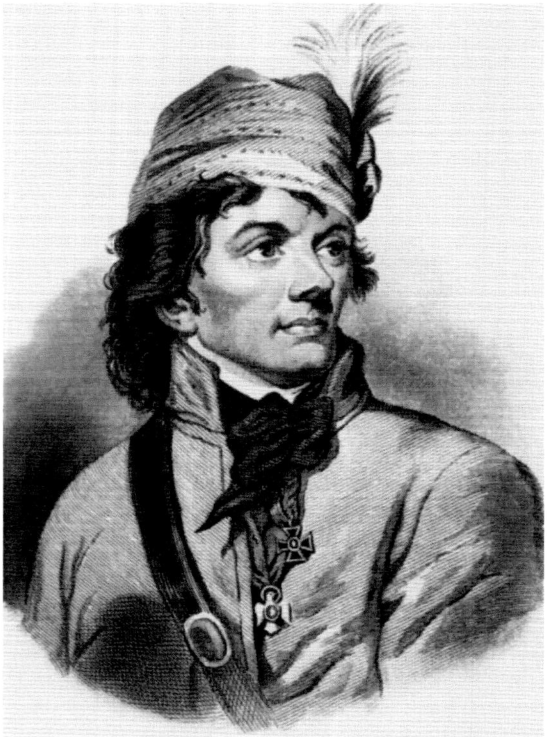

Kosciusko, a native of Poland, received most of his military training in France. Upon hearing of the outbreak of war in America, he moved to the colonies and joined the Continental Army as a colonel. He was immediately tasked with constructing the defenses of Philadelphia. Kosciusko would ultimately become the chief engineer for the Continental Army. In August 1777, under the command of Gen. Philip Schulyer, Kosciusko constructed a series of fortifications on the northeastern and northwestern sides of Peebles Island. This was done in anticipation of General Burgoyne's impending invasion of Cohoes and Albany. These fortifications, still visible today on Peebles Island State Park (below), were never used, as it was decided to surprise Burgoyne at Saratoga. In 1783, Kosciusko was given the rank of brigadier general by the Continental Congress. (Left, courtesy of the Library of Congress.)

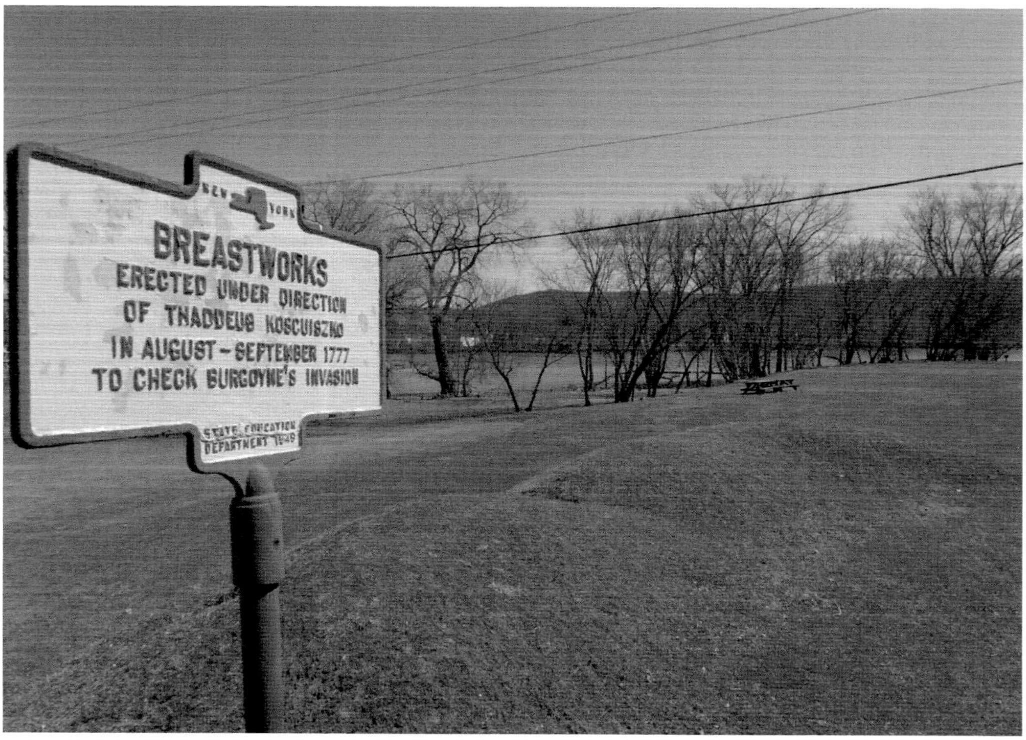

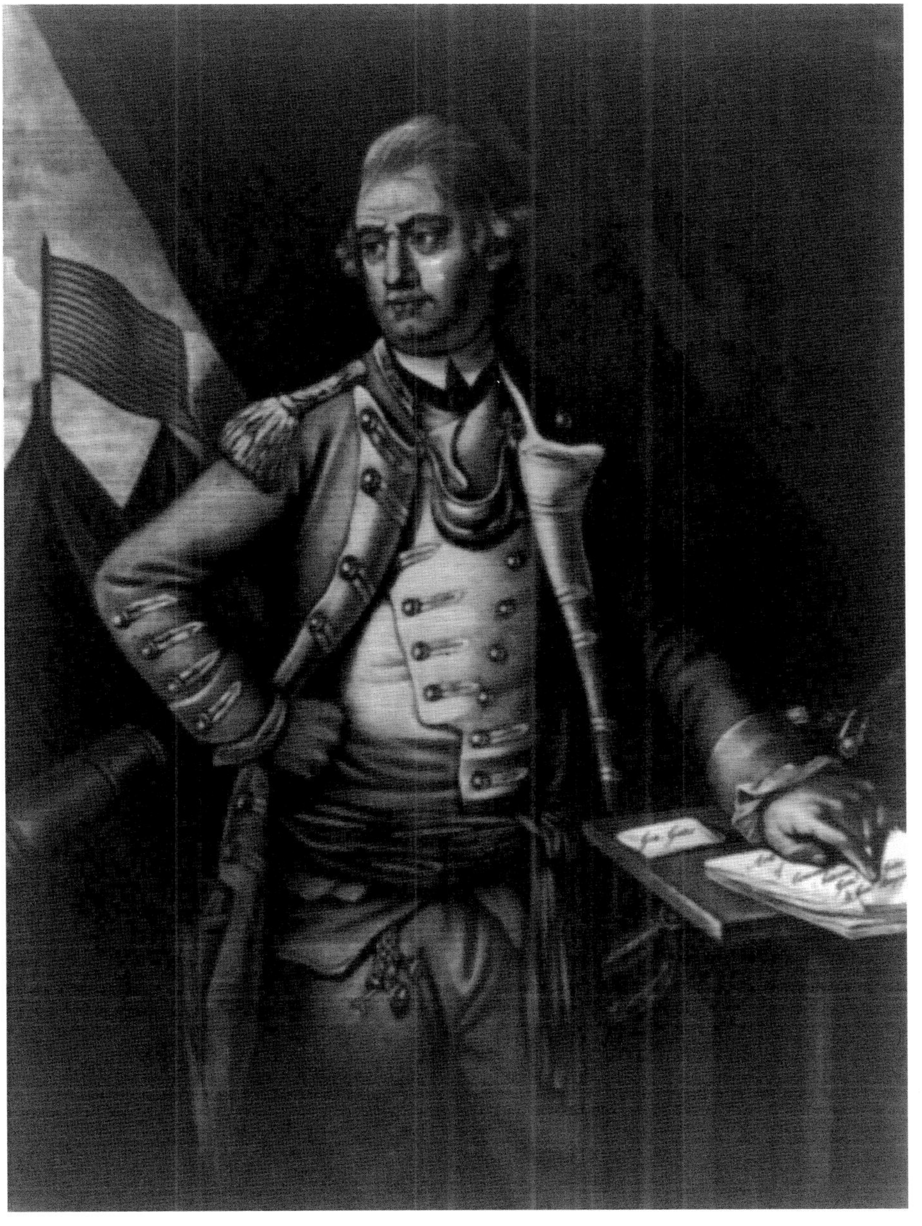

A retired officer in the British Army, Horatio Gates, frustrated by his lack of advancement, joined the Colonial effort in 1775 at the outset of the war. He was given the rank of major general in 1776. In August of the following year, Gates assumed command of the Northern Department of the Continental Army, which was encamped on Van Schaick Island. It was anticipated that the British, led by Gen. John Burgoyne, were on their way south to capture Albany. Gates, not intending to wait, decided to march to Saratoga on September 9 and surprise Burgoyne. On September 19, the Battle of Bemis Heights was fought, led by Gates and his army of local militia. Complete surrender was had on October 17, 1777, a turning point in the Revolutionary War. (Courtesy of the Library of Congress.)

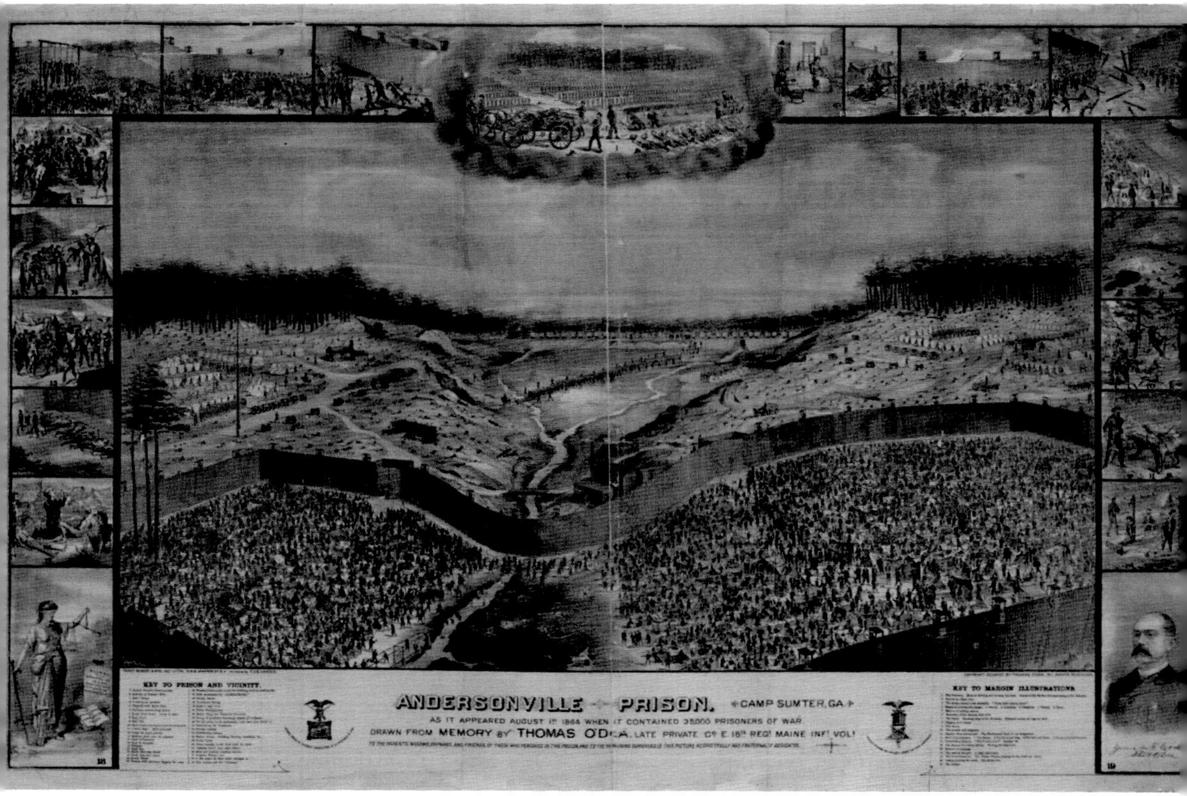

In the summer of 1864, Thomas O'Dea, a young infantryman from the 16th Regiment Maine Volunteers, was captured by Confederate troops and sent to the infamous Andersonville Prison. The camp, located in central Georgia, operated during the remaining 15 months of the war. It housed some 35,000 prisoners, nearly 13,000 of whom died. Conditions were deplorable, with little food and no clean water. Dysentery and other diseases swept across the prison, and most men died of starvation. O'Dea managed to survive and was released in February 1865. He moved to Cohoes in the early 1870s and became a bricklayer. He then became a union leader, serving as general secretary of the Bricklayers and Stone Masons Union of America. In 1879, from his home on Summit Street, after grueling days of laying bricks, Thomas O'Dea began to sketch the grim scene that was forever seared into his memory. At that time, the full story of the horrors of Andersonville had not been made known. O'Dea wanted the world to understand the totality of the disease, starvation, and death that took place. He finished the print in 1885, and it became a national sensation. By 1887, O'Dea had established a full-time business selling lithograph copies for $5 each from his home on Walnut Street. He returned to Andersonville in 1914 for the 50th anniversary of his capture. O'Dea died in 1926 and is buried in St. Agnes Cemetery in Cohoes. Shown here is O'Dea's famous print of the Andersonville Prison. (Courtesy of the Library of Congress.)

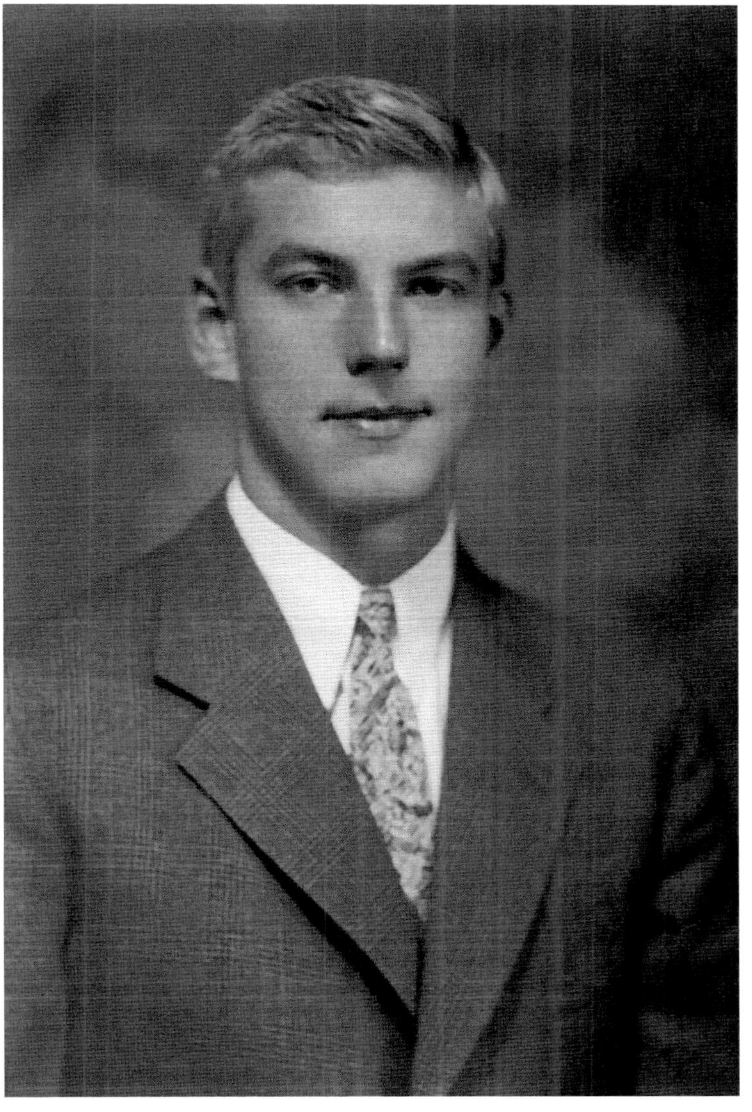

Carlson was dubbed by correspondents during World War II as one of the "fightingest men" in the Marine Corps. Born and raised in Cohoes, he was the brother of E. Iver Carlson. William attended Cohoes High School and went on to Wesleyan University. He became a lay preacher in the Methodist Church and enrolled in divinity school in Denver. During school, he became a student pastor at a small Methodist church outside of Denver. In July 1942, Carlson left divinity school with just one year left before ordination to enlist in the Marine Corps. He was commissioned as an officer one year later. He turned down the offer to become a chaplain, instead choosing to lead on the front lines of battle. He led the 6th Division Marines on many battles in the Pacific, primarily in Okinawa. He had caught the attention of war correspondents when he conducted church services in between battles. Dispatches out of Okinawa read "preacher packs a terrific punch." Carlson was killed leading the charge on Oroku Peninsula on Okinawa's west coast. In 82 days of fighting, the 6th Marines secured Okinawa and suffered 8,226 casualties. (Courtesy of the Plowman family.)

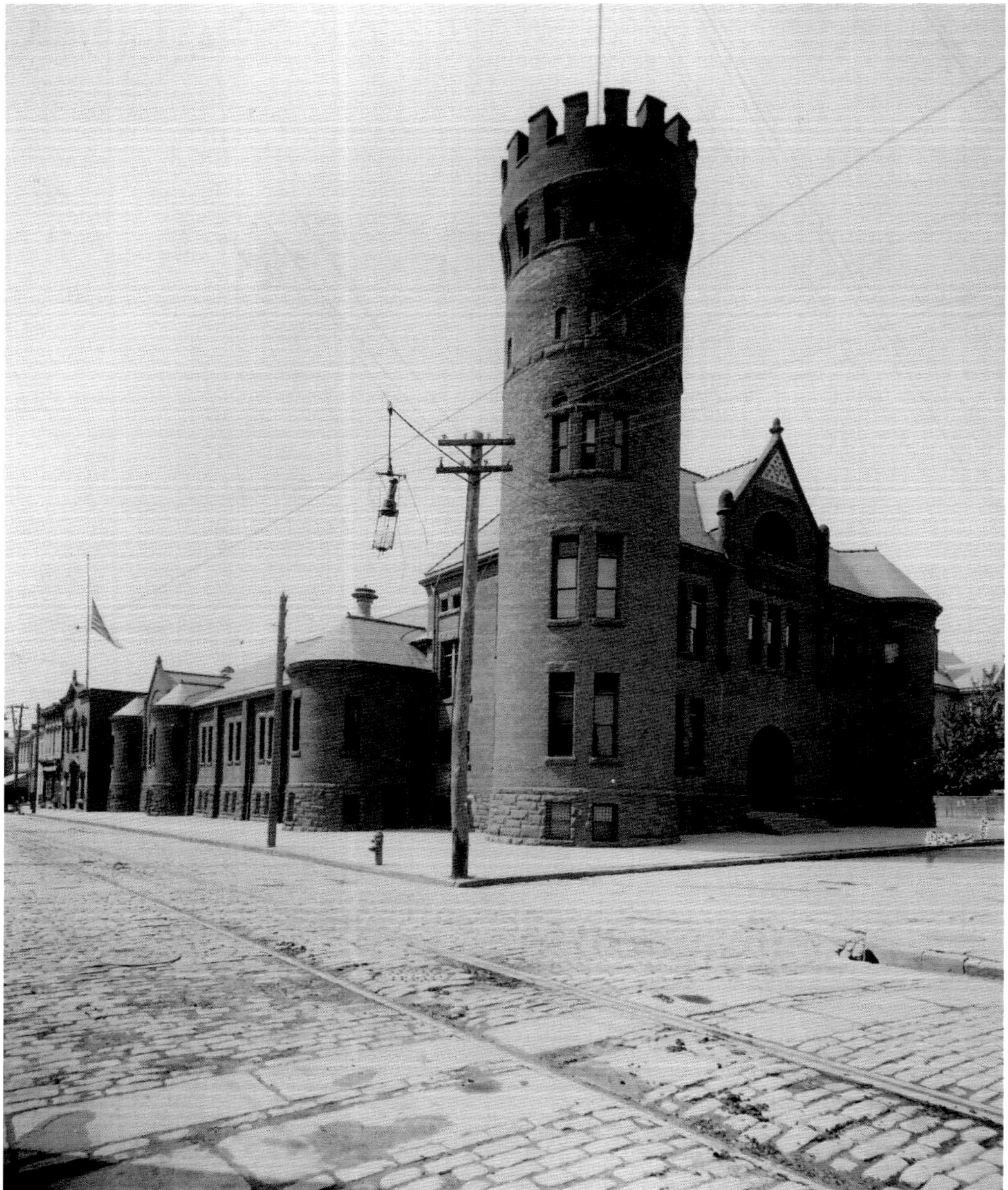

The 105th Infantry Regiment, Company B, was organized in February 1876. Some of its first assignments were to quell union riots in Cohoes and Troy. It was not regimented until the outbreak of the Spanish-American War in 1898. During World War I, the unit was deployed to the front lines in Belgium and won many awards. During World War II, the company participated in the attack on the Gilbert Islands and the capture of Okinawa. During that conflict, the unit won three Congressional Medals of Honor and the Distinguished Unit Citation. Shown here is the Cohoes Armory, home of the 105th Regiment from 1893 to 1964. (Courtesy of the New York State Military Museum.)

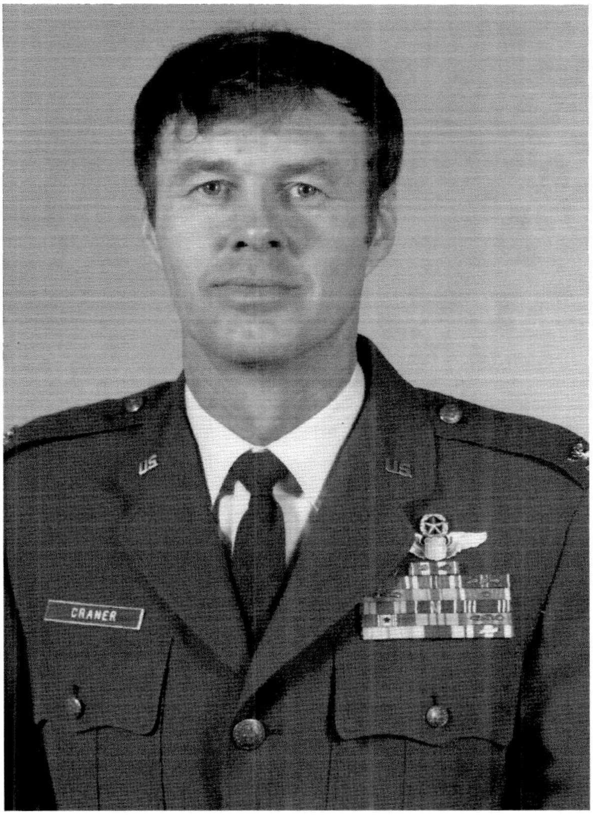

On September 4, 2008, at the Republican National Convention, Sen. John McCain, the Republican nominee for president, told the nation about his friend Bob Craner. "The good man in the cell next door to me, my friend, Bob Craner, saved me." McCain, along with Craner, were held as prisoners of war for nearly six years at the infamous Hanoi Hilton in North Vietnam. Craner, an F-100 fighter pilot, was shot down over North Vietnam in 1967. Bob Craner was born in 1933 and grew up in the Orchard section of Cohoes, near what is now Craner Park. He attended Catholic Central High School and went on to the University of Nevada and Arizona State University, where he majored in Russian studies. He received his navigator and pilot training in 1953 and served as a weapons instructor at Nellis Air Force Base in Nevada. Craner was on his second volunteer tour in Southeast Asia when he was shot down. During his captivity, he endured severe beatings and was kept in relative isolation. For three years, he occupied the cell next to McCain's. The two developed a friendship through tapping on the wall adjoining their cells. It was this friendship that kept both men from giving up hope and losing their sanity. Craner was released on March 14, 1973, returning to Cohoes a week later. March 23, 1973, was declared Lieutenant Colonel Robert R. Craner Day. A motorcade met Craner at the Albany Airport, and he was escorted to city hall for a ceremony at which he was presented keys to the city by Mayor Virginia McDonald. Devlin Park in the Orchard section of the city was rededicated as Craner Park. He was the recipient of two Purple Hearts, two Silver Stars, the Distinguished Flying Cross, and the Bronze Star. He remained in the Air Force upon his return home and earned a degree from the College of the Holy Cross in Worcester, Massachusetts. In 1980, Craner died of a heart attack and was buried with full honors at Arlington National Cemetery. He was only 47 years old. Today, the memory of Bob Craner lives on in the form of the Robert R. Craner Service Medal, an award presented to military veterans from Cohoes on Memorial Day and Veterans Day. (Courtesy of the Spindle City Historic Society.)

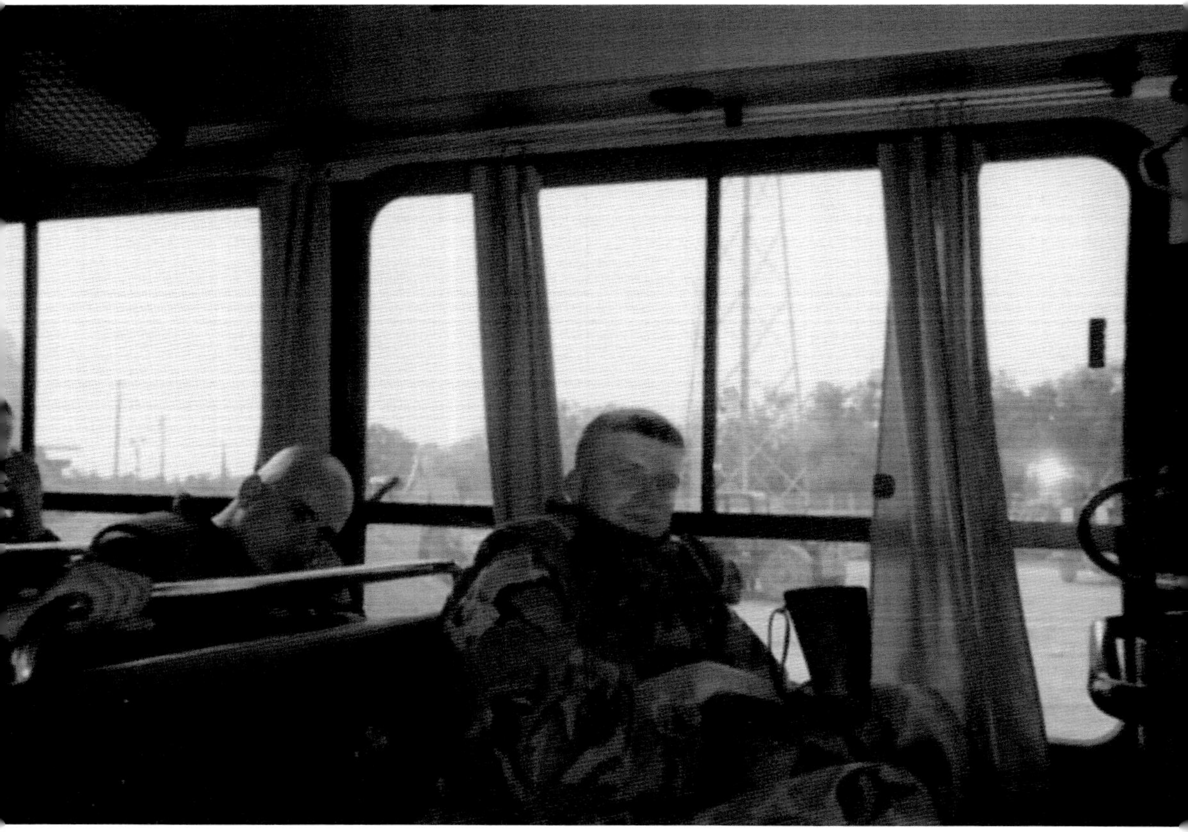

Born and raised in Cohoes, Matt Stevens represents the current generation's sacrifice in service to their country. Entering the Army soon after graduating high school, Stevens was sent to Kosovo in the spring of 2001 as part of an ongoing peacekeeping mission. In the summer of that same year, the events of September 11 plunged the nation into what would be known as the War on Terror. Stevens was sent to Kuwait in preparation for the invasion of Iraq in the winter of 2003. On March 20, Stevens and Bravo Company 369 crossed the border. Stevens and those troops who took part in the early days of the war saw some of the heaviest fighting. A gunner on an Abrams tank, one of Stevens's first missions was to secure the Baghdad airport. Stevens and his company were relieved and came home on July 5. A decade after the war began, Stevens, like many other combat veterans, continues to adjust to civilian life, as the scars of war run deep. While questions remain as to the justification of the war, Stevens is proud of his service, and Cohoes is proud of him. (Courtesy of Matt Stevens.)

Entertainers and Sportsmen

Throughout the decades, there have been those who, it seemed, were destined to be in the spotlight. For some, that stage was a ball field; for others, it was an opera house or movie set. The individuals chronicled in this chapter are not military heroes. They are not great industrialists or political figures. But their contributions to the community are no less consequential. In fact, some of these individuals have made an impact far beyond Cohoes, with an entire nation embracing their talents. Some were local celebrities. But all have, to some extent, provided an escape from life's toils and strains. Whether they performed on the playing field, in the boxing ring, on the stage, or on the screen, these men and women are proof that talent runs deep, even in small communities like Cohoes. This chapter highlights those who may be long forgotten and those whose fame is still going strong.

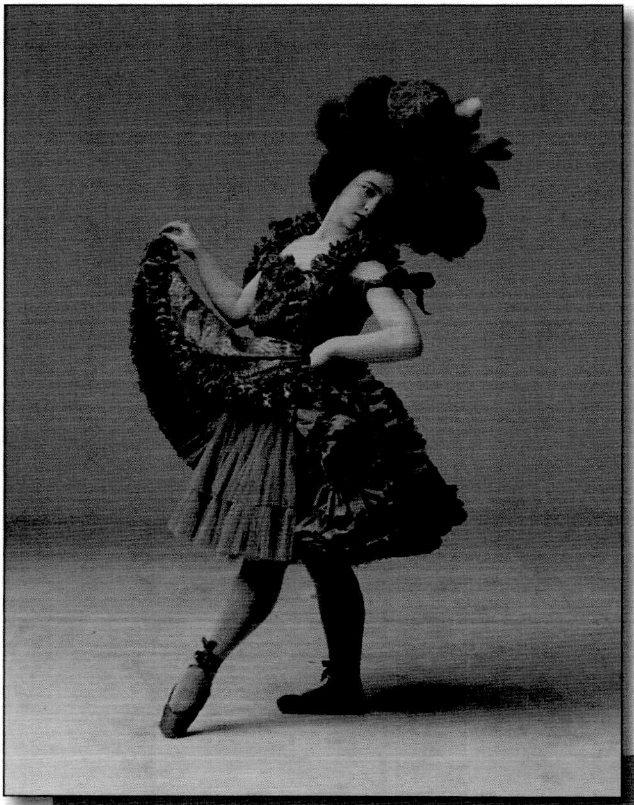

Adelaide Dickey started dancing at the early age of five. The Dickey family lived at the top of Imperial Avenue, in a house (below) built by her father, William James Dickey. Billed as "La Petite Adelaide," Dickey's first documented local performance was in 1893 at the Cohoes Music Hall. She would go on to a highly successful career in Vaudeville and then film, beginning with her first movie in 1898. But Dickey would become most known for her talents as a dancer. In 1910, she partnered with J.J. Hughes, and they became a highly successful and popular dance team. Adelaide and Hughes opened their own dance studio and performed in various nightclubs in New York City. When Hughes died in 1927, Adelaide retired from dancing. She remained active in the New York social scene and died in 1960 at the age of 78. (Left, courtesy of Paul Dunleavey.)

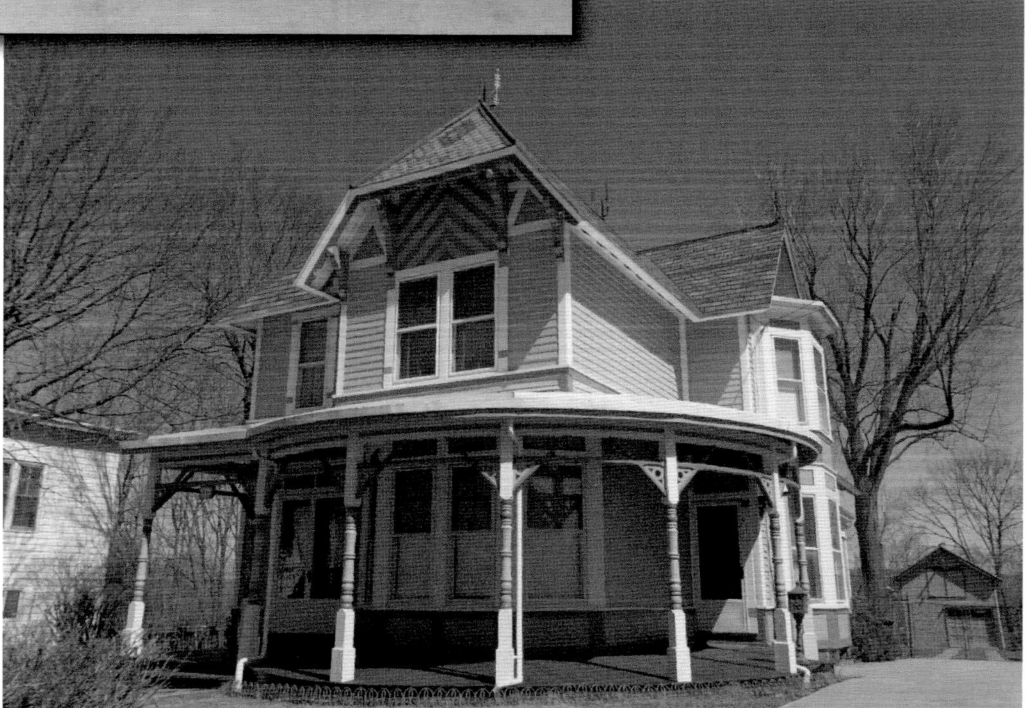

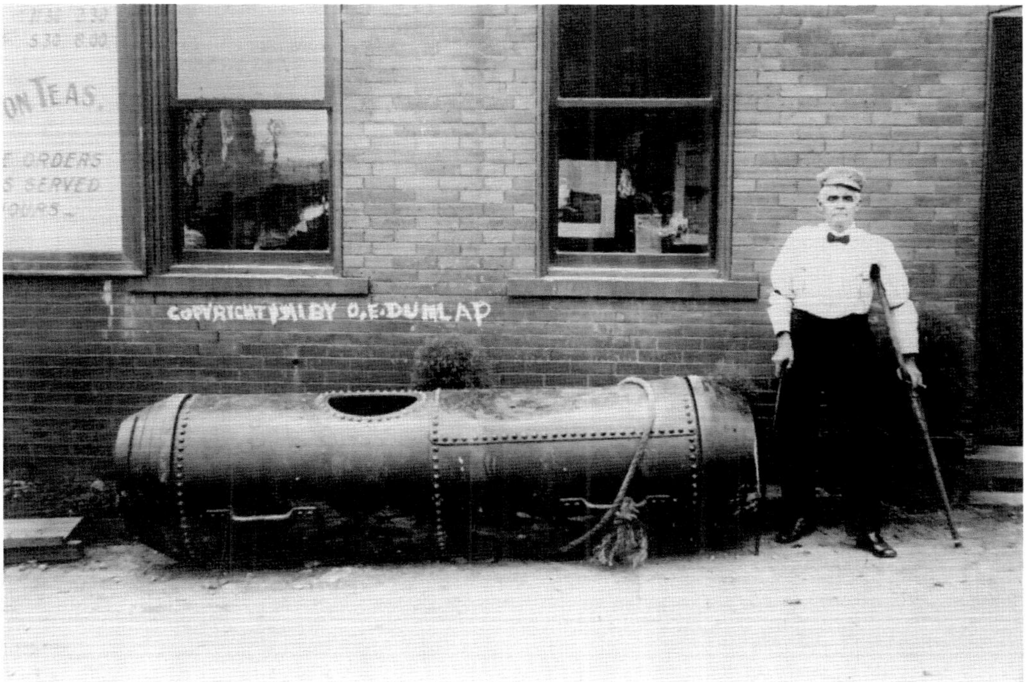

On April 15, 1899, to the delight of some 10,000 spectators, Bobby Leach crawled into a barrel and entered the swift and mighty current of the Mohawk River. He then tumbled over the torrents of the Cohoes Falls. In the process, one of the straps of the barrel broke. Leach was recovered several minutes later, suffering from a laceration to the scalp. His death-defying feat was one of the greatest spectacles in the city's history. It would be another 12 years before Leach and his barrel made a similar attempt, at Niagara Falls. That stunt caused more serious damage, landing Leach in the hospital for six months. (Courtesy of the Library of Congress.)

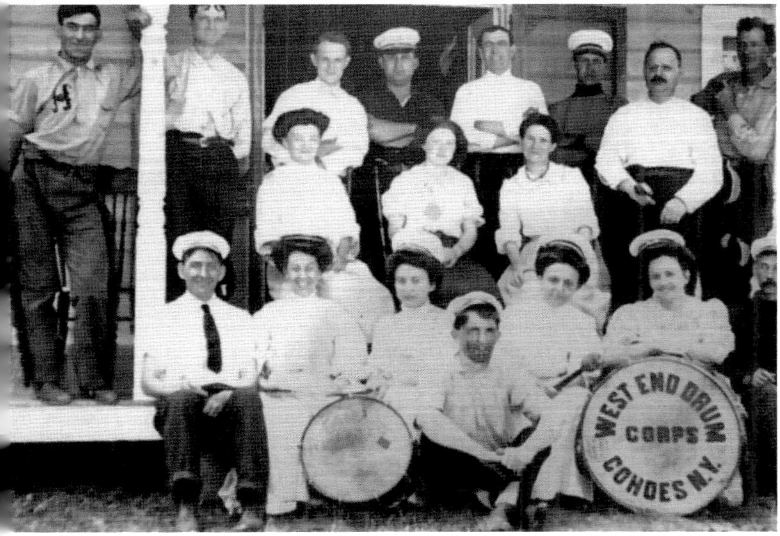

Before television or even radio came into being, people often spent their days listening to and participating in drum corps as a source of entertainment and civic participation. The Cohoes Drum Corps was mostly made up of residents from the west end of town. This photograph was taken in 1910 at a competition on Saratoga Lake. (Courtesy of Sue Baird.)

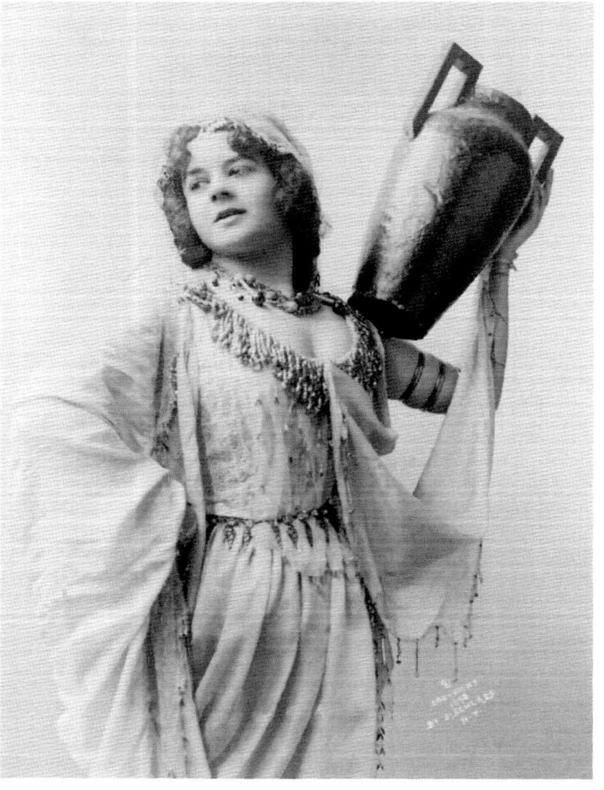

It could be said that Eva Tanguay was the Lady Gaga of the early 20th century. She was outrageous, she was glamorous, and above all, she was extremely entertaining. She once wore a dress completely covered in pennies and proceeded to peel them off and fling them at men in the audience. Tanguay was born in Marbleton, Quebec, in 1878. Her family immigrated to the United States seeking employment in the burgeoning textile industry and settled in Holyoke, Massachusetts. While local legend claims that Eva grew up in Cohoes, there is no historical evidence to support the claim. She may have lived with family on Congress Street for a brief time when she was a young girl. What we do know for certain is that she performed as a child actress at both the Cohoes Music Hall and the Cohoes City Theatre. Eva struggled during these early performances but soon found her distinctive style. In 1901, she landed a part in the Broadway musical *My Lady*. But it would be Vaudeville in which Tanguay would truly shine. In 1909, she was brought in to star in The Ziegfeld Follies, a series of elaborate theatrical productions on Broadway. By 1918, she had become one of the most successful Vaudeville performers in the country, earning between $2,500 and $3,500 a week, which was great money in those days. But the more Eva earned, the more she spent. Her gowns cost between $500 and $1,500. By the late 1920s, Vaudeville was losing its appeal as silent movies became the new rage. When the stock market crashed in 1929, it is estimated that Tanguay lost nearly $2 million. Bad times continued for Eva in 1933 when, at 55 years of age, she went blind. She would spend her remaining days in relative seclusion in her apartment in New York. But even though she was blind and riddled with arthritis, she managed to maintain a positive outlook. In January 1947, she suffered a stroke and died. She was 68. While the world has long since forgotten the showmanship of Eva Tanguay, in Cohoes, her spirit lives on in more ways than one. It is said that she has made several appearances at the Cohoes Music Hall in the decades since her death. Her presence has been described as a "whimsical, playful spirit." Even in death, Eva Tanguay continues to entertain the people of Cohoes. (Courtesy of the Library of Congress.)

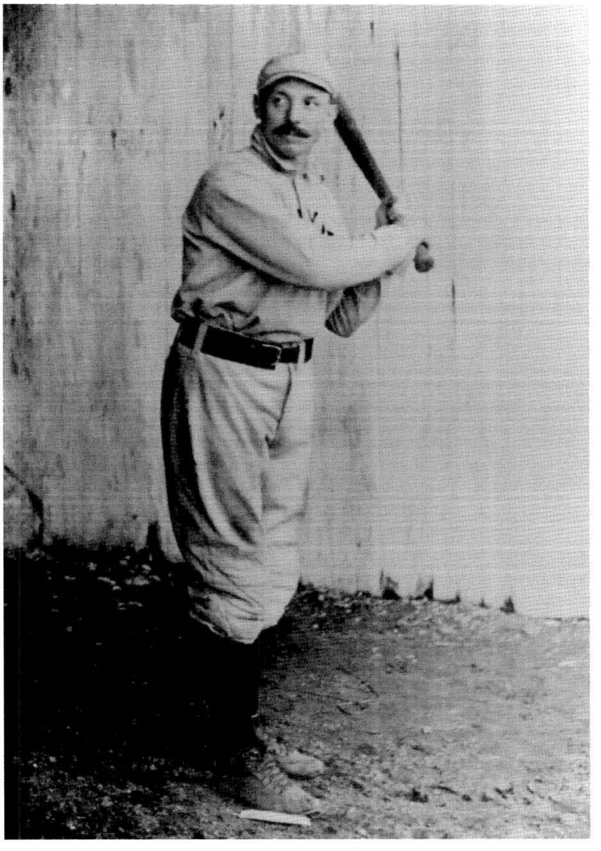

George Davis was born on August 23, 1870, to Abram and Sarah Davis. The family lived at 8 Main Street, in a two-story wood frame structure just west of Remsen Street and just east of the Erie Canal. Davis attended the White Street School until his mid-teens, when he joined his uncle's teamster business. He began playing baseball at an early age, mostly with local youth teams, including the YMCA team. He soon caught the attention of professional scouts and, at age 19, was signed by the National League's Cleveland Spiders. In just two years with Cleveland, he rose to the top of the league, being ranked seventh in runs batted in. Davis was quickly becoming known as a great all-around player. In 1892, he was obtained by the New York Giants, where he spent the next nine years at shortstop. For the Giants, Davis hit over .300 and set all-time franchise records. In 1902, due to a corruption-plagued National League, he joined the Chicago White Sox. However, a decision to move back to New York forced Davis to sit out the 1903 season when the White Sox fought the move and won. From 1904 until the end of his career, Davis would become known for his exceptional defensive play. During his time with Chicago, the team was always in the top three in league standings and won the World Series. Davis retired in 1910 and became a manager of a minor league team in Des Moines, Iowa. Managing, however, proved unsuccessful, and Davis moved back to New York City, where he became manager of a bowling alley. In 1917, he became a coach for the St. Louis Browns, but lost the job after only one year. He then became employed by the Ford Motor Company as a field inspector of Ford agencies throughout the Midwest. In 1932, Davis and his wife moved to Philadelphia, where he died in 1940. Many decades later, through the efforts of Cohoes city historian Walter Lipka, Davis was rediscovered as one of the best shortstops to have played the game. In 1998, Davis was inducted into the National Baseball Hall of Fame in Cooperstown, New York. (Courtesy of the National Baseball Hall of Fame and Museum, Cooperstown, New York.)

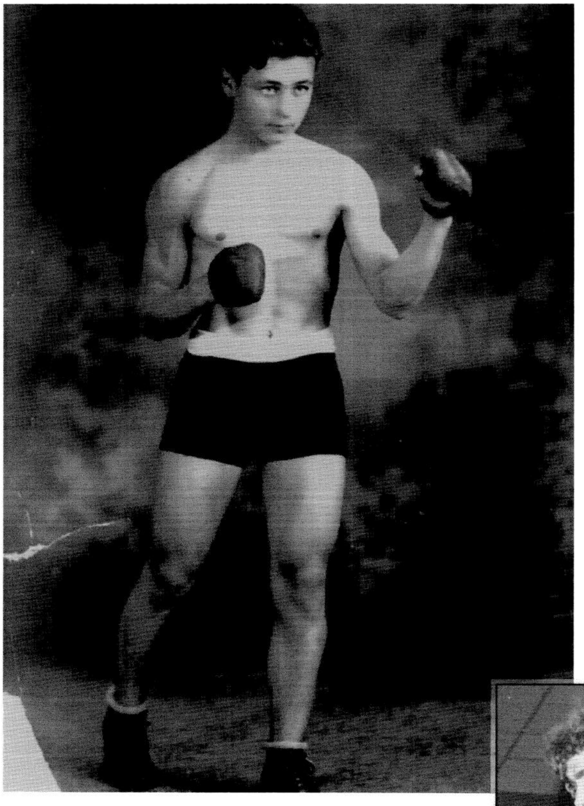

Joe Nocella was a lifelong resident of Cohoes. He owned and operated the Mobil service station at the corner of Main and Remsen Streets for 44 years. Prior to that, Nocella was a professional boxer who was known locally and throughout New England during the 1920s. Nocella fought in Madison Square Garden, winning all four of his featured fights. After his retirement, Nocella remained active in the community until his death in 2007 at the age of 95. (Courtesy of Michael J. Brooks.)

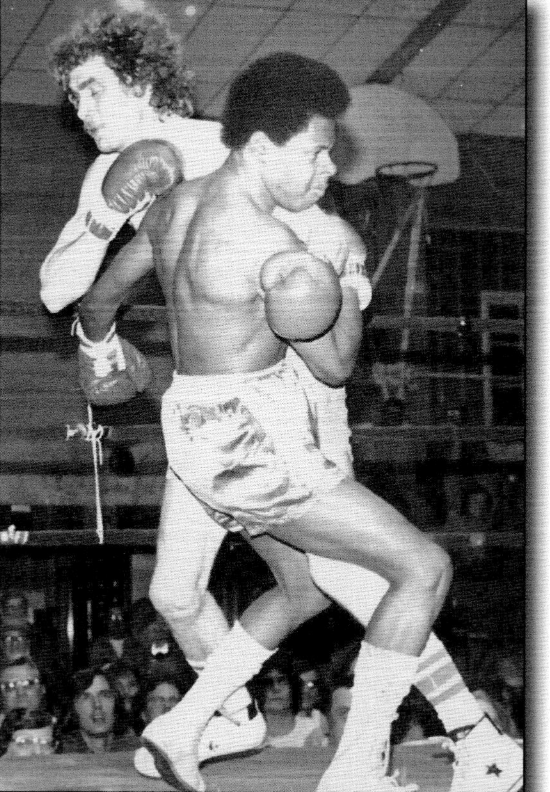

Darrell "Clyde" Beattie started his amateur boxing career in 1973. In 1979, he fought his first professional bout, defeating Malcolm Gordon. Beattie went on to a professional career, compiling a record of 16 wins, 13 losses, and 2 draws. He was at one time ranked eighth in New York state. Beattie retired in 1991 and has spent the last 20-plus years as a coach, trainer, referee, and judge. For the last 10 years, he has headed up the Cohoes Youth Boxing League. Beattie (rear) is seen here in his fight against Malcolm Gordon. (Courtesy of the *Troy Record*.)

Born in Austria in 1907, Mike Mazurki came to Cohoes with his family, settling into a tenement apartment on Olmstead Street. Mazurki, at six feet, four inches tall and weighing well over 200 pounds, became an athlete on the professional wrestling circuit. But his facial features caught the eye of Mae West, who saw his photograph in a newspaper. She hired him to be a bodyguard. Mazurki starred in his first film, *The Shanghai Gesture*. He then went on to roles in *Dick Tracey* and *Night and the City*. By the mid-1950s, Mazurki turned his attention to the small screen, with roles in hit shows like *I Dream of Jeanie*, *Bonanza*, *Gunsmoke*, and *Gilligan's Island*. As famous as Mazurki became, he always gave back to Cohoes. He starred in two productions at the Cohoes Music Hall, including *Of Mice and Men* (below). Mazurki died in 1990, but remains a beloved figure in his hometown. (Below, courtesy of the Cohoes Public Library.)

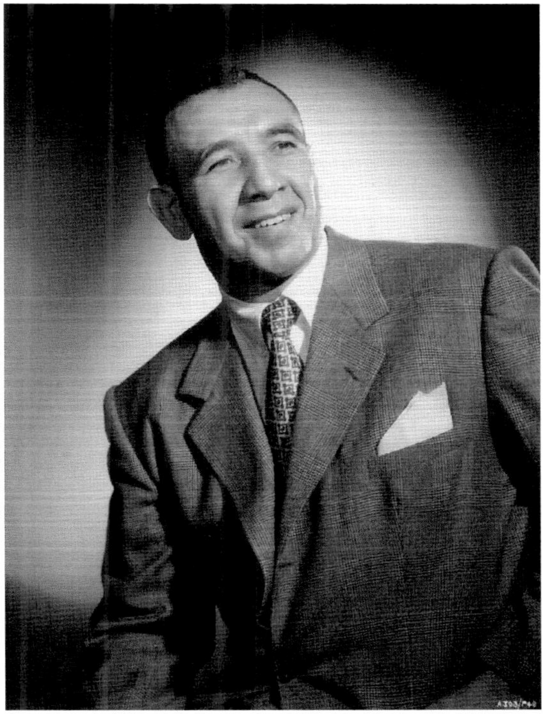

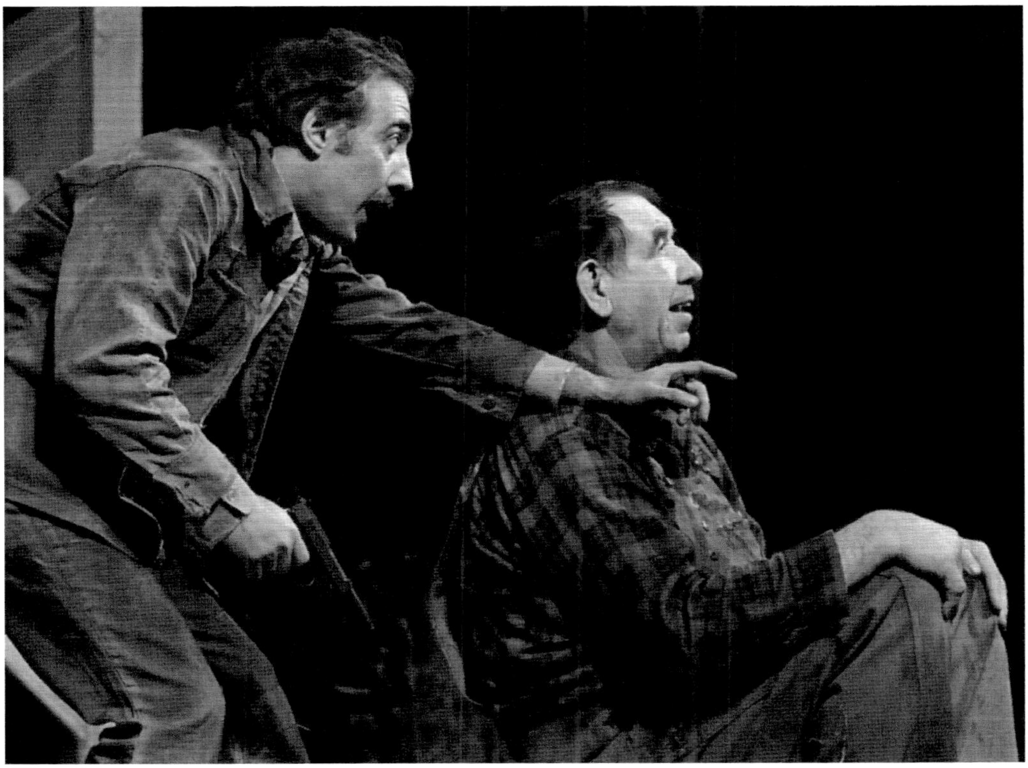

The Rymanowski Brothers Orchestra was started in 1947 by John and Alex Rymanowski. Throughout the remainder of the 1940s and during the 1950s, the nine-piece orchestra recorded with several labels, including Lamb and Decca Records. During the 1960s, John's sons Dennis and Gerry joined the band, which was then scaled down to a five- and six-piece orchestra. Now in their sixth decade as a family band, they have stayed true to their Polish roots, remaining primarily a polka band. The Rymanowski Brothers play numerous venues across the Capital Region, including an annual concert in their hometown of Cohoes. In 2010, they recorded the album *It's about TIME*, which proved an immediate hit. At left is the band around 1950, with Alex and John Rymanowski in the front row, third and fourth from left. Below, today's band members are, from left to right, Dennis Rymanowski, Gerry Rymanowski, Jerry Romanowicz, Joe Rycaz, and Bob Drozd. (Courtesy of the Rymanowski family.)

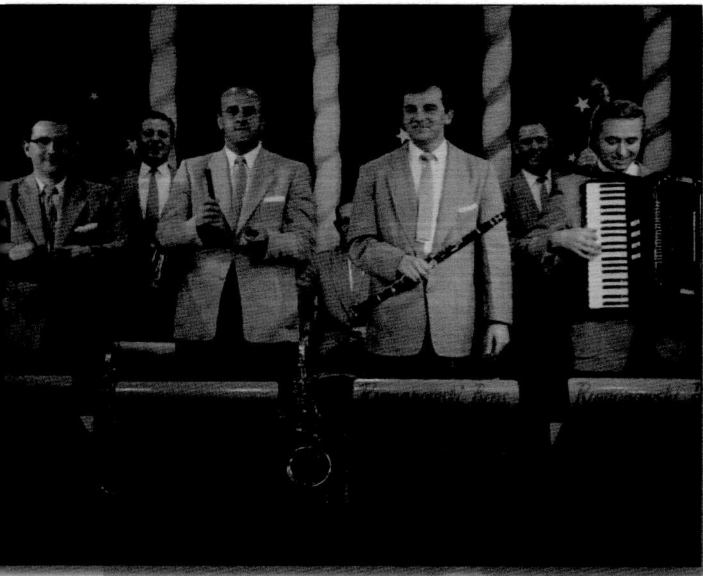

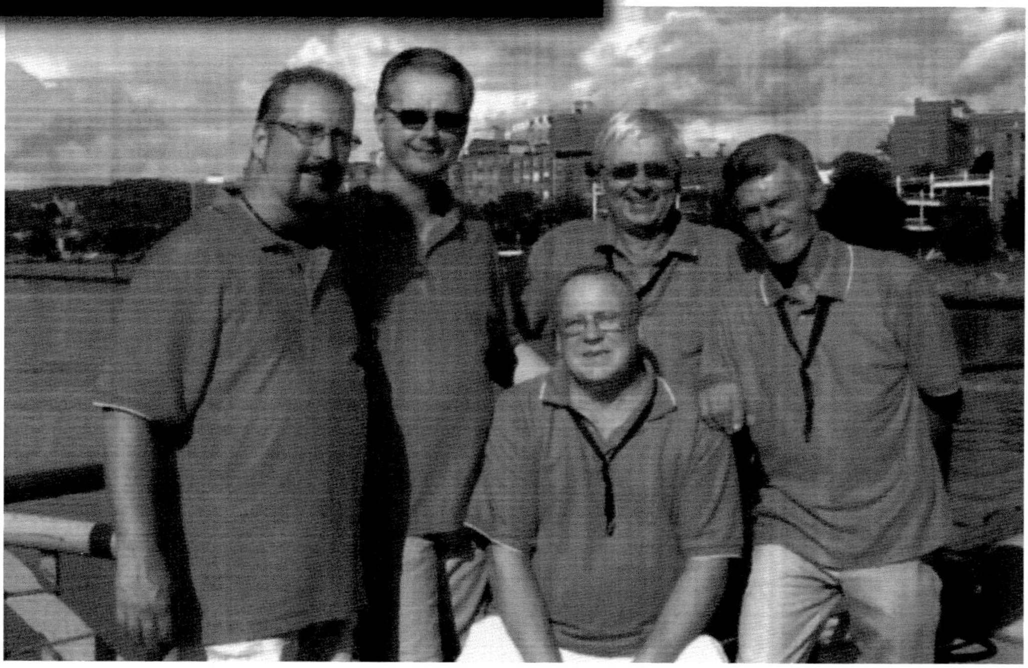

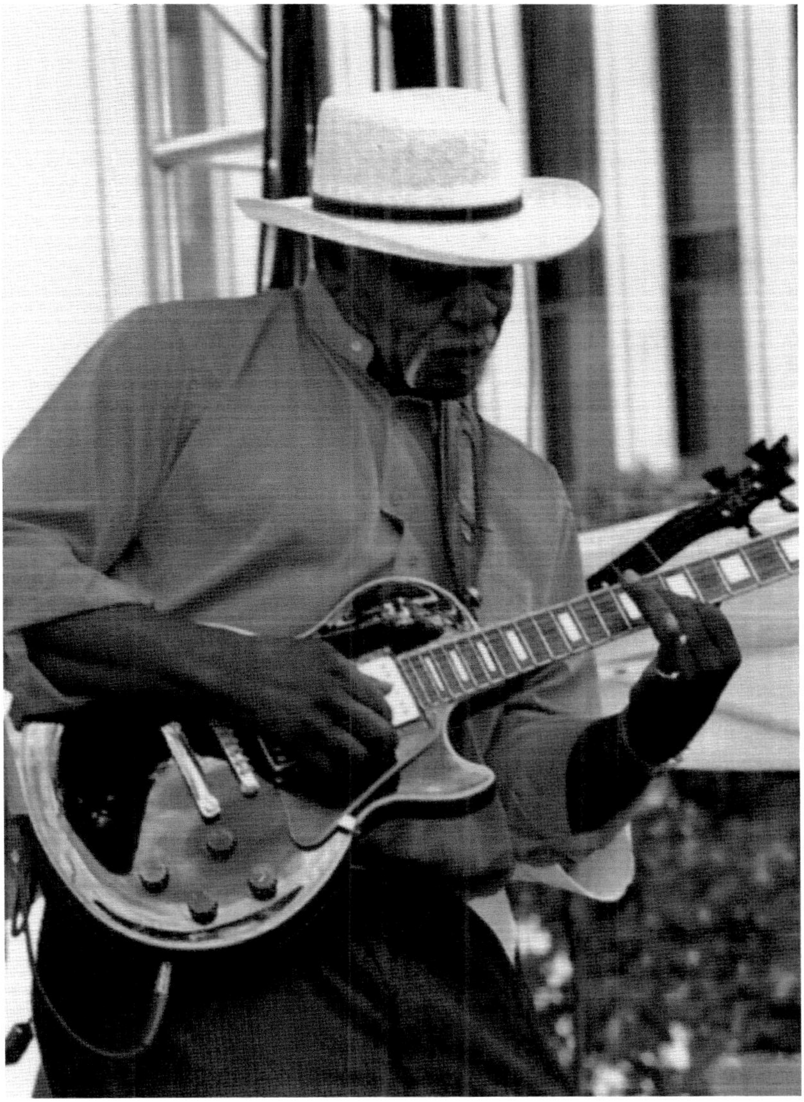

In 1938, Ernie Williams, 13, was living in a shack on a Virginia plantation. He would spend the long, hot days picking tobacco, but at night, he would lose himself playing the blues on an old six-string guitar. At the age of 19, Williams was able to save enough money for a one-way ticket to Harlem. Once in New York City, Williams would play as many as seven nights a week, going from club to club, from one end of the city to the other. One of his early highlights was playing amateur night at the Apollo Theater. Williams moved north to the Albany area in the 1960s and worked a number of odd jobs to support his family. Determined to not give up music, Williams made himself a fixture in the Albany blues community during the ensuing decades. He released six albums and opened for the likes of B.B. King. Williams loved playing and loved people, which was especially evident when he played at local community events, such as the Falls View Park Festival and the Canal Square Concerts in his adopted hometown of Cohoes. Williams died in 2012, making music until the very end. His music will certainly live on for generations to come. (Courtesy of Mike Carey.)

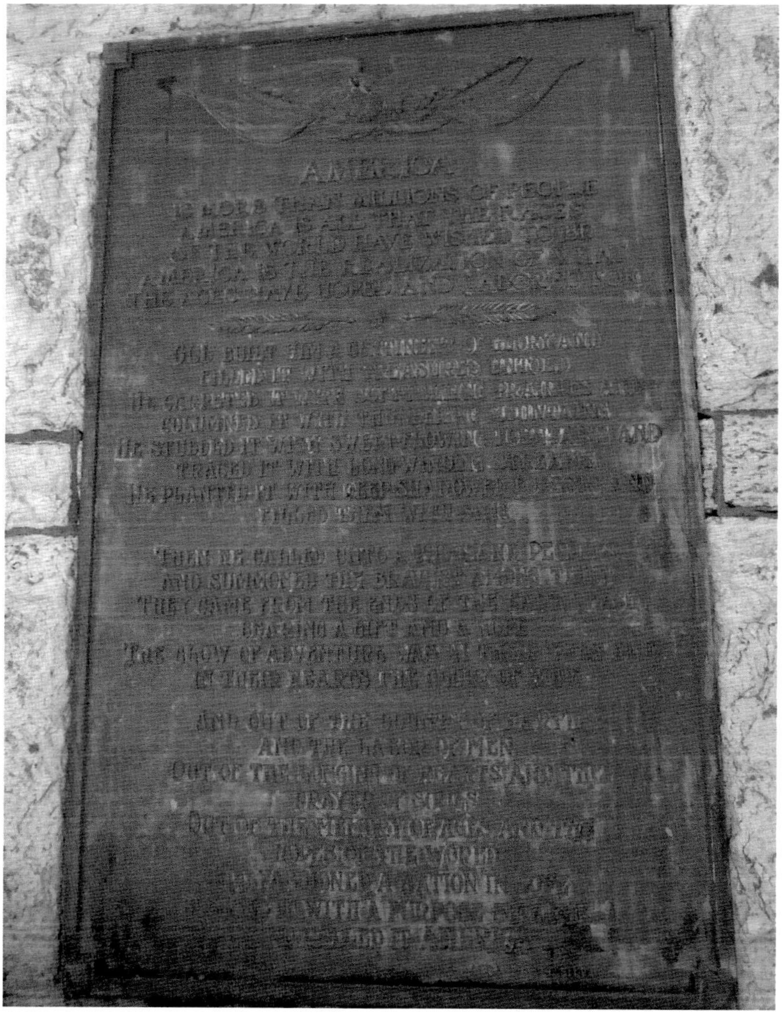

Silver was not from Cohoes. He never lived in Cohoes or set foot in Cohoes, for that matter. Silver was a rabbi and an early proponent of the Zionist movement in the United States. He was also a poet; in 1926, he wrote a short patriotic poem called "America," which has graced the front entrance to Cohoes City Hall for many decades. It is not known exactly when it was placed there, or by whom. But after reading the poem, it becomes evident why it was put there. It is the perfect summation of this book. "America is more than millions of people / America is all that the races of the world have wished to be / America is the realization of what the ages have hoped and labored for / God built him a continent of glory and filled it with treasures untold / He carpeted it with soft rolling prairies and columned it with thundering mountains / He studded it with sweet flowing fountains and traced it with long winding streams / He planted it with deep shadowed forests and filled them with song / Then he called unto a thousand peoples and summoned the bravest among them / They came from the ends of the earth, each bearing a gift and a hope / The glow of adventure was in their eyes and in their hearts, the glory of hope / And out of the bounty of the earth and the labor of men / Out of the longing of hearts and the prayer of souls / Out of the memory of ages and the hopes of the world / God fashioned a nation in love / Blessed it with a purpose sublime / And called it America."

Berstein, Peter. *Wedding of the Waters*. New York: Norton and Company, 2005.

Biskin, Miriam, Mabel Gilman, Frances Levy, Beatrice Poinsel, Mary Sausville, Ruth Sanford, eds. Cohoes: *The Cohoes Centennial*, 1969.

Light, Sally. *Canals and Crossroads: A Sesquicentennial History of the Albany Diocese*. Albany, NY: Albany Catholic Press, 1997.

Masten, Arthur. *The History of Cohoes, NY, From its Earliest Settlement to the Present Time*. Cornell, NY: The Cornell University Library, 1995.

Phelan, Thomas, Thomas Carroll. *Hudson Mohawk Gateway*. Sun Valley, CA: American Historical Press, 2001.

Robinson, Frank. *Albany's O'Connell Machine*. Albany, NY: The Washington Park Spirit Inc., 1973.

Spindle City Historic Society. *Cohoes*. Charleston, SC: Arcadia Publishing, 2001.

———. *Cohoes Revisited*. Charleston, SC: Arcadia Publishing, 2005.

Walkowitz, Daniel. *Worker City, Company Town*. Chicago: University of Illinois Press, 1981.

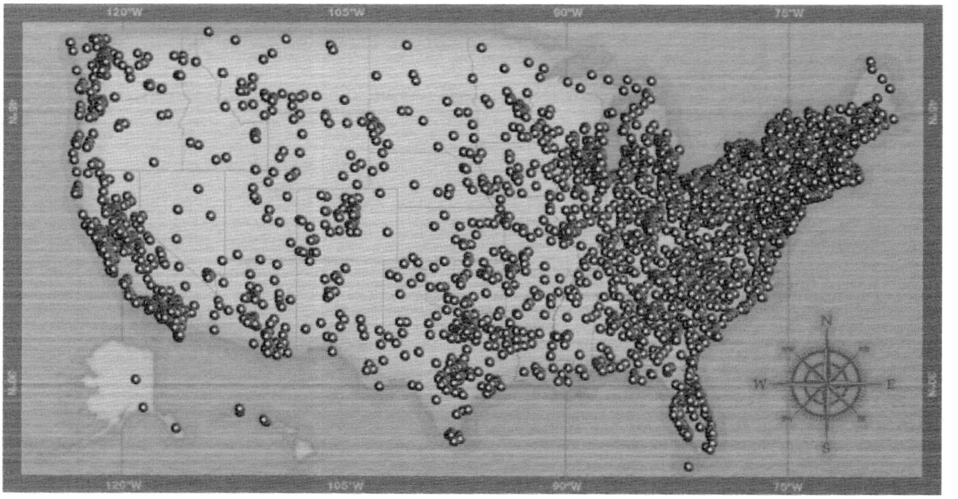